AF600670

TRACY W. McGREGOR

Great Lakes Books

A complete listing of the books in this series can be found online at wsupress.wayne.edu

TRACY W. McGREGOR

Humanitarian, Philanthropist, and Detroit Civic Leader

PHILIP P. MASON

Wayne State University Press
Detroit

12 11 10 09 08 5 4 3 2 1

Library of Congress Cataloging-in-Publication Data

Mason, Philip P. (Philip Parker), 1927–
Tracy W. Mcgregor : humanitarian, philanthropist, and Detroit civic leader / Philip P. Mason.
p. cm. — (Great Lakes books)
Includes bibliographical references and index.
ISBN-13: 978-0-8143-3376-1 (hardcover : alk. paper)
ISBN-10: 0-8143-3376-1 (hardcover : alk. paper)
1. McGregor, Tracy W. (Tracy William), 1869–1936. 2. Detroit (Mich.)—Biography. 3. Philanthropists—Michigan—Detroit—Biography. 4. Civic leaders—Michigan—Detroit—Biography. 5. Homeless men—Services for—Michigan—Detroit—History—20th century. 6. Charities—Michigan—Detroit—History—20th century. 7. Libraries—Michigan—Detroit—History—20th century. 8. Detroit (Mich.)—Social policy. I. Title.
F574.D453M35 2008
361.7'49092—dc22
[B]
2007024243

♾ The paper used in this publication meets the minimum requirements of the American National Standard for Information Sciences—Permanence of Paper for Printed Library Materials, ANSI Z39.48–1984.

To Mildred White, whose loyalty to Tracy McGregor and the McGregor Fund made this book possible

CONTENTS

ACKNOWLEDGMENTS

The staffs of the following archives and libraries assisted in identifying and sharing relevant material on the life and times of Tracy and Katherine Whitney McGregor: the Burton Historical Collections of the Detroit Public Library, the Bentley Library of the University of Michigan, the State Library of Michigan, the State Archives of Michigan, the Grosse Pointe Historical Society, the Liggett School Archives, Goodwill Industries of Greater Detroit Archives, and the Alderman Library of the University of Virginia.

At the Archives of Labor and Urban Affairs at the Walter P. Reuther Library at Wayne State University, which is the repository of the Tracy McGregor Collection, the Associated Charities of Detroit and its successors, the United Community Services and United Way of Metropolitan Detroit, and the Merrill-Palmer Institute, I wish to thank Michael Smith, the director; staff members Margaret Raucher, Elizabeth Clemens, and Thomas Featherstone, curator of its extensive photograph and audiovisual collections. I owe much to them for their help in locating and providing reproduction of relevant photographs in a timely manner.

The staff of the William L. Clements Library of the University of Michigan, with which McGregor was closely associated, was most helpful, including Don Wilcox, Clayton Lewis, and Laura Daniel. I owe a special debt of gratitude to my friend and colleague, John C. Dann, its director. As one of the nation's premier rare book librarians and prominent colonial historians, he provided invaluable insights on Tracy McGregor's remarkable success as a collector of Americana. He also shed light on McGregor's close association with Randolph Adams, director of the Clements Library, and on McGregor's crucial role on the library's Committee of Management in the 1930s.

At the Manuscript Division of the Library of Congress I received special help from the late Mary M. Wolfskill, head of the Reference and Reader Service section. She provided access to the records of the American Historical

Association, the McGregor Plan for the Encouragement of Book Collecting by American College Libraries, and the James Couzens papers.

Several of my colleagues were especially helpful. Stanley D. Solvick graciously shared his research on the Merrill-Palmer Institute. James Norton, former research director of United Community Services of Metropolitan Detroit, made available to me his extensive research files on the Associated Charities of Detroit. Caroline Scholfield, formerly on the staff of the State Library of Michigan, located valuable and often obscure reports and documents relating to McGregor's leadership role in reforming Michigan's mental health, prison, hospital, and public housing programs. Kathleen Mutch, my research assistant, located numerous important sources.

Mark and Catherine Phillips, Susan Mason, and Evan Burkholder utilized their genealogical and legal expertise in finding relevant information on the early life of the McGregor family and relevant court records. Beth Whitney provided information on the Whitney family history.

The trustees and staff of the McGregor Fund of Michigan have played an important role in this study. William J. Norton, the distinguished social worker McGregor brought to Detroit to head the Detroit Community Union in 1917 and who served on the McGregor Fund Board of Trustees from 1925 to 1968, shared with me his memories of Tracy McGregor as well as the oral histories he conducted in the 1950s with Murray McGregor, Pliny Marsh, and staff of the McGregor Mission. Trustees Lem Bowen, Douglass Dow, and Elliott Phillips gave their enthusiastic support for a biography of McGregor. Norah M. O'Brien, director of Finance and Administration, provided valuable information on the fund and assisted in locating and reproducing photographs of McGregor and the mission. I owe a special thanks to C. David Campbell, president of the McGregor Fund, for his continuous support for the biography, his many helpful suggestions that have greatly improved the manuscript, and especially his understanding of the need for careful research to produce a definitive book.

As explained in the introduction, I owe special thanks to Mildred White, assistant to Tracy McGregor from 1934 until his death, and subsequently executive secretary of the McGregor Fund until she retired in 1973. She recognized the need to collect and preserve the official and personal family papers of McGregor before they were lost and to make sure that a biography of McGregor would be completed. She expressed her hope that I would someday undertake such a project, and to that end she gave to Wayne State University the voluminous collection of McGregor family papers that she had accumulated.

Several colleagues and friends gave advice and helpful suggestions on the contents and scope of the biography—especially the late John Fraser, first and longtime director of the McGregor Memorial Conference Center; Father James C. Wolf, OFM/Cap, archivist at the St. Bonaventure Capuchin Monastery in Detroit; Paul Ganson, historian of the Detroit Symphony Orchestra; David Miller of the Ruth Mott Foundation; and the late Alma H. Young, dean of the College of Labor, Urban, and Metropolitan Affairs at Wayne State University.

I greatly benefited from the advice and scholarly insights of several colleagues who read earlier drafts of the manuscript, including historians Norman McRae, Arthur Woodford, JoEllen Vinyard, John Dann, and C. David Campbell; Peter Thurber of the McGregor Fund also made helpful suggestions on the manuscript.

To Jeffrey Abt, associate professor of art and art history and a member of the editorial board of the Wayne State University Press, I owe a special debt of gratitude. His careful review of the manuscript and his recommendations to emphasize in more detail McGregor's role in the political, cultural, and philanthropic life in Detroit helped me change the focus of the manuscript in a meaningful way.

Kathryn Wildfong, acquisitions editor of the Wayne State University Press, has been most helpful with her many suggestions for improving the manuscript.

I was fortunate to have the continuous and indispensable assistance of Alberta Asmar during the several years of research and writing. She helped locate relevant archival and photographic sources, and she spent countless hours in typing the several drafts of the manuscript.

And, finally, my profound gratitude to my wife, Marcia, my "editor in chief." She was involved in every stage of the biography; she shared her skills as an editor to provide invaluable insights and suggestions. My heartfelt thanks.

Tracy McGregor examining one of his rare books, ca. 1932. Courtesy McGregor Fund.

TRACY W. McGREGOR

INTRODUCTION

TRACY W. MCGREGOR PLAYED a vital role in one of Detroit's most critical periods, from the time it emerged as one of the nation's leading urban, industrial centers in the 1890s until it arose as the world's leader in automobile manufacturing in the 1920s.

By 1910, McGregor was recognized as one of Detroit's major charitable contributors. He operated a successful Mission for Homeless Men, was a trustee of the Associated Charities of Detroit, and later led the campaign for the new Detroit Community Union. In 1925 he established the McGregor Fund of Michigan, one of the state's first major charitable foundations.

Tracy had also become one of Detroit's most influential civic leaders and, under the auspices of the Thursday Noon Group, which consisted of the city's top business, cultural, and community leaders, helped reshape public policy relating to elections, housing, mental health, the court system, and improvement in the infrastructure of the metropolitan area.

McGregor's leadership of the Mission for Homeless Men made him acutely aware of the need to work through the political organizations of the city in order to accomplish his goals. In the early 1900s he joined Joseph L. Hudson, founder of the Detroit Municipal League, to reform Detroit's election system and to campaign for prohibition. In 1904, with the aid of Hudson, Dexter M. Ferry Jr., James Ingles, and other community leaders, he founded and financed the Provident Loan and Savings Society to fight the usurious loan rates inflicted on Detroit's working class. He actively supported Henry Leland's Detroit Citizens League and organized a group of public officials to establish public housing in Detroit. The reforms championed by McGregor significantly improved the city's political, educational, and legal systems as well as its citizens' quality of life.

Despite the satisfaction McGregor enjoyed from the reforms he championed, it was his work with the Mission for Homeless Men, renamed the McGregor Institute in 1911, that remained the central focus of his life. At the age of twenty-one, following the sudden death of his father, Thomas, Tracy took over the reins of the new mission and almost single-handedly turned it into one of the most prominent missions of its kind in the nation. For forty-five years, until it closed during the Great Depression, the mission served more than seven hundred thousand men.

After 1901, following his marriage to Katherine Whitney, one of Detroit's wealthiest heiresses, he was able to expand his influence in the community and charitable life of Detroit. His sudden wealth enhanced his acceptance by Detroit business and community leaders and enabled the McGregors to become leaders in the charitable activities of Detroit; yet they differed from major Detroit philanthropists in that they not only gave significant grants to Detroit's major charities but also actively participated in the daily work of these charities. Before making a financial commitment, Tracy and Katherine visited the charities, reviewed their plans and mission statements, and gave their donation in installments, which facilitated a regular involvement in the work of the organizations. For example, when Katherine established an orphanage in Highland Park in 1904, she not only financed its operation but also spent several days a week, often accompanied by Tracy, at the orphanage to assist in supervising the children.

Tracy's active leadership of the Associated Charities of Detroit mirrored this approach. He visited the various affiliated charities, reviewed their administrative and financial operations, and gave generously to the charities. In 1917 he chaired the commission to reorganize the Detroit charitable movement, which led to the establishment of the Detroit Community Union and the Detroit Patriotic Fund. McGregor helped select William J. Norton as director of the Detroit Community Union, and the organization heralded a new approach to federated giving.

In 1925 Tracy and Katherine decided to establish the McGregor Fund to carry on their charitable work, with the specific objective "to relieve the misfortunes and promote the well-being of mankind." Tracy selected several trusted colleagues, including William J. Norton, Frank Sladen, Kirby White, and Henry S. Hulbert, to serve with him on its board of trustees. He and Katherine provided several million dollars to underwrite its funding priorities. At the time of his death in 1936, he was widely known as Detroit's premier philanthropist.

McGregor's interest in the cultural life of the community was another important focus for him. He always regretted that he had had to leave Oberlin before completing his degree in history, the classics, and music, but even after the long hours and rigorous demands at the mission, he took time to study history and pursue his love of music. When he planned the new facilities for the mission, especially the structure on Brush Street, he included a large library and reading room for the mission men. All of the evening chapel sessions included musical performances, and at the weekly meetings of the Mission Brotherhood and other mission clubs, speakers were invited to discuss the cultural life of Detroit. Tracy and Katherine also gave generously to the Detroit Symphony Orchestra and other cultural organizations.

In 1918, following the death of Lizzie Palmer, the wealthy widow of Senator Thomas Palmer, McGregor was appointed by the Wayne County Circuit Court to serve on a commission to establish a special training program for young women. After his appointment as president of the Merrill-Palmer Institute, a position he held from 1918 until 1936, he worked closely with its director, Edna Noble White, to establish one of the most prestigious educational institutions in the United States.

The McGregors also had a special interest in the public libraries in the Detroit area. In 1918 they gave to the city of Highland Park the Stevens's homestead, formerly the site of the McGregor orphanage, which would become the impressive McGregor Public Library.

The McGregors loved books, especially those on literature and history, and had accumulated a small collection of rare editions. But in 1925, Tracy began to develop a more extensive collection of Americana, and with the assistance of Randolph Adams, director of the Clements Library, and collectors such as Lathrop Harper of New York, he brought together in eleven years one of the finest rare Americana collections in the United States. He derived a great deal of personal pleasure in building up the library, but his long-range plan was to place his library in a university not associated with a major research center, where it could be used by young students to enrich their understanding of American history. He tentatively selected the University of Virginia, where he planned to move and administer the library, but his sudden death in May 1936 interrupted these plans.

McGregor formulated another innovative initiative to encourage colleges and universities to develop their own rare Americana collections. With the sponsorship of the American Historical Association, he provided funds for annual matching grants to a selected group of about thirty colleges and universities.

McGregor's close association with Randolph Adams, director of the Clements Library, resulted in his appointment in 1933 to the prestigious Committee of Management of the library. This decision proved fortuitous for the library, because its founder, William Clements, had lost his fortune in the stock market crash of 1929 and had decided to sell his personal collection of papers. McGregor interceded in the delicate negotiations, persuaded the Clements family to reduce their price, and authorized the McGregor Fund trustees to give the university more than $100,000 for the collection. With McGregor's inspired leadership, the Clements Library was able to acquire some of the most important research collections, including the papers of Sir Henry Clinton, Governor George Clinton, Lord George Germaine, and Generals Nathaniel Greene and Thomas Gage.

Given Tracy McGregor's remarkable accomplishments in shaping Detroit's political, philanthropic, charitable, and cultural history, it is surprising that so little is known about him today. This was the problem I faced when I first learned about Tracy and Katherine McGregor. In 1958, shortly after my appointment at Wayne State University as archivist and professor of history, I attended the dedication of the Tracy and Katherine McGregor Memorial Conference Center. Built by the world-renowned architect Minoru Yamasaki, the conference center was the most striking and beautiful building on the campus, a distinction it still enjoys fifty years later.

Within days of the dedication, the archives received a steady stream of inquiries from community leaders, faculty, and students requesting information about Tracy and Katherine McGregor. Interest in this couple has continued to this day, prompted by visits to the center by thousands who have been impressed by the beauty of its sculpture court and the exterior and interior of the memorial building.

These inquiries prompted me to learn more about Tracy and Katherine Whitney McGregor. I found the Whitney family relatively easy to study. David Whitney Jr., Katherine's father, was one of Michigan's most prominent and successful business leaders, a pioneer in lumbering, shipping, and real estate. The accounts of his successful career appeared in the Detroit press and other local publications. Carolyn Patch's biography of another of his daughters, Grace Whitney, *The Story of an Abundant Life*, provides valuable family information about Grace's humanitarian endeavors in France following World War I.

However, information about David Whitney's youngest daughter, Katherine, is scarce. Despite her great contributions to scores of charitable institutions, including the McGregor Fund, little is available in print about her humanitarian interests and accomplishments. Several Detroit newspapers featured stories about her shortly after her marriage to Tracy McGregor in 1901, but little else is available. The reasons for this absence are understandable. She carefully guarded her privacy and refused interviews with journalists and other writers. Even before her marriage, she avoided any involvement in the local social scene to which her wealth and family status entitled her or, indeed, that was expected of her. Katherine was also extremely shy about photographs or other likenesses of herself. Only one clear photograph of her has been preserved, taken about 1901. Following her husband's death in 1936, she systematically destroyed all other existing photographs as well as her personal papers.

Tracy McGregor also preferred anonymity and avoided, whenever possible, newspaper interviews and any personal accounts of his life. His active role as superintendent, and later managing director, of the McGregor Mission for Homeless Men and the recognition and accomplishments of this institution inevitably brought his name before the public. The important positions he held as the leader of the Thursday Noon Group, as president of the Merrill-Palmer Institute, as one of the officers of the Associated Charities of Detroit, and as the founder of the Detroit Community Union and the Detroit Community Fund were given broad coverage in the local press as well as in the numerous business and community magazines. Tracy McGregor also received limited attention in various books about Detroit, written for the most part by local journalists.

Few academic historians have devoted attention to Detroit's history, except for those writing during the more recent decades of the twentieth century. Silas Farmer's comprehensive *History of Detroit* was published in the 1880s before the McGregor family moved to Michigan. Melvin Holli's distinguished studies of the political history of Detroit, especially the biography of Mayor Hazen Pingree, do not address the social and philanthropic areas in which McGregor was active. Neither Frank and Arthur Woodford's *All Our Yesterdays: A Brief History of Detroit* nor Sidney Glazier's *Detroit: A Study in Urban Development* gives attention to McGregor and his accomplishments, due to their broad scope. Oliver Zunz's *The Changing Face of Inequality: Urbanization, Industrial Development, and Immigrants in Detroit, 1880–1920* does devote considerable attention to the political, demographic, and social developments of Detroit that surround the McGregor years. Shirley and Norman McRae's *Detroit: The First City of the Midwest* also covers the work of the McGregors' Helping Hand Mission, and especially the critical role of the Thursday Noon Group, in spearheading a variety of civic endeavors. Sidney Fine's monumental biography of Frank Murphy was an invaluable resource in understanding the decades of the twentieth century during which McGregor was active in civic and charitable affairs.

The most comprehensive account of Tracy McGregor was written by Henry S. Hulburt, his close friend and a trustee of the McGregor Fund, on the occasion of the dedication of the McGregor Library of Americana at the University of Virginia in 1939. Another colleague, William J. Norton, provided a touching reminiscence of McGregor following his death in 1936. W. C. Richard's lengthy biographical essay, which appeared in *Detroiter* magazine in May 1928, provides the best information on his family and their early life in Ohio and the program of the Mission for Homeless Men. William Lovett's *Detroit Finds Itself* and James J. Ingles's *A Sketch of My Life* give the best account of the work of the Detroit Civic League and the Thursday Noon Group and their critical role in reforming the political and judicial systems of Detroit. The annual reports of the various organizations and charitable groups with which McGregor was associated in a leadership role or as a major financial contributor also contain valuable information about his accomplishments and influence. The minutes of the board of trustees of the McGregor Fund, which was established in 1925, describe in great detail the philosophy and priorities that governed McGregor's life.

Several archival collections proved to be valuable research sources on Tracy McGregor. The Burton Historical Collection of the Detroit Public Library, which is the official depository for the public records of the city of Detroit as well as the personal papers of hundreds of Detroit political, business, and community leaders, contains a number of collections relating to McGregor or the organizations with which he was associated. The voluminous files of the Detroit Civic League, which led the campaign for reform of Detroit's political system, contain information on McGregor's important leadership role as well as his financial support of the league. The Bentley Library at the University of Michigan has a number of relevant collections, especially the papers of William J. Norton, relating to his work as head of the Detroit Community Union and as a trustee of the McGregor Fund from 1925 to 1968, and later the Children's Fund of Michigan. The William Clements Library of the University of Michigan holds the papers of several colleagues of McGregor, including those of Dr. Randolph Adams, the director of the library from 1925 to 1951. Adams was McGregor's mentor in the development of his magnificent Americana collection. McGregor's role as a major financial benefactor to the University of Michigan, as well as the critical role he played in acquiring several major manuscript collections for the Clements Library, is reflected in this collection.

The Archives of Labor and Urban Affairs at Wayne State University acquired several major collections documenting the activities of McGregor, including the official files of the Associated Charities of Detroit, dating back to 1870, and its successor agencies: the Detroit Community Union, the Detroit Community Fund, the United Community Services, and the United Way of Detroit. The Merrill-Palmer Institute Collection contains valuable material relating to McGregor, who served as its president from its founding in 1918 until his death in 1936. McGregor's plan to encourage and subsidize colleges to establish rare book collections is covered in detail in the records of the American Historical Association Collection in the Library of Congress.

These sources, both printed and archival, were extremely important in my initial research on the life and times of Tracy and Katherine McGregor. They shed light on this amazing team of philanthropists as well as provided a general idea of their activities in support of local charities and national social movements. But despite the valuable information they provided, the sources also raised a number of questions about the McGregors, which identified areas that required further research. For example, what role did both Katherine's and Tracy's families have in nurturing their humanitarian interests? What role did Tracy's sudden wealth, resulting from his marriage to Katherine Whitney in 1901, have on the influential position he soon gained in the Detroit community, and in what ways did he use his financial resources to aid the destitute and needy? What role did the Mission for Homeless Men, later called the McGregor Institute, have in helping Detroit's homeless and transient men? How did McGregor go about reorganizing the Associated Charities of Detroit into one of the nation's leading urban social welfare agencies? How did McGregor, in fewer than ten years, develop one of the most important collections of Americana in the United States? The existing sources do not fully answer these questions, nor do they address in sufficient detail the important contributions of Tracy and Katherine McGregor.

In my own research I discovered the answers to many of these compelling questions about the McGregors when I developed friendships with William J. Norton, Lem W. Bowen, Douglass Dow, and Paul T. Rankin, all of whom served as members of the board of trustees of the McGregor Fund and had known Tracy McGregor. I also met Mildred White, who joined the staff of the McGregor Fund in 1934 and served as its executive secretary until her retirement in 1973. Following McGregor's death in 1936, Mildred carefully collected and preserved all of Tracy McGregor's personal papers located in his Washington, D.C., and Detroit offices. From Murray McGregor, Tracy's younger brother, she acquired the early family papers as well as the official files of the McGregor Institute. She contacted McGregor's high school friends and asked for their written reminiscences. The orphans who lived at the McGregor orphanage in Highland Park were asked to describe the impact that Tracy and Katherine McGregor had upon their lives. Not satisfied with just collecting material on the McGregors, White spearheaded a plan for a biography of Tracy McGregor. With the assistance of William J. Norton, who was then president of the McGregor Fund, she persuaded the trustees to undertake an oral history project, which would include persons who knew and worked with Tracy McGregor.

My association with Mildred White gave me a unique opportunity to learn more about the McGregors and to fill in many of the gaps missing from the meager written accounts. It also gave me an opportunity to persuade her that the voluminous files that she had collected should be placed in an established archive where they could be preserved according to archival standards and made available to qualified researchers. Mildred was receptive to this proposal. She recognized the historical value of the collection she had put together, not only as it related to the McGregors but also how it shed light on Detroit and its history. She was motivated also by her concern that, after her retirement, the staff of the McGregor Fund and some of the trustees who had never known Tracy McGregor might not recognize its value or give the collection its proper care and might even authorize its destruction.

The McGregor Collection consisted of about fifteen cartons of records generally arranged by subject. The papers covered such topics as the McGregor family and its early history and the Toledo Helping Hand Mission, the forerunner of a similar institution in Detroit, which later became the McGregor Institute. The mission records were extensive, including detailed financial accounts, reports, newsletters, information on the chapel services and women's workshops, and biographical data on scores of the men who lived there between 1891 and 1935.

The files that Mildred White preserved and collected contain valuable information about the formation of the Provident Loan and Savings Society and the important activities of the Thursday Noon Group, both of which I discuss at length in this volume.

The collection also covers in detail McGregor's role as president of the Merrill-Palmer Institute, the Associated Charities of Detroit, the Detroit Community Union, and the Detroit Community Fund. In addition, McGregor's business activities are documented, including his leading role in the Whitney Realty Company and the Warren Farms and La Salle subdivisions.

For the last decade of his life, McGregor devoted most of his attention to two projects—the development of a plan for the McGregor Fund and the collection of rare books on Americana. Despite failing health and his concern about Katherine's mental condition, he found solace in these two enterprises. The records make clear that he was successful in reaching both goals.

The McGregor archival collection, unfortunately, contains only limited information on Katherine Whitney McGregor. It does reveal her early interest in helping the needy and the destitute of Detroit. The information relating to her charitable contributions is readily available in the financial records, which her husband maintained, but little is known about her personal life and interests. She had occasional contacts with other members of her family, but she appears to have been closer to Tracy's brother, Murray McGregor. She avoided public meetings, receptions, and other community affairs even when Tracy McGregor was the guest of honor.

Tracy McGregor, conversely, was a true collector and to some degree a pack rat. He kept meticulous records of all of his activities from his youth to a few days before his death. His diaries and journals contain details of his daily activities, including frequent introspective accounts of his concerns and doubts and periods of depression. Of special interest also are copies of the sermons he delivered at the nightly mission chapel meetings. They reveal his deep Christian faith, which influenced his whole life, and show how these values dominated his work on behalf of numerous community and charitable organizations. The McGregor papers also make clear his style of philanthropy. He did not establish the McGregor Fund to avoid the pressures of responding to the hundreds of organizations, churches, charitable groups, and individuals who came to him for financial assistance. On the contrary, even after the fund was established in 1925, Tracy and Katherine responded generously to such requests. As noted earlier, their procedure for evaluating requests from charities differed from other philanthropists. Tracy and Katherine always carefully investigated the work of a charitable institution before giving financial aid, and once they approved, they visited that agency to determine if the funds were being properly spent. They set the model for "participating philanthropy."

After reviewing the archival collection, as well as the limited number of publications that described the spiritual, philanthropic, and civic contributions made by Tracy and Katherine Whitney McGregor, I realized that a lengthy and comprehensive account of their lives was long overdue. The McGregor Memorial Conference Center on the campus of Wayne State University in Detroit, Michigan, and the McGregor Library of Americana at the University of Virginia are both fitting testimonials to the works of these two remarkable citizens. But the McGregors also chose to share their wealth through charitable gifts and civic crusades that made lasting contributions to Detroit during the vital era when it was emerging from a growing town to a major urban metropolis. They made a difference in the character of the city and should be recognized appropriately.

PART I

The McGregor Family

1

The McGregor Family and Mission

TRACY MCGREGOR'S ANCESTORS first settled in the United States in 1830 when John M. McGregor, a Presbyterian minister, migrated from Perthshire, Scotland, to St. Lawrence County in upstate New York. Here he found a large settlement of Scottish families, mostly farmers who had been attracted to the rich agricultural land of the area. Within a few years of his arrival, the Reverend McGregor established parishes in several of the surrounding communities, including Hammond, Oxbow, and Rossie, New York. Few records have survived relating to his work in the church, except for a brief statement in an early history of Oxbow, which called attention to his "stately form and dignified demeanor."[1]

Although he was a respected and influential minister, life was not easy for the Reverend McGregor and his family. His modest salary barely accommodated a family of six children. He supplemented his meager income by purchasing a farm in Oxbow, which provided food and additional financial support.[2]

The youngest of John's children, Thomas, was born on December 23, 1840, in Oxbow. Thomas attended local public schools and spent his spare time working on the family farm. In March 1864 he married Elizabeth Taitt, the daughter of a prosperous neighboring farmer, James Taitt. After spending two years in the Oxbow area, Thomas and Elizabeth decided to move west to start a new life. They contacted friends who had preceded them westward and selected Berlin Heights, a small village near Sandusky, Ohio, for their new home. In the coming years they had three children—Tracy, born in 1869, Murray, in 1879, and Ruth, in 1881.[3]

Thomas, no longer interested in farming, took a job in a local music store specializing in pianos, organs, and sheet music—a decision that proved to be a wise choice. He enjoyed meeting and talking to people and relished the challenge of convincing them that they needed music in their homes. His business partner, W. J. Perman, later reflected on Thomas's successful approach to their business: "His energy was something wonderful. . . . I have known him to close up seven sales in one day."[4]

Thomas's success as a salesman, however, did not fully satisfy him. He loved music and was proud of his accomplishments in the business world, but he found something "missing in his life." He confided to a friend that he had "come to believe that God had special work for me" and that it was not the business of selling pianos and organs. He later recalled, "This belief grew in intensity and power as the years went by."[5]

His change of heart took place after he reached the age of forty. Although he had been brought up in a deeply religious setting and was active in church affairs, it took some years after settling in Ohio before he "converted to Christianity." Prior to the conversion, however, Thomas had already developed a "deep sympathy for all underprivileged beings, both people and animals." Thomas's son Murray later recalled an early childhood experience when his father took him and his young sister Ruth "on Christmas Day to one of the poorest sections of Toledo . . . insisting we divide our Christmas candy with those whom Christmas had passed by." Murray also remembered instances where his father was "approached on the streets by begging men with whom he would stop and talk." He also brought young waifs home "and kept them until he could contact their parents."[6] On another occasion a policeman observed Thomas "kneeling at the door of a home. This occurred several times, until thinking he was ill, I spoke to him. 'My good man, you are not well. May I take you home?' Thomas replied, 'No thank you, I am all right. I was so burdened for the souls of some of my friends that I could not sleep and must get up and come to their homes to pray for them.'"[7]

According to Murray, his father's conversion to Christianity had led to a "mental conflict between his conviction that he must devote himself entirely to the service of the unfortunate men and the financial need to continue a business career."[8] Thomas agonized over this dilemma for several years. In 1887 he made his decision and announced to a surprised business colleague as they were returning home from delivering a piano in Port Clinton, Ohio, "I have decided to give up the piano business and serve the Lord."[9] He explained further, "I want to start a mission for the unfortunate in Toledo, and if only I can talk to the men I can win them for Christ."[10] His wife and their children reacted with shock at his decision to suddenly quit his job, especially as the family had no other source of income and little in savings. Nevertheless, they accepted Thomas's explanation that "the Lord would take care of them."[11] Murray later said, "It was only through a courageous faith in God that finally he gave up selling pianos and organs and, without visible means for the support of his family, turned to the new Calling."[12] Fortunately, Thomas also received support from his many friends at the Washington Street Congregational Church in Toledo, where the family had a membership and where he and Elizabeth had served as trustee and deaconess, respectively, for nearly a decade.

Finally, in November 1888, Thomas founded the Bethany Mission in a downtown Toledo building called the "Wigwam." On Sunday, "two hundred young scholars" attended Bible classes at the mission. During weeknights the mission was used "for meetings of wild boys and young men."[13] The success of the mission pleased not only Thomas and Elizabeth but also the leaders of many local churches who did not have the facilities to meet the needs of this segment of Toledo's young population, which mostly numbered among the lower economic class.

Thomas created four separate units of operation to handle the work of the mission. The first supervised the meals, the lodging, and the washing and fumigation of clothes. The second unit was described as "a Christian home for those who are converted, who feel the need of good influences to help them in the path of life after they are converted." The third unit operated a Bible school "where they are taught the word of God," and the fourth was responsible for finding work for the mission men. Another feature unique to the Toledo mission, and also later adopted in Detroit, involved the staffing of the mission. Thomas believed strongly that "nearly all of the work is done by men who have come out of the gutter of crime and drunkenness themselves."[14]

The Bethany Mission was well received in the Toledo community, but the McGregors soon became aware that its size could not accommodate their plans to provide living facilities for the growing population of young men who were coming by the hundreds from Europe, from the mining region of northern Michigan, and from rural areas of the Midwest in search of jobs in the factories of Toledo. The sudden rise in the population, along with the severe "boom and bust" economic cycles that were striking the industrial centers of

America, periodically left Toledo with thousands of unemployed and destitute men without food or housing.

During the winter of 1889, McGregor responded promptly to the crisis. He began to look for new facilities that would not only accommodate the mission schools but also provide housing for the homeless. He found a suitable building available for lease on St. Clair Street in Toledo. After limited renovations, it opened in February 1889 as the Toledo Helping Hand Mission, which provided free lodging and meals for any man who sought assistance.[15] During the first eight months of operation, the Helping Hand Mission achieved an impressive record. It served thirty-nine thousand meals, provided lodging for 15,574 men, and held two mandatory gospel services each day for all lodgers. Of the twenty-three thousand persons present at these services during the same eight-month period, Thomas reported that 2,492 individual prayers were offered and 3,721 testimonials given.[16]

As founder and superintendent of the Helping Hand Mission, McGregor not only managed the mission and its various programs but also had to raise the necessary funds for food, equipment, supplies, and other support to keep it running. This involved daily solicitations for food, clothing, and other items needed at the mission from business, community, and church leaders as well as from local restaurants, hotels, and retail operations. He raised $2,309.58 from such sources and an additional $429 from lodgers who had found jobs and paid for their meals and sleeping accommodations during the first eight months. The McGregor family's meager savings provided the remainder of the needed funds to keep the mission in operation.[17]

Despite the impressive achievements of its first few months, the mission had its local detractors from "almost all classes both in the Church and out of it."[18] Some church leaders argued that the Helping Hand Mission was not equipped to provide sound Christian lessons and that the lay ministers at the mission lacked the appropriate training as spiritual leaders.[19] Business leaders opposed the mission on the grounds that free meals and lodging only encouraged "idleness and bad habits."[20] The press added their negative assessment of the mission, suggesting that it was a "haven for criminals and a resort of thieves" and that "it was held in ill-repute by the police officials and ministers of the city."[21] McGregor responded to his critics promptly and forcefully. He met with them, challenged their negative assessments, and requested that they visit the mission to examine firsthand its programs. Church leaders were invited to attend and participate in the gospel services.

Others voiced support of McGregor's efforts. In one letter to the editor in the *Toledo Commercial* early in 1889, when the mission was only a few months old, an irate resident, familiar with the work of the Helping Hand Mission, challenged the critics. He charged that the dissenters "never saw the inside of the Mission" and were guilty of "willfully misrepresenting a noble enterprise." The writer observed that the "Helping Hand Mission is for the poor; it is for the wretched; it is for the degraded; it is for the outcast; it is, yes, it is for the unworthy." He continued, "It takes in everyone who is needy. It gives him a meal and a night's lodging. It asks him no questions. Will a man listen to a lecture on morality and religion when he is starving?" The writer concluded his argument with the plea that "the malingerers of the Mission should investigate the real methods before criticizing one of the noblest charities ever organized."[22]

The second annual meeting of the mission held at the First Congregational Church in the spring of 1891 witnessed more positive accounts of its programs and work. Distinguished social worker H. H. Hadley, the director of the St. Bartholomew's Rescue Mission in New York City and the featured speaker, applauded McGregor for "doing the greatest work of any man in the country in conducting helping hand missions" and said McGregor "had accomplished more good, relieved more misery and suffering with the limited means at his disposal, than any two like institutions in the country." The pastors of the First Congregational and Central Congregational churches of Toledo also commended McGregor for his work.[23]

The strong support from these local churches as well as the praise from Hadley meant a great deal to Thomas and his wife. Despite the difficulties they faced in operating the Bethany and Helping Hand missions and the criticism of this work from some segments of the Toledo community, they were not discouraged. In fact, Thomas considered the mission so successful and the work so rewarding that he decided to establish a series of such missions for the homeless in other Great Lakes cities. In the summer of 1890 he visited Buffalo and met with community and church leaders to determine the need for and feasibility of opening a mission there. Although he found hundreds of homeless and destitute on the streets of Buffalo, he decided that the time was not ripe for such a venture.[24]

Thomas's next choice was Detroit, some fifty miles north of Toledo and already a major industrial center. Here, in November 1890, he followed the same approach as in Buffalo. He met with community leaders and the heads of several charitable institutions and discussed with them his plans for a mission in Detroit. While in Detroit he also witnessed the hundreds of unemployed and destitute young men living on the streets and in the alleys of the downtown business district. Without adequate clothing and food, and with winter approaching, Thomas was acutely aware of the need for a proper facility for these men.[25] During his brief visit he was invited to address several religious meetings and talk about his experiences in Toledo. He made a very favorable impression not only among the church parishioners but also among the clergy. "There was about him the air of one who had a mission and a tone of certainty that God would [support] such an objective. . . . Here was a man," they observed, "who was forgetting himself [and] who was aflame with desire for others."[26]

The visit convinced Thomas that Detroit was the ideal site for his next mission and that he must act at once. He located a vacant three-story building at 69 East Larned Street, near Cadillac Square in the center of the downtown business district. The structure was twice the size of the Toledo Helping Hand Mission, measuring sixty by forty feet, with fourteen-foot ceilings. He signed a fifteen-year lease and secured the agreement with a five-hundred-dollar down payment for five months, at the rate of one hundred dollars per month. He reported later that he depended upon the generosity of several "dear Christian brothers" for the payment and was deeply moved by a local "Christian lady who gave me $50 without even being asked." This supportive response only reinforced his decision to select Detroit as the site of his second homeless mission.[27]

Within hours of the lease signing, Thomas started work on the renovation of the Larned Street facility. Even though the building had once been used for lodging, it required major repairs before it would meet new city building standards. All of the walls had to be stripped and repapered, new stairways constructed, plumbing and heating systems installed, kitchen and bathroom facilities rebuilt, and the structure repainted inside and out. Also included in Thomas's new design was a chapel large enough to seat four hundred persons, a reading room, staff offices, and a special living section for men who could pay for their room and board. A special facility and equipment for fumigating clothes was also essential, especially as so many of Detroit's destitute had been sleeping in vermin-infested alleyways and deserted buildings in the city.[28]

The recruitment of experienced workers for the new mission was accomplished overnight. As soon as the news spread on the streets of downtown

Detroit that a Mission for Homeless Men was being established nearby, scores of young men rushed to the site to offer their services. They brought their skills as artisans and craftsmen, and, with encouragement from Thomas, they offered their services as painters, carpenters, paperhangers, steamfitters, and mechanics. Even those without skills were recruited for routine jobs such as carrying trash from the building and transporting the gifts of supplies and food staples from Detroit merchants. In return for their work in renovating the building, they were allowed to camp inside the building, usually with only straw and newspapers as beds.[29]

Finding the needed equipment, supplies, and other building materials to renovate the mission building presented a serious challenge to McGregor. With limited financial resources, he had to rely on donations from local merchants, and daily visits to the stores and homes of merchants were required to curry favor and plead his case. To some he stressed the "Christian" need to aid the homeless and needy; to others he argued that the mission would keep destitute beggars off the streets and from bothering customers and shoppers. Whatever the arguments he may have encountered, and due in large part to Thomas's sincere personality, his efforts met with eventual success. Several hardware stores gave him carpenter's tools and nails, a local mill provided a gift of lumber and firewood, and other local firms donated paint and wallpaper.[30]

A more critical problem faced by McGregor was heating the building while it was under construction. The Detroit winter of 1890–91 was particularly harsh, with several heavy snowfalls and days of frigid cold. Before the furnace was purchased and installed in March 1891, the building was on some days so cold that the men had difficulty working. They couldn't hold the cold metal tools, and on some nights, even with the small stoves placed on each floor, the men had great difficulty sleeping. Some of the workers later recalled that they had "to move about constantly in order to keep warm."[31]

Providing meals for the men also proved daunting. Because there were no funds for food, Thomas had to depend on donations from local stores, restaurants, and hotels. Often the gifts were barely edible. The first supply of bread given to the mission by a local bakery was so hard that it could not be cut with knives—it had to be chopped up with an ax. Soup, usually the main fare of lunch and dinner, left much to be desired. One of the men later remarked that "if you were to spill it on the finest silk dress you ever saw, it would not soil it any more than water or starch." But, he added, "it was warm enough to combat the cold of the building."[32]

On some winter days, however, even the bread and the necessary ingredients for soup were not available, and the men went without a meal. On these days, work on the building was delayed due to the lack of sustenance. "When we went to bed at night—one hundred and fifty of us," one worker later observed, "there wasn't a nickel in the Mission and not enough food to bait a mouse trap." He continued, "along about eight o'clock in the morning, a man came in and asked about the condition of things. Mr. McGregor told him, 'Well never mind boys, we will see what the Lord will do for us.' Shortly thereafter, a local merchant brought in an armful of bread which we divided up."

McGregor fully understood what the men were going through. He not only spent hours each day in the building but also ate many meals with them. On many occasions, when there was insufficient food, Thomas told the men he "wasn't hungry." "I have seen the tears fall from Mr. McGregor's eyes many a time because we were not more comfortable," one of his colleagues later recalled.[33]

During this food shortage, McGregor daily walked the streets of downtown Detroit visiting merchants and requesting their assistance. One of his colleagues who often accompanied him on these trips described his approach.[34] "He would simply sit down and tell them what he was doing, and they would ask him 'What is it you need?' and they would give him something. Even when his pleas were turned down he would not become discouraged."[35] On one occasion, when a merchant abruptly told him, "I can't be bothered with hearing you," McGregor responded, "I only want to tell you what I am doing, I don't ask for a cent of money." Before he left the store he was given what he needed.[36]

Thomas's long days continued after the work ended and dinner was completed. At seven o'clock each evening he conducted a chapel meeting. On the day he opened the doors of the mission in December 1890, he conducted a chapel service for twenty of the men. During the week after the first service, "twenty men testified and prayed" and announced their "conversion to Christianity." As more and more of the men began to attend the daily chapel services and listen attentively to his sermons, Thomas remarked to a close friend, "My preaching has more impact on hungry men."[37]

The renovation proceeded slowly during those winter months, but the slowdown did not discourage Thomas. At one of the chapel meetings in March 1891 he told the men about a dream he had the preceding night. He described himself standing on a hill and seeing men marching four abreast, then fifty abreast, and then he heard a voice. "These are the men who have been saved through the instrumentality of the Mission."[38] When men in the meeting asked him about the shortage of funds and food, he replied, "When God gets me where he can trust me, I'll have money a foot deep."[39]

The efforts of the Detroit mission would have been enough for most men, but Thomas had other responsibilities as well. He continued to handle the operation of the Helping Hand Mission in Toledo, which he had opened in 1889. In his absence, his wife took charge of that program, but frequent crises involving money and personnel often required him to rush back to Toledo after work for an evening meeting and return to Detroit early the following morning in time to supervise the renovation of the mission.[40]

Thomas's schedule also had an impact on his family life. He and Elizabeth and their three children—Tracy, a student at Oberlin College in 1890, Murray, and Ruth—all assisted at the Helping Hand Mission. Murray often accompanied his father to Detroit to help on the renovation. In reviewing this hectic schedule one might wonder how Thomas maintained such a rigorous pace. Perhaps his sister Kate had the answer when she observed, "If Thomas made up his mind to do something nothing was able to stop him. . . . As a young man," she continued, he was "by nature very generous, very enthusiastic, very energetic and unselfish." These qualities and characteristics were certainly evident when he undertook to build the mission for homeless men in Detroit.[41]

McGregor had planned to formally open the Mission for Homeless Men early in March 1891 but was faced with delays in obtaining needed building materials and kitchen appliances, and the official opening was postponed until April 3. On that day, hundreds arrived to join the workers and residents of the mission in celebrating the official proceedings. Tours of the facility were given, followed by a chapel session in the auditorium.[42]

Unfortunately, after all his hard work and planning, a severe cold and respiratory illness prevented McGregor from participating in the festivities. He was present at the celebration in spirit, however, and those who attended were fully aware of his indispensable role in making the mission a reality. Ironically, his illness had been caused by his commitment to the mission. A week earlier, while supervising the repair of a sewer pipe in front of the mission, he had stood and watched workers struggle with the difficult task. After a few minutes he turned to a colleague and announced, "I will go down and dig awhile with the boys, and it will encourage them and it won't hurt me any. I am used to hard work." He set aside his coat, grabbed a shovel, and jumped into the water-filled trench to help. After several hours in the freezing water he rushed across town to meet with a prospective donor. Tragically, he didn't take time to change into dry clothing, and by early evening he had developed a cough and high fever. He was so weary and sick the following day that he returned to his home in Toledo to recover from his illness. In the days that followed he was attended by several physicians, but their treatments failed to cure him. On April 24, 1891, Thomas died, leaving as his major legacy the Mission for Homeless Men.[43]

Tracy McGregor received word about his father's death while attending classes at Oberlin. Without hesitation, he began packing his belongings and made arrangements to return to Toledo. In response to his roommate's question, "What are you going to do now?" Tracy replied, "I am going home to take up the work left by my father."[44] He returned to Toledo to be with his mother and siblings and to assist the family in handling the funeral arrangements. Within hours of his return to Toledo, Tracy realized the size of the task he faced. At age twenty-two he now had the responsibilities of caring for his family—a mother, a thirteen-year-old brother, and a nine-year-old sister—and, despite very limited financial resources, of operating the Helping Hand Mission in Toledo and the mission in Detroit. With practically no administrative experience, he nonetheless accepted the responsibility immediately.[45]

Although both missions needed attention, McGregor decided that his priority must be given to the mission in Detroit. The Toledo mission had been in operation for two years, and although it continued to face serious financial problems, it was serving several hundred men each week and was becoming more accepted by the community.

Tracy McGregor, of course, had a general idea of his father's plans and was certainly familiar with some of the problems Thomas had faced in the renovation of the Detroit mission building and especially the difficulties in securing financial support. He had spent hours with his parents discussing their work at the Helping Hand and Bethany missions in Toledo, and he had come to Detroit on several occasions to assist his father in the renovation of the facility there. He shared his parents' commitment to helping the homeless and indigent and to facilitating their conversion to Christianity.[46]

It had been obvious to Thomas McGregor that Tracy would step into the breach if necessary. Several months prior to his death, one of Thomas's Detroit friends said to him, "Mr. McGregor, you're getting along very nicely with this work, but it's a new type of work[,] probably nothing just like it in the country. You may not live very long; what's going to happen to your work if you die? You're not training anybody else to carry on?"[47]

Thomas's reply was prompt. "Oh, Tracy will take my place."

Tracy," his friend replied, "but he's only a boy. This is a difficult kind of work. You wouldn't expect him to do it."

"You don't know Tracy!" was Thomas's reply.[48]

In retrospect it is clear that Thomas did have a profound understanding of his son and of his tremendous potential. They always had shared a close relationship and the same deep religious convictions. Tracy's early life had prepared him for the challenges of supervising the mission.

Tracy McGregor was born in Berlin Heights, Ohio, a rural farming area near Sandusky, on April 14, 1869. He attended public schools there, and in 1883, he enrolled in Toledo High School after his family moved to that city. His classmates remembered him as being "austere, but it never prevented him from having a lot of fun . . . drinking and smoking, even cards and dancing being taboo."[49] He was an excellent student and served as historian and valedictorian of his class. According to one of his classmates, he was "always very popular and beyond question the most beloved member of the class."[50] Another classmate remembered his interest in music: he had a "fine baritone voice, sang in a school quartet and at church events."[51]

Harriet Gleason, a close friend and high school sweetheart, described Tracy: "He was well built" and had "thick wavy, dark hair, large expressive eyes, and a full generous mouth." She related "one of the most unforgettable memories of the Tracy McGregor of that period." Harriet, Tracy, Elliott Talmadge, and their friends loved to go skating on the Maumee River, but Harriet was ashamed to wear her old rusty wooden skates in public. Her widowed mother had four young children to raise, and new skates did not fit into the family budget.

On one of their skating dates, Tracy and Harriet, carrying a new skating bag her mother had made, arrived at the river. Tracy, in his typical gentlemanly way, insisted on putting on her skates. When she looked down at her feet, she saw "the most wonderful new skates." He had conspired with her mother to "remove the old skates and put the new ones in my bag."[52]

Outside of high school, the Washington Street Congregational Church was the focal point of Tracy's life. He attended church and evening chapel services regularly, taught Sunday school classes, played the organ, and participated in citywide religious programs.[53] He was "converted to Christianity in 1884" when he was fifteen years old.

In the summer of 1887, after graduation, McGregor attended a two-week "College Students Summer School" in Northfield, Massachusetts. Although the session was brief, it helped him prepare for college and gave him the opportunity to meet and talk to the main instructors, Dr. Henry Drummond, Dwight L. Moody, and Henry Clay Trumble. He was "greatly impressed and deeply moved by this experience," and it reinforced his plans for a career in social service.[54]

While in high school McGregor joined the Toledo Young Men's Christian Association (YMCA) and became interested in its programs to aid young men. Immediately on graduation in the summer of 1886, he accepted a position as assistant secretary there and did such an outstanding job that he soon assumed the responsibilities of acting secretary as well, while the trustees sought a suitable candidate to fill the position. As one observer noted, "This was a heavy task for a boy not long out of high school, and showed the confidence the Board of Trustees had in his ability, judgment and character."[55]

Although challenged by and satisfied with his work at the YMCA, McGregor had always planned to go to college, and soon he made the decision to leave his position at the end of the summer and enroll in Park College in Parksville, Missouri. It isn't clear why he selected this school, but it was probably due to financial limitations. He worked four hours each day waiting tables, which paid for his tuition and board. He later recalled that the meals served were limited: "No butter, little sugar, cake or pie at meals." The only sweets he had came from his mother each week.[56]

Though Park College was affordable, McGregor was not fully satisfied with its educational program. In 1888 he transferred to Oberlin College, which was closer to his home in Toledo and gave him frequent opportunities to visit his family and his friends. He enrolled in the liberal arts curriculum there and took courses in ancient history, rhetoric, Greek, Horace, analytical geometry, trigonometry, and English literature. He also selected courses in the school's Conservatory of Music. He proved to be an outstanding student and attained grades ranging from "good to excellent."[57]

When Tracy left Oberlin and went to Detroit in early May 1891 to carry on his father's work at the mission, he faced a big challenge. Although the mission had formally opened early in April, much work remained. Many of the rooms had not yet been painted, the sewer system required attention, the cellar needed to be cleaned and whitewashed, and piles of rubbish, unusable building materials, and old kitchen equipment were awaiting a trip to the city dump. The lodging areas that housed 100 to 150 men each night also needed attention. Bunks and metal beds, along with sheets, blankets, and pillows, had to be found to replace the piles of newspapers and clothing that had served as mattresses and pillows. Stoves and other kitchen equipment, lamps, tables, chairs, and furniture for the chapel were also at the top of the mission's "want list."[58]

Food for the daily meals was continually in short supply and depended on daily donations from local restaurants, hotels, and grocery stores. After Thomas McGregor's illness in the spring of 1891 and his return to Toledo, the situation rapidly deteriorated. No one on the mission staff had the experience, the energy, or the local contacts to replace Thomas. In fact, when Tracy arrived, a group of the staff urged him to close the mission or transfer it to another local social agency. Without the leadership of Thomas McGregor, whom they admired and respected, even idolized, the staff did not see how the mission could survive. They were less than enthusiastic about Tracy, a twenty-two-year-old college student who did not seem to have the charisma or the leadership qualities of his father.[59]

McGregor's response was prompt and decisive. The mission would not close, nor would it be transferred to another agency. His father had given his life for this mission, and Tracy now saw it as his responsibility to see that it succeeded as a memorial to his father. That night, after resolving the controversy with the staff, he wrote to his mother, who had remained in Toledo running the Helping Hand Mission there. "Pray for me Mama. All is well now and God is with us."[60]

2

Tracy McGregor and Katherine Whitney

THE FIRST DECADE of operation for the Mission for Homeless Men presented continuous challenges to Tracy McGregor.[1] He worked long hours seven days a week, improving its facilities, raising funds for its operation, and marshaling community support for its programs. By 1900 the mission was widely recognized by Detroit business and community leaders and the numerous charitable agencies represented by the Associated Charities of Detroit. McGregor had reason to be pleased with the progress he had made.

A blossoming friendship with Katherine Whitney also gave McGregor cause for a positive outlook on life. Katherine was the youngest daughter of David Whitney Jr., one of the wealthiest men in Michigan. How Tracy and Katherine met and became close friends is unknown, for no letters between them have survived, and he refused to discuss the relationship with anyone, even his mother and brother. Perhaps they met during one of his meetings with her father at Whitney's palatial residence on Woodward Avenue to obtain financial assistance for the mission. He must have made a good impression, for Whitney was generous in his support and thought highly of the young superintendent of the mission.

Katherine's stepmother, Sara, shed some light on the friendship when she confided to a friend that Tracy visited their Woodward Avenue home often, even after her husband had given McGregor money for the mission. "He began to call," she observed, "when there seemed no reason for calling."[2] Mission records reveal also that Katherine often came to the mission with a group from the First Presbyterian Church and volunteered to work on different projects. For at least a year she played the piano and sang at some of the evening religious services. It was during these visits that McGregor discovered how much they shared in common, especially their love of music and interests in charitable activities.

By 1900 Katherine recognized that, as one of Detroit's wealthiest heiresses, she was under constant pressure to become more involved in the social activities in the city—the dances, receptions, and debutante balls. But, increasingly, as she became more active in church and other charitable activities, she realized that she didn't have time for both, "so," she later recalled, "I made my choice, and having at length convinced my family that I was perfectly settled and sincere in my own way of living, I was happy and contented." She credited her father in helping her decide. "He gave me the opportunities to do good."[3]

David Whitney's decision to support his daughter was not out of character. In his roles as a successful businessman and one of Detroit's wealthiest citizens, he had recognized his own obligation to assist the needy and for years had been active in supporting Detroit's charitable organizations and church groups.

Like so many of Detroit's business leaders who had migrated from New England and New York, David Whitney brought with him an ethic of responsibility toward the less fortunate. One of four sons born to Catherine and David Whitney in Westford, Massachusetts, he began his business career as a clerk in a lumber firm in nearby Lowell. It didn't take long for him to master every aspect of the business, and after three years he was rewarded with an appointment as superintendent of the company. In 1857, at twenty-seven years of age, along with his brother Charles, he relocated to Detroit, attracted by the lumbering opportunities in Michigan, which was the national leader in the production of white pine lumber. Huge stands of timber, ideal as building material, covered much of the lower peninsula of Michigan and supplied the housing needs of many cities in the Midwest.

With his extensive knowledge of retail lumber operations, he founded the firm of C. and D. Whitney Jr., later expanded to Whitney, Skilling, and Barnes. The partnership soon became the largest lumber company in the United States, with business extending as far as Pennsylvania, Ohio, and further into the Midwest. The Whitney firm supplied much of the white pine lumber that rebuilt Chicago after its disastrous fire in 1871.

When the partnership dissolved in 1877, Whitney turned his attention to investments in the pinelands of Michigan, Wisconsin, and, later, Oregon.

With the very substantial profits realized from these business ventures, he purchased a number of steam vessels and soon commanded one of the largest fleets on the Great Lakes. Whitney also invested heavily in a number of profitable Detroit business firms.[4]

He then moved into real estate. Even before he became active in this business venture, however, he had purchased a substantial number of prime Detroit buildings and tracts of land. In 1877, under the supervision of the Detroit architect Gordon W. Lloyd, he built a major structure at Woodward and Park streets. Equally well known to generations of Detroiters was the home he built in 1894. Located at Woodward and Canfield avenues, this palatial Romanesque revival-style mansion still stands and has served as the headquarters of the Wayne County Medical Society and the Visiting Nurses Association and, since 1988, has housed a prestigious Detroit restaurant.[5]

David Whitney and Flora Ann McLauchlin married in 1860 and had four children. Grace was born in 1862, followed by David Jr. in 1867, Flora in 1869, and Katherine in 1873. In 1882, when his wife died, David married her sister, Sara Jane McLauchlin.

David was disappointed that his first child was not a boy, but Grace soon became the "apple of her father's eye." At the age of thirteen she was enrolled in Hellmuth College in London, Ontario, near her mother's childhood home. This school was run by the Reverend John Liggett and his sister Ella, who later established the famous Liggett School in Detroit. After three years in the Ontario school, during which she served as "class historian," Grace became concerned about her mother's illness and returned to Detroit to complete her education.[6] In Detroit, with her father's encouragement, Grace soon became actively involved in several Detroit charities.[7]

Katherine, eleven years younger than Grace, followed in her sister's footsteps. She too attended the Liggett School after it had moved to Detroit, and she also took an active part in charitable work. As early as 1890, while she was still in school, Katherine and several of her friends volunteered their services at the Infants Ward Association of the Children's Free Hospital. She also shared her "pin money with unfortunate families" and, later, with financial assistance from her father, supported a number of local charities including several Presbyterian church programs, the Florence Crittenden Mission, and the Phyliss Wheatley Home. Her other special interests included aiding the "mountain whites" of rural Appalachia that had migrated to the Detroit area and the "educational programs of the Negro." In fact, Katherine spent so much time on these endeavors that her father tried to place some restrictions on the hours she devoted to charity. Katherine later recalled that her father insisted that "if her days were given up to charity she must devote her evenings to social pleasures."[8] She tried to abide by her father's entreaties but was unsuccessful. On one occasion, she reported that she was sitting at "the tea table after having spent a wearisome day among the poor when the telephone rang and she was summoned to talk to a Methodist minister in the western part of the city." The minister brusquely announced that a local elderly couple was ill and alone, "without food or fire." As she rushed out, her father stopped her and said, "Why, Katherine you are so tired. I would far rather pay a man to attend to these things than having you wearing yourself out over them." Katherine disagreed and hurried to the family's home, accompanied by a doctor and a nurse. After she "attended to all of the woman's wants" she returned home, exhausted but satisfied.[9]

On one occasion when Tracy commented on Katherine's personal wealth, she responded that it was merely "a trust of funds to be used for the benefit and relief of the less fortunate section of mankind." Revealing how much they shared in common, Tracy replied, "It is an inspiration to me how your heart goes out to the unfortunate."[10]

Although they shared common values, their courtship faced obstacles. McGregor initially would not consider marriage with one of Detroit's wealthiest women because of his modest resources and income. As long as he could not "provide" for her properly, marriage had to be postponed. Katherine, however, was not satisfied and turned to her father for advice. She told him that she was deeply in love with McGregor and wanted to be his wife. Her father, who also held McGregor in high regard, agreed to intercede. He called on McGregor and discussed the future of the mission and McGregor's plans. Whitney's solution was straightforward. He donated an endowment of twenty-five thousand dollars to the mission and gave McGregor a substantial grant of money to travel to Europe to study the problems of the homeless there.[11]

On his return from Europe in 1899, Tracy's friendship with Katherine blossomed further, and they made definite plans for marriage but decided to wait until the new mission building was completed and in operation. Katherine recognized also that her father, who had become seriously ill, needed her constant attention. In the meantime, they kept their marriage plans to themselves. Murray McGregor, Tracy's younger brother, recalled, "Tracy was very quiet about it. . . . I don't believe that Mother knew very much about it."

In fact, Murray first learned of his brother's marriage plans when he opened a telegram by mistake. "It gave the secret away," he remembered, "but he [Tracy] would not talk about it."[12]

After the dedication of the new mission facility in June 1901, Tracy and Katherine announced their wedding plans. She did not want it to take place in Detroit, especially as her father had died on November 28 of the previous year. Neither of them wanted to be in the limelight, which such a local ceremony would have resulted in, and Tracy was still concerned about the publicity regarding the disparity in their personal wealth. The couple chose San Francisco as the site for the wedding, which took place on November 20, 1901, at the First Congregational Church. Katherine was accompanied by her stepmother, Sara Jane Whitney, and joined by her aunt, Mrs. James Smith, a resident of San Francisco. "There were no attendants," the *Detroit News-Tribune* reported, and "the bride was gowned very richly but simply in white satin and carried white orchids. Her gown was trimmed with lace and sprays of orange blossoms and a wreath of the same flowers fastened in her hair." The Reverend Mr. Adams performed the ceremony.[13]

Following the wedding Tracy and Katherine spent several months traveling through California before returning to Detroit. Tracy was exhausted from the pressures of raising funds and building a new mission facility and had needed the rest and relaxation in California. In the spring of 1902, the couple returned to Detroit and resided temporarily in the Whitneys' residence on Woodward Avenue. Within a few months they leased a flat in the Pasadena Apartments on East Jefferson Avenue.[14]

The successes of McGregor's endeavor and the sudden change in his financial status brought even greater pressures on him, however. Now, as one of Detroit's wealthiest men, he was "plagued" with requests for assistance from the leaders of Detroit's churches, charities, and other needy citizens. On some days a constant stream of visitors arrived at his office in the mission to talk about their projects and request financial support from him. His personal involvement in many of Detroit's charitable institutions also took their toll and began to affect his physical and mental health. In his diary entry of May 20, 1907, he confessed, "After years of mission service, I needed leisure to think, to grow and to rest worn nerves. God knew this and through 'K' [Katherine] gave me the opportunity. This, I have been slow to perceive. I fretted at the thought of letting go the aggressive and large work which I considered all-important." Then, with typical humility, he added, "I have been a dull scholar. Now that my eyes are opened I pray that this vision may be preserved."[15] His self-doubts continued to plague him, nonetheless. In one entry he wrote, "Father, help me to retain and to obey the gifts of truth I am prone to forget. I chide the Mission men because they are overcome by drink time after time, yet how often I too fail in other points—impatience, ambition, and selfishness."[16]

In response to the mounting pressures of his work, McGregor traveled often, visiting Chicago, Cincinnati, Washington, D.C., New York, Boston, and other east coast cities. He welcomed these trips because they gave him an opportunity to leave Detroit and visit and study what other communities were doing to aid the poor and unfortunate. During these trips he visited other missions and community organizations and met with their leaders. These excursions not only gave him excellent ideas on how other charitable organizations were run but also confirmed that the Mission for Homeless Men in Detroit was efficiently operated and served more needy men than any others in the United States.

The trips also gave Tracy and Katherine—on those occasions when she joined him—time to enjoy other personal pursuits. He took up bird watching and kept detailed accounts of his sightings. In his diary he recorded a view near the U.S. Treasury Building in Washington. "I looked up into a clump of shrubbery when a birdsong full of joy and melody stirred me with delight."[17] He later referred to this experience as one of the highlights of his visit, along with sojourns at local libraries and bookstores, which planted the seed for his later passion of book collecting. In one entry, commenting on his visits to Cincinnati and Washington, he wrote, "I read plenty of books . . . and have in mind the great thoughts of others. I am stimulated. . . . The flatness of life is dispelled and the restlessness also."[18]

Despite the pleasures of travel and the enjoyment of meeting others with mission interests, Tracy continued to feel torn about his future. After attending an Easter service at the Central Methodist Church in New York City in April 1907, he wrote in his diary, "It is strange that one who has known deep and positive religious experiences should be troubled by doubt and uncertainty." He continued to suffer from waves of depression, as his diary entries revealed. He analyzed his moods and negative views and came to the conclusion that his frequent trips away from Detroit were responsible. "When isolated from work," he confessed, "the mind is free to dwell upon the morbid thoughts which a nervous condition of the body arouses." Later, in a more positive vein, he proclaimed, "Keep a goin! Grit your teeth, pray, sing, but keep a goin.

Whatever comes it's all a part of life and leads somewhere. Resist the apathy, the depression, the soul paralysis. . . . Let each day be a part of eternity. Do not put off joy until circumstances are ideal. Live now, the best is yet to be."[19]

McGregor's periods of mild depression and self-doubts continued to plague him for the rest of his life. He had difficulty reconciling his enormous wealth with the poverty and sacrifices he had made during much of his early life. On one occasion he told his brother that he wished Katherine had been penniless rather than being a wealthy heiress. He did, however, recognize the great contributions he and Katherine could make to charitable and other social causes with their wealth.[20]

Interestingly, these frequent periods of "mental depression" were followed by experiences of "unusual exaltation of mind with intense peace and joy." Motivated by a need to analyze those mood changes, he often sought an answer through meditation. On one occasion while in New York City, he recorded in his diary that "after sundown, I spent an hour in Central Park for the purpose of silence and meditation," an experience that helped clear his thoughts. "Darkness, seclusion, proximity to nature have been contributing causes to these moods," he wrote, "but so also has a sense of need and a desire for moral and spiritual help." He became more aware of the "reality of the spiritual world" during these experiences, and the meditation seemed to help bring him out of his bouts of depression. He wrote, "Occasions of supreme joy . . . followed as the pendulum sometimes swings farthest in the opposite direction."[21]

In 1915, after concerted pressure by Katherine and some of his closest friends, Tracy finally decided to step down as superintendent of the McGregor Institute.[22]

3

The Final Years

By 1921 McGregor suffered from serious health problems. He was having increasing difficulty sleeping and experienced constant pain in his neck and back. Acting on the advice of his close friend, Dr. Frank Sladen, physician in chief of Ford Hospital, he went to New York City for several weeks of treatment with Dr. A. B. Clark, an osteopathic specialist. Dr. Clark diagnosed his problems as "a slight misplacement in the sacrum" and "rigidity in the dorsal region about the head and neck."[1] The treatment was successful, and McGregor reported in his diary that he "felt better, more bodily and mental stability and poise." He also noted that he "had been taking leisurely walks in Central Park, which doubtless have been healthward."[2]

His condition showed a marked improvement during the summer of 1921, but when he celebrated his fifty-third birthday on April 14, 1922, he noted that "during the past winter my vitality seems to be less than before" and "shortness of breath and extreme depression more frequent." The back and neck discomfort resurfaced in 1923, and on this occasion he went to the Kellogg Battle Creek Sanitarium for treatment with Dr. James A. Raymond, "a spine specialist."[3] When this treatment failed, he sought the advice of Dr. Curtis Lee Hall, an orthopedic specialist in Washington, D.C., who diagnosed his problem as "mild arthritis" and prescribed a series of massage treatments during the following month. These treatments were apparently helpful, because during his stay there he played golf several times a week and met with several members of Congress and federal officials to discuss personal health reform legislation.[4]

McGregor continued to be deeply concerned about his health. On his fifty-sixth birthday, in 1925, he recorded in his diary that his "chief desire during whatever life remains is to have better health and to adjust my circumstances that I may be able, with more calm and equipoise to perform any work I am suited to do."[5] Apparently, however, there was little improvement, and in April 1926 he returned to Baltimore for an extensive medical examination at the Johns Hopkins Medical Center. After a week's visit with heart and orthopedic specialists, they diagnosed an "asthemic state with low vitality, insomnia, and anxiety about his wife's poor health, under nourished . . . moderate arthritis in lumbar spine and myosites in the neck region, slight bradycardin or shortness of breath on exercise."

McGregor was advised to "enter Johns Hopkins Hospital for a few weeks' upbuilding," including "a certain amount of rest . . . massage three times a week . . . biking and exercises for the arthritic condition."[6] McGregor was unable to follow Dr. Barker's advice because of other pressing commitments, including a series of board meetings of the Detroit Community Union and Fund, the Provident Loan and Savings Society, the Merrill-Palmer Institute, and the Wayne County Training School. He carefully considered Dr. Barker's recommendation, but added that he hoped "meditation and relaxation" would help him "recover his poise."[7] His general health improved during the summer and early fall of 1927, but by December he suffered a setback and on the advice of Dr. Sladen entered Ford Hospital on Christmas Day. He was diagnosed with insomnia, "below normal blood pressure and sub-temperature . . . and lack of thyroid."[8] After ten days of analysis and treatment by a group of hospital specialists, which involved violet ray treatments and daily massages, he was discharged and returned to his busy schedule. He did observe that "this temporary break with work and all connections and the opportunity to rest are very welcome."

It is obvious from his daily diary entries that the pressures of his heavy schedule were affecting not only his physical condition but also his mental health. In May 1928, he confided that he was "daily possessed by depression" and that "all spirit and courage seems to have gone out of me."[9] In addition to frequent stays at Ford and Johns Hopkins hospitals, McGregor curtailed many of his public meetings and, in August 1929, moved his office from the McGregor mission to the Colonial Apartments on Parker Avenue. In his new office, located on the east side of Detroit, he wrote: "Am hoping that relief from downtown rush, noise and callers will bring more peace of mind and inward cheer and thus delay the further breakdown of health."[10]

Katherine McGregor's health also caused her husband concern. Although she did not retain her medical records, her husband often left notes in his diary about her condition. As early as 1914, he noted that she began visits to the Battle Creek Sanitarium every year, sometimes for weeks at a time. In 1921 McGregor reported that Katherine was suffering from "severe headaches" and that her "abdominal pain continued."[11] His frequent business trips and, after 1920, his absences to play golf, caused her bouts of severe depression. In one diary entry in 1921 he observed that "perhaps her most evident symptom of illness is her dread of having me absent from her even for a short time that is required to play golf."[12]

Similarly, Katherine also worried about Tracy's health. In an undated letter to him, written in the 1920s and addressed "For my darling to remember," she listed a number of personal pressures "for the man who has passed middle age" to avoid. They included "running, walking rapidly, walking and talking against the wind, all sudden muscular effort, carrying articles of heavy weight as traveling bags and reaching too high for books." She discouraged his habit of reading during evenings with the advice that "active brainwork should be given up an hour before bed time, even if it be but the reading of a book of essays on history which requires concentration and thought." She also urged that "no one suffering from a weak heart should live through the winter months in a climate where he is subject to the rigours of severe cold."[13]

Katherine strongly disliked social events such as debutant parties, weddings, receptions, and so forth and seldom entertained anyone in her home. By the 1920s she had became even more of a recluse and rarely left her home except with her husband. Tracy was deeply concerned about her declining health and decided to spend several months each winter in Florida and Washington, D.C. New York City was also on their itinerary, where they enjoyed the theater, the opera, the symphony, and other musical performances.

Golf became McGregor's main diversion from the pressures of work. He played occasionally before 1920, but in that year he took a serious interest in the sport. In June he met Carleton Wells, a young graduate student in the English department at the University of Michigan, who was also the state golfing champion of Michigan. They developed a warm friendship and played golf often at the Barton Hills Golf Club in Ann Arbor and the Detroit Golf Club.[14] McGregor also played several days a week when he vacationed in Florida and when he visited New York, Baltimore, and Washington, D.C. The sport was more than a mere game to McGregor. "Golf," he wrote, "is like the finer qualities of one's inner self. Perfection comes through relaxing. Poise accompanies quiet."[15]

McGregor also loved nature. On every trip to New York City he spent hours in Central Park; in Washington, the wooded areas along the Potomac River were among his favorite haunts. At Barton Hills in Ann Arbor, he spent hours walking through the wooded area, even when snow covered the ground. From his home in Barton Hills he wrote in his diary, "Looking out of the window . . . I could take the landscape in my arms and caress it. Towees, chick-dees, kinglets, juncos were associates of the outing."[16] Tracy's love of nature provided him with a respite from the burdens of his personal and professional life.

The onset of the Great Depression brought even greater pressure and heartaches to McGregor. The Mission for Homeless Men could no longer provide the needed services for Detroit's transients, homeless, and unemployed and, as noted, closed in 1935. The numerous charities and public institutions in which the McGregors were actively involved were all facing severe cutbacks and even closures. They were constantly being contacted by these organizations for financial support and counsel. The trustees of the McGregor Fund faced similar pressures.

Organized charities were not the only ones who turned to the McGregors for financial assistance. Starting in 1930, as the Depression worsened, a steady stream of business associates, community leaders, friends, and even complete strangers contacted them asking for grants, gifts, or loans. McGregor recognized that this intrusion on his already busy schedule was jeopardizing his health, but he found it extremely difficult to isolate himself from these contacts. He devoutly believed, with a deep religious conviction, that it was his "Christian duty" to assist the needy and disadvantaged. He shared the views of Andrew Carnegie, who believed that "the rich had an obligation to share their wealth in ways which benefited the public and that the wealthy must be a trustee for the poor."[17]

In keeping with this philosophy, McGregor gave loans and outright gifts to scores of Detroit's needy citizens and families. The staff of the McGregor Mission for Homeless Men and the men who lived there before it closed received assistance, as did numerous local families who needed a down payment on a house or money for medical or funeral expenses. McGregor's own experience in financing his education encouraged him to give generous grants to students who needed such support to enter college. Even total strangers sometimes received financial assistance from the McGregors.[18]

McGregor's detailed financial records reflected his generosity. He not only entered a notation for each loan in a ledger but also kept a signed agreement for each, specifying the terms and schedule for repayments. This procedure was somewhat misleading, for he never planned to seek repayment for each loan. As Kathryn Slagle, his assistant, explained, McGregor "intended to let the loan recipient struggle awhile thinking it might be good for them, but I knew his general idea was opposed to burdening people with debts." Slagle added, "Mr. McGregor always preferred to make gifts rather than loans."[19]

McGregor was also extremely generous to some of his close friends and associates. In December 1932, for example, when he learned of the financial difficulties facing his longtime friend, Fred Butzel, he sent a very substantial sum with a personal note: "I am taking the liberty of sending the enclosed to help in supplying your personal exchequer in view of all you have done for Detroit and for humanity in general. You may think of it, if you wish, as a contribution to you as an institution rather than a private individual."[20]

Butzel's prompt response reflected his appreciation and the great admiration and respect he felt for McGregor. "Words fail to describe my extraordinary astonishment and pleasure occasioned by your letter and stupendous check," he wrote. "Your contribution certainly solves lots of problems for me as I do find it awfully hard to hold up my end and the misery of old friends is hard to contemplate. . . . I am only sorry that you are not here so that your wise counsel could be tapped."[21]

A year later, William J. Norton, another close friend of Tracy's whom he had hired in 1918 to take over the directorship of the Detroit Community Union, received a similar check from McGregor. The gift enabled Norton "to push forward the education of my children, a purpose that is very close to my heart." Norton added: "My appreciation is great and deep, too deep for many words." Norton closed his personal letter with an evaluation of Tracy as a friend and mentor: "It is your spirit of devotion, and your kindly tolerant wisdom that have endeared you to Detroit. I wish it might place you in some detached place here, where you could inculcate all who serve this community with the same spirit and understanding."[22]

By 1934 McGregor's hectic schedule was beginning to take its toll on his health again, as well as on his relationship with Katherine. Despite annual visits to Ford Hospital in Detroit, Johns Hopkins Hospital in Baltimore, and related health clinics in Atlantic City and New York City, he continued to be plagued with back pain, indigestion, and depression. Katherine's health also continued to decline. She suffered from severe headaches, abdominal pain, and emotional problems, and despite treatment from physicians in Detroit and Washington, D.C., there was little improvement. Over the years she had become reclusive, refusing to attend parties, receptions, and public events. In a diary entry in September 1929, Tracy noted: "Katherine is running down in health. Her burdens are too much for her."[23]

Katherine was aware of her health issues and the burdens she faced, but to her, the main problem was her husband's hectic schedule and the pressures he faced each day. She recognized his deep commitments to the McGregor Institute, the Detroit Community Fund, the McGregor Fund, and the Wayne County Training School. She shared his concern for Detroit's homeless and disadvantaged, but she also witnessed what the pressures of these associations were doing to her husband's health. On one occasion when he was away on a business trip, she shared her concerns with him in a letter: "You must get out from under the pressures that will kill you and drive me to suicide. I cannot see you shrivel and get gray and stiff and aged because other people use you and sap the last of you. . . . I cannot see you going on, giving your last vitality to the life-sucking friends to whom your health will mean nothing." She ended: "But when your strained heart stops someday unexpectedly what in the world can comfort me?"[24]

Tracy apparently did not answer Katherine, or at least no letter survives, but he also felt obligated to complete projects that he had inaugurated and for which he had accepted a leadership role. On his sixty-first birthday on April 14, 1930, he noted, "There are a lot of things to finish before I get through. Hope I shall not kick off before the job is done."[25] This emphasis on his responsibility for unfinished work became a recurring theme in his diary entries and in his correspondence to friends. In a letter to his brother, Murray, in April 1934, he confessed, "I am not ready to drop out chiefly because of the jobs to be attended to before that event."[26]

McGregor did try to reduce his daily pressures by limiting his hours at his Brush Street office, which usually were taken up with visits from former "mission men" and representatives from local charities, churches, and friends who requested loans.

Despite McGregor's hopes, the move to a new east Detroit office in 1929 did not accomplish these objectives.[27] The location of his new headquarters was soon a matter of common knowledge, especially among his business and community associates, and those seeking financial assistance and counsel visited his office daily. After the crash of the stock market in 1929 and the onset of the economic downturn, Tracy's situation grew worse. Katherine was aware of his stressful schedule and continued to plead with him "to give up your outside responsibilities and service to others." She noticed the impact it had on his health and cautioned him, "You are frail and broken now and prematurely aged. You do not sleep, you cannot eat, and your faculties are failing."[28] Although there is no indication that Tracy responded to his wife, he may have attempted to curtail some activities and projects. But it is clear that he continued to devote several days a week to his favorite charities, the McGregor Fund, the Clements Library, and the public commissions and boards on which he served. Nor did McGregor cut back on the development of his Americana collection. Hardly a day passed without contact with Henry Stevens, Lathrop Harper, and other collectors and dealers. After 1934, he gave even more attention to the McGregor Plan, which encouraged the establishment of rare book collections in colleges and universities.

McGregor did make one major concession to Katherine by agreeing to her demand that they leave Detroit and move their residence to Washington, D.C. In her mind, Detroit, with all his business and community associations, was the cause of his declining health. Furthermore, she no longer felt that Detroit was her home. In January 1931, Tracy agreed to the relocation and made arrangements to move his residence, the headquarters of the McGregor Fund, and his book collection to the U.S. capital. He leased offices at 1901 Wyoming Avenue, and the move took place in May. He and Katherine took up residence in the nearby Wordman Park Hotel.

Katherine and Tracy also continued to travel, especially during the hot, humid days of the summer. They went to New York City often to attend the theater, the opera, and various musical events and during the winter months continued their sojourns to Florida. McGregor visited Detroit often, usually every month to attend board meetings of the Community Fund, the Merrill-Palmer Institute, the McGregor Fund, the Provident Loan and Savings Society, the Clements Library, and the Wayne County Training School. He also gave special attention to the housing projects of the LaSalle Land and Warren Farms companies.

McGregor's travels to Detroit gave him an opportunity to see his physician and close friend, Dr. Frank Sladen, and make lengthy visits to the Henry Ford Hospital for complete physical examinations and tests. These hospital sojourns, however, were different from those experienced by most patients.

He did undergo thorough examinations and therapy, but on most days he left the hospital for several hours to attend meetings and conduct business. During his five-day stay at the hospital in November 1934, for example, his schedule included meetings at the offices of the First Michigan Bank, the Wayne County Medical School, the Sigma Gamma Clinic, the Health Committee of the Community Union, the McGregor Fund, the Wayne County Training School, the Merrill-Palmer Institute, the Provident Loan and Savings Society, the Detroit Community Fund, the McGregor Institute, and the Committee of Management of the Clements Library. Interspersed were meetings with David Whitney, Judge Henry S. Hulbert, Cleveland Thurber, William J. Norton, Alexander Ruthven, and Carleton Wells. The University of Michigan Observatory at Lake Angeles, which the McGregor Fund had helped establish, was also on his itinerary.[29]

The periodic Detroit visits also gave McGregor an opportunity to spend time with family. He met frequently with his brother at the McGregor Institute and often entertained him and his wife, Jessie, and their children at the Detroit Club. He also saw his sister, Ruth, and her husband, George Brown, and their family at their home in Highland Park. He gave special attention on these visits to his nephew, Douglas McGregor, and his wife, Caroline. He developed a close friendship with Douglas, whom he had gotten to know when Douglas had worked with his father, Murray, at the McGregor Institute. After Douglas graduated from the College of the City of Detroit in 1932, Tracy financed his graduate education at Harvard University, which awarded him a Ph.D. in experimental psychology in 1935. McGregor was especially proud of his nephew and his academic accomplishments, and after Douglas's graduation, he contacted a number of college presidents who were participating in the McGregor Plan and asked for their assistance in finding Douglas a teaching position. As it turned out, Tracy's influential contacts were not needed. Harvard hired Douglas as an instructor in 1935 on his own merits. Before Douglas retired from academic life in 1954, he had attained a record of which his uncle would have been proud. He taught psychology at the Massachusetts Institute of Technology and in 1948 was appointed president of Antioch College.[30]

McGregor took advantage of his residence in the nation's capital to pursue his longtime interest in aiding the homeless, destitute, and unemployed. He met often with officials of the newly established Department of the Homeless of the U.S. Emergency Relief Association and other government agencies that dealt with the nation's disadvantaged. He actively served on the board of trustees of the National Commission on the Care of the Homeless and Transients, often traveling to New York City to meet with fellow board members. In addition, at McGregor's urgency, the McGregor Fund gave generous grants to the national commission's programs. The National Conference of Social Workers, the National Mental Health and Hygiene Commission, the Family Welfare Association, the National Probation Association, the Travelers' Aid Society, and the International Migration Service also received his personal attention and financial support.

By 1933 McGregor was recognized as a national leader in these fields and was invited to be a keynote speaker at the National Conference of Social Work. His presentation, which took weeks to prepare, was well received and was published as *Toward a Philosophy of the Inner Life*.[31]

It was soon evident to McGregor that his move to Washington had neither lessened his workload nor improved his health. He did not have to meet with a constant line of visitors who wanted financial assistance as he had in Detroit, and he had a loyal staff to help with his Americana collection and the administration of the McGregor Fund, but his habit of micromanaging these projects took its toll. By 1935 he began to plan for the future, and on one of his visits to Detroit in the fall of 1935 he visited the Woodlawn Cemetery in Detroit "to look into buying a lot."[32] He also devoted attention to placing his financial affairs in order. He advised his colleagues on the board of trustees of the McGregor Fund that in the event of his death they should devote special attention to certain projects such as the McGregor Institute, the American Historical Association Americana committee, and organizations aiding the homeless and transients.[33]

While he was developing plans to leave Washington in the spring of 1936, his health continued to decline. On April 7, 1936, Katherine confided in Murray and his wife that "her heart was filled with concerns about our darling Tracy." She reported that he was getting the "absolute rest under doctors' and nurses' supervision and care that he should have been given sooner, even years ago." She continued that Tracy's "life long habit of constant work with little consideration for himself is hard even now to control."[34] She added that "we do not want the word that he is ill to get about."[35]

McGregor's hectic schedule in April when he was under constant medical supervision seems somewhat of a contradiction. His plans to move to Charlottesville, Virginia, by the fall of 1936, and the hiring of two key assistants to work with him, were undoubtedly influenced by his own recognition of the seriousness of the breakdown in his health. Late in April, he entered Garfield Hospital in Washington, D.C., "for rest and observation," undoubtedly at the urging, even the insistence, of Katherine. He was still able to conduct business, for, as late as April 30, he was sending letters to friends, business colleagues, and potential candidates for the two positions he wanted to fill. His condition worsened, and at 8:00 A.M. on May 6, 1936, with Katherine at his bedside, he succumbed to the effects of a fatal heart attack.

His death came as a shock to many of his friends and associates, especially in Detroit. Although his health had noticeably declined during the past year, his hectic schedule had not changed. All of the Detroit newspapers carried extensive coverage about his career and his contributions to charity and philanthropy in Detroit.[36]

His funeral was held in the First Presbyterian Church on Woodward Avenue and Edmund Place in Detroit on Friday, May 9, 1936. Three ministers participated in the memorial service—the Reverend Joseph A. Vance, pastor of the First Presbyterian Church; the Reverend Benjamin Bush, pastor of the Westminster Presbyterian Church; and the Reverend Warren Wheeler, pastor of the First Congregational Church. Fifty of Tracy's friends and community and business colleagues served as honorary pallbearers and nine as official ones, including Cleveland Thurber, Frank Sladen, Richard Webber, Kenneth Moore, Frank Perley, Renville Wheat, Frank D. Eamon, Nathan Viger, and Edward S. Reid. Those attending the ceremony witnessed lengthy eulogies, citing his long history of dedicated service to the homeless and disadvantaged.[37] Judge Henry Hulbert, who was a close friend of Tracy's for nearly three decades, penned one of the most eloquent and poignant tributes.[38]

> Tracy McGregor was a distinguished man who looked the part. His white, wavey hair crowning a thoughtful, kindly face made him stand forth in any group of people. There was purpose and stability of character in his large, firm features and the reflection of a very active, clear mind in his eyes. These also revealed a heart that was deep and broad in its human sympathies. They were tired eyes for he toiled long and hard for the solution of numberless problems that baffled folks whom he loved sincerely. Above his soft, deep-set, penetrating eyes were the shaggy brows and forehead of a natural leader of men. A strong face, one would exclaim, and a good face.

On June 9, 1954, eighteen years after the death of her husband, Katherine Whitney McGregor died at the age of eighty-one. Despite the McGregors' move to Washington, D.C., in 1931, she never regained her health, and after McGregor's death she developed even more serious mental problems. McGregor's friends and especially his brother and members of the board of trustees of the McGregor Fund kept in close contact with her and provided advice and assistance when needed. As her mental condition deteriorated, she was committed to the Craig Psychiatric Hospital in Beacon, New York, in 1944, where she lived for the rest of her life. Her funeral services were held in Detroit on June 12, 1954, followed by burial at Woodlawn Cemetery.[39]

The trustees recognized the important role Katherine had played in providing major financing not only for the McGregor Fund but also for its programs. In addition to paying tribute to McGregor as "a humanitarian of magnitude and a great civic leader," they also acknowledged that "Katherine Whitney McGregor quietly behind the scenes made possible much of his service and always loyally and faithfully supported and encouraged him."[40]

PART 2

The Mission

4

The Mission for Homeless Men

Tracy McGregor's first task when he left Oberlin College in April 1891 was to assist his mother, Elizabeth, in planning the funeral and memorial service for his father. He then turned his attention to the mission. After carefully inspecting the mission building and holding meetings with key staff members, McGregor developed a plan of action. He gave highest priority to fund-raising and donations of food, clothing, equipment, and needed supplies. Without such assistance it was obvious that the services of the mission would have to be seriously reduced or even closed. Fortunately, Thomas McGregor had kept detailed records on the individuals, organizations, and churches that provided funds and on the restaurants, hotels, and stores that donated food. Tracy's father had disliked asking people for money because he felt it was "disloyal to his religious convictions . . . and dishonoring to God."[1] Tracy, conversely, felt that devoting so much of his time to contacting people for funds did not dishonor God, although it did take up precious time needed to provide religious services to the homeless men. If only he could raise sufficient funds to ensure long-range planning or even secure an endowment, he could devote more of his time to working directly with the men and their problems.

McGregor turned first to several community leaders who were familiar with the work of the mission and especially with the dedicated and tireless efforts of his father. The David Preston family, for example, had from the beginning been one of the most active benefactors and supporters of the mission and its work. Not only did they provide funds, but also several family members helped in the renovation of the building and in organizing and directing its religious programs. Miss Minnie Preston, who was active in the Central Methodist Church and who greatly admired and respected Thomas, was one of the first to contact Tracy and pledge her assistance with an initial gift of $250. She also used her influence to persuade the Deaconess Society of the Central Methodist Church to provide financial assistance and to help with the daily religious services for the homeless men.[2]

By the end of his first week in Detroit, Tracy was very satisfied with the public response to his efforts. In a letter to his mother he wrote, "God is blessing us. . . . Fifteen dollars, three hundred chairs, and a large box of dishes have been received during the past week from unexpected sources."[3] The next week he reported gifts of stools, wash basins, and an oil stove.[4]

These gifts and the moral support of religious leaders were indispensable to keeping the mission operating, but it was evident to Tracy that he also needed the active involvement of Detroit's business leaders. Later he told his brother, Murray, about one of his first meetings with some of them. When, as he was explaining the work of the mission and its importance to local business firms, his host interrupted him and angrily shouted, "Damn you and your whole Mission. I wish you were at the bottom of the Detroit River."[5]

McGregor's response was controlled, quiet, and reasoned. He explained how the mission was aiding Detroit's business firms by reducing vagrancy, begging, and drunkenness on the streets, as well as helping the men improve their lives. After these brief remarks, he got up to leave and that same business leader replied, "Say McGregor, if you can do things like that, it's all right. Here's a hundred dollars." That was the first of many donations McGregor received from this Detroiter.[6]

McGregor followed in his father's footsteps by being at ease with "drunkards and rowdies, course and unclean men" as well as by being accepted by the wealthy and educated. His contemporaries described McGregor as "well-bred, gentle-voiced and orderly in dress."[7]

By the end of the mission's first year of operation, on March 31, 1892, McGregor proudly reported that the mission had received $547 in cash donations and $2,628 in subscriptions. In addition to the substantial gifts of food, equipment, clothing, and supplies, these funds provided an adequate income for its operation. McGregor then announced a fund-raising plan for the second year's budget. His plan showed that he needed to add four business firms or individuals at twenty-five dollars a month and ten churches, societies, or guilds and twenty individuals, each at five dollars a month. He announced also that he had hired the respected Detroit banker, Edward W. Pendleton, to audit the mission's financial records and to serve as treasurer for its board of trustees.[8]

Once the mission was able to operate on a sounder financial basis and provide adequate meals and lodging for its guests, Tracy turned his attention to the religious programs of the institution. Following his parents' lead, Tracy believed missions should do more than merely provide a place to sleep and eat or to recover from drinking binges. The men needed more than a few hours, or even days, at the missions; they needed assistance in adopting a new way of life. Tracy firmly believed that "no power was equal to the religious inspiration for reforming men." This philosophy became the cornerstone of the mission's forty-five years of operation.[9]

The linchpin of the mission building, as designed by Thomas McGregor, was the chapel, which held from 250 to 350 persons. It held religious services for the workers who lived there even before the mission was opened. After Tracy arrived on the scene, he opened the gospel and prayer services to the residents of the mission and to the community at large. The service included a sermon by Tracy followed by testimonials of those who had been converted to Christianity.[10] Tracy, who had a beautiful singing voice, led the singing, often performing a vocal solo. His brother played the piano at the nightly religious meetings from age thirteen on.[11] On some evenings, local pastors participated in the services, and later Edward Carrabin was appointed the mission's chaplain and directed many of the evening programs. Tracy's mother also led some of the services.

In order to avoid any misunderstandings about the responsibilities of the men who sought assistance from the mission, upon arrival "a slip [was] given to each man" that listed the following instructions:[12]

1. *Do Not Frequent Saloons or Drink Intoxicating Liquors*
2. Observe a gentlemanly conduct in the building and be willing to assist in keeping it in order
3. Attend the service held each night at 7:30 and be present at its beginning
4. Be earnest in your search for work
5. Do not spit tobacco on the floor
6. Do not loiter about the front of the building, or use the chapel as a sitting room. In pleasant weather the fourth floor will be open at 10:30 A.M. and at 3:00 P.M.

At the end, McGregor added: "The Superintendent will always be glad to talk with you. We wish to aid you in becoming a true man. Remember there is a better life for you, and that God loves you."[13] After each religious service, McGregor met with the men who wished to talk with him about their beliefs and the problems they faced.

Bible classes were also held each day either before the prayer services or in the afternoon. Local clergy and "Christian teachers," mostly women from the church guilds, as well as Tracy's mother, taught these classes. They were always well attended, especially by "converted men who were not working." Bible classes were also held every Sunday from 8:00 A.M. to 10:00 A.M. Although attendance was not required of the residents, there was considerable peer pressure to attend.[14]

A local *Detroit Free Press* reporter, who had attended one of the first chapel services, described the atmosphere there. In the first row he observed a "big, awkward boy—probably twenty-five years old with tattered, patched clothing—a blind fellow and an Indian, sitting next to several well dressed men, crying during most of the sermon." The reporter explained that the work of the mission was nonsectarian and interdenominational and that the motto of the chapel was "The Hope of the worst lies in loving contact with the best."[15]

The mission's first annual report, issued in April 1892, also stated the importance of these religious programs. McGregor reported the following statistics for that first year:[16]

Gospel meetings sponsored	353
Average number in attendance	87
Number of professed seekers	2211
Number of Sunday School Sessions (9:00 A.M.—Men only)	40
Average number present	51
Weekday Bible Classes	48
Average attendance	12

The work of the mission progressed rapidly after the first year's operation. The building was completely renovated, the finances were placed on a sound footing, and the number of indigent men served by the mission increased steadily. In fact, it had become so successful that it soon outgrew its facilities and McGregor began a search for new quarters. By the middle of the year he found a suitable facility—a four-story warehouse, located on Cadillac Square in downtown Detroit, only a few blocks from the mission's current location on Larned Street. With financial backing from several major local citizens, he rented it and immediately commenced its renovation. A new furnace and boilers were installed, five large bathrooms with showers and a laundry were added, and equipment for fumigating clothes was purchased.[17]

The ground floor of the new facility was converted into a chapel large enough to hold four hundred persons. McGregor also designated a room on the first floor with twenty-five beds for newcomers during their first night at the mission and added a barbershop. A kindergarten for forty needy children was also established.

The second floor housed an assembly room, a library containing books and four local daily newspapers donated by area citizens, and offices for the superintendent and his staff. Separate rooms were provided for a limited number of "true Christians who had been at the Mission for some time."[18]

The third floor contained sleeping accommodations that included iron bed frames with straw mattresses, feather pillows, and white pillowcases. The top floor was set aside for the kitchen, storerooms, and a dining facility consisting of ten long tables, each seating ten persons at a time. Many of these changes and improvements reflected the lessons learned from the shortcomings of the Larned Street facility.

The mission's new location in Cadillac Square, which was surrounded by numerous saloons and taverns that attracted the destitute, was very appropriate. McGregor had become familiar with this area of downtown Detroit and had witnessed firsthand the homeless who roamed the streets by day and slept in doorways and empty buildings by night. It was these men he wanted to attract to the mission.

Although the religious services continued to be a priority, McGregor soon recognized that finding gainful employment for the men was essential if they were to change their indolent habits and become useful citizens. The establishment of a mission employment bureau in 1891 was designed to meet this need. As a first step, the mission sent out notices to community, church, and business leaders announcing the availability of mission men to do housecleaning, yard work, and the "beating of carpets" as well as to work in the manufacturing and industrial firms in Detroit.[19]

The anonymous gift in 1891 of a five-acre farm located on the outskirts of Detroit provided immediate employment for a number of mission men who planted potatoes and other vegetables for the mission kitchen. A few years later McGregor expanded these facilities by acquiring one hundred acres of farmland on Plymouth and Schaefer roads in Detroit. Because so many of the mission men had grown up on farms, it was not difficult to recruit experienced workers. Furthermore, McGregor decided that the location of the farm was ideal for men with serious drinking problems. By transferring them out of downtown Detroit, where they were near the taverns and bars and in constant contact with their alcoholic friends, he helped them break their drinking habits.[20]

For mission men who had difficulty finding outside employment, work was organized within the mission. These jobs included caring for the beds, doing the laundry, cooking, tending the stoves and furnace, and collecting donations from hotels, stores, and restaurants. Those men with tailoring experience mended clothes, cobblers fixed shoes, carpenters repaired furniture, and several barbers worked in the new barbershop.[21]

A major innovation of the mission's employment bureau was the establishment of a wood business. In the 1890s and early 1900s, most Detroit families heated their homes with wood and used smaller pieces in their kitchen stoves and fireplaces. McGregor soon recognized the potential for such a venture. Not only would it provide jobs, but also it would make a profit for the mission. In 1893 he made arrangements with a lumber mill in northern Michigan to ship by rail to Detroit a large supply of the hemlock slabs left over from the production of boards and other building supplies. McGregor rented property on Fort Street to store the wood, which was then transported to the mission where the men cut it into seven-inch lengths, split it into kindling, and placed it into canvas bags and barrels. Another crew of men loaded the containers of wood into the mission's wagons and delivered them to Detroit homes. The charge was twenty-five cents a bag of kindling, delivered, into cellars, sheds, or up one flight of stairs. A single barrel cost fifty cents; seven barrels, a dollar.[22]

The success of the kindling wood sales led the mission to expand its operation to include hardwoods. Surplus beech and maple trees were purchased from northern Michigan mills, shipped to Detroit by rail, and stored until needed at the mission's Fort Street facility. These were cut into eight-, twelve-, and sixteen-inch lengths, split and sold at $6.50 a cord, delivered. As the demand for the wood grew, the mission purchased a buzz saw and increased their delivery capacity to five horses and five wagons, which, with the "McGregor Mission for Homeless Men" sign emblazoned on the side, were a common sight on the residential streets of Detroit.[23]

The wood sales operation did pose some minor problems, however, because of questionable practices by some of the delivery men. Occasionally customers were overcharged, and sometimes the men did not turn over all of the money collected. According to one mission staff member, "he constantly came up against human nature of the men. A few of the men did not have a too high type of ethics, and sometimes, were light fingered." One scam involved the deliverymen selling their own mittens and gloves that were issued to them. After a number of these items turned up missing, Edward Carrabin, the "canny Scotsman" who supervised the wood business at the time, gave the men "two different colored mitts" so, he predicted, "they couldn't be pawned." This plan proved successful, but it apparently confused at least one of the delivery men, who, when asked by one lady customer why his gloves were of different color, replied: "Lady, it's so we can tell our right hand from our left."[24]

After his first two years as superintendent of the mission, Tracy developed a new set of house rules to govern the residents. The first night at the mission would be free; after that the men were asked to pay ten cents each for meals and lodging. If they were unable to find work, they were expected to work three and a half hours a day at the mission in return for meals and lodging. For those men who obtained full- or part-time employment and wanted to remain at the mission, a charge of two dollars a week was levied for room and board. These workers were assigned special quarters, sometimes a private room on a separate floor. This practice reflected McGregor's conviction that workingmen should be housed separately from the indigent and alcoholics.[25]

Mission men, of course, were strongly encouraged not to frequent saloons or drink intoxicating beverages. If they appeared drunk while trying to enter the mission, they were not allowed admittance. In fact, one test given those who appeared inebriated was to walk a straight line up the high stairway leading into the mission. If they failed, they were told to leave and return when they were sober. House rules also called for the use of "proper language and observing a gentlemanly conduct in the Mission building."[26] Spitting tobacco on the floor or smoking in the mission were also forbidden.

These rules served dual purposes. They established standards that governed the behavior of the men while in the mission and provided specific regulations governing dismissal. They also challenged the sharp criticism of some local citizens who charged that the mission encouraged laziness and indigency.

In response to the negative attacks on the mission, as well as to better understand the needs of the mission men, McGregor kept detailed records of the registrants, especially those who remained for longer periods of time. In a survey conducted between May 1893 and March 1894, McGregor developed an excellent cross section of the men. Of the 3,972 served during that period, 2,661 were born in the United States, 312 in England, 291 in Canada, 232 in Ireland, 208 in Germany, 148 in Scotland, 23 in Sweden, 10 in Denmark, and the remainder from various parts of Europe, Asia, and Central America. The majority, 3,834, were described as "drinkers." The religious backgrounds of the men varied: 2,278 were Protestant, 1,555 were Catholic, 1 was Jewish, and 138 professed no religion. Of the total, 3,940 were white and only 32 "colored." Single men represented the majority, 3,548; 191 were married and 233 were widowers. The age breakdown revealed that 20 were older than 15 years of age; 389 between 15 and 20; 1,647 between 20 and 30; 1,137 between 30 and 40; 479 between 40 and 50; 205 between 50 and 60; and 95 men were older than 60.[27]

The data accumulated also revealed the occupations of the men. For the year ending March 1893, the largest occupational groups were sailors, numbering 472; followed by painters, 166; fireman, 158; molders, 30; machinists, 98; cooks, 83; carpenters, 75; blacksmiths, 62; hostlers, 62; clerks, 61; shoemakers, 61; cigar makers, 56; boiler makers, 50; teamsters, 49; printers, 45; tailors, 39; bricklayers, 37; waiters, 37; plumbers, 32; barbers, 31; stonecutters, 31; butchers, 30; tinners, 23; coopers, 20; gardeners, 17; lumbermen, 17; polishers, 17; coremakers, 16; ship carpenters, 16; steamfitters, 16; tinsmiths, 15; broom makers, 14; jockeys, 13; plasterers, 13; agents, 12; horseshoers, 12; peddlers, 12; glassblowers, 11; coachmen, 10; confectioners, 10; masons, 10; miners, 10; switchmen, 10; and upholsterers, 10. In addition, the mission listed 106 additional occupational groups, which represented 9 or fewer of the men.[28]

By 1899, when McGregor had completed his first nine years as superintendent, he had reason to be proud of the mission's record and its accomplishments. He reported with great satisfaction that during this period, 7,719 men had been assisted with 40,325 lodgings and 115,139 meals. Nearly half of the men served, he reported, were younger than thirty years of age, reflecting the increased number of young men migrating to Detroit from the rural areas of Michigan and Europe. The employment bureau had assisted 1,240 men in finding "permanent and temporary situations," and he reported also that the mission men had repaired and sold three thousand garments and one thousand pairs of shoes.[29]

James Redhouse was typical of the men who became closely associated with the mission. Born in Sanilac County in 1872, Redhouse attended Ferris

Institute for four years, then came to Detroit in 1892 to find his fortune in the business world. Unfortunately his arrival coincided with the beginning of a severe depression, and he was soon out of work and without funds. He later recalled that he "walked the streets of Detroit for two weeks trying to find something to do." In desperation, he walked into the mission and was met at the door by McGregor. Redhouse told him about his situation: he had no money, was starving, and "hadn't had anything to eat for two days and . . . didn't know how to beg."[30] After patiently listening to Redhouse, McGregor responded, "Well, here's your choice. . . . You run upstairs to the kitchen, and the cook up there will take care of you." Redhouse not only received a special dinner but was also hired to work in the kitchen for his room and board. Soon after, McGregor approached him and told him, "We need a man to superintend the work of the wood yard down on Fort Street. Prove to me you could do that job and I will pay you a dollar a week," in addition, of course, to providing his room and board. After four weeks at the woodyard, Tracy asked Redhouse to run the mission's farm on Plymouth and Schaefer roads.[31]

The farm was extremely successful and helped the mission in a variety of ways. It not only provided work for mission men "away from the evils of local taverns" but also supplied the mission with a supply of vegetables for the dining room and feed for the horses used in delivering wood.[32] After a few years at the farm, Redhouse returned to the mission in Cadillac Square where he was assigned various part-time jobs. In November 1897 he was working for a local Detroit druggist, George N. Whipple, located at 222 Orleans Street. Whipple sent a letter to McGregor that was not only a testimony to the character of Redhouse but also a tribute to the mission's employment services:[33]

> Last Saturday I had occasion to employ temporary help and telephoned to the Mission for a man. A young man, James Redhouse, was sent me and I thank you kindly for sending me such a good man, the work was hard, and plenty of it, and my impression when I saw the young man was that he would not want it. But the way he threw off his coat with the remark "I'm your man" gave me a very good opinion of him. I know he is willing to work, and I think him worthy of all you can do for him.

By 1896, the annual budget of the mission had risen to $11,031, raised by gifts and the contributions of the mission men who held jobs. The future of the mission was no longer tenuous; it had become an established institution in Detroit. It had a sound financial base, and even though it needed additional funds, at least it was not in jeopardy of closing. The increasing number of men, young and old, that it served was impressive, and to McGregor, the number of those who were converted to Christianity helped justify his exhaustive efforts on their behalf.

McGregor also took great pride in the religious programs of the mission. Chapel meetings were now attracting an average of 225 men each evening; the weekly women's religious meetings averaged 110 attendees; the children's Sunday school, 109; and the girls' sewing classes, an average of 60.

But it was obvious to McGregor and his colleagues at the mission that men were not the only group of Detroiters who needed lodging, meals, and special assistance. The city also attracted thousands of young women who flocked there from the rural areas and small villages of Michigan and the Midwest to seek employment and a new life in the city. Detroit also had its share of young widows whose husbands had been the victims of fatal accidents in foundries and factories. The case files of the Detroit Association of Charities provide detailed testimony to the plight of these young women, often with large families to support and no source of income.[34]

Earlier, Thomas McGregor had recognized the plight and special needs of women during his brief residence in Detroit while supervising the renovation of the original mission building. The difficulties facing many Detroit women were similar to those in Toledo, with whom he and Elizabeth McGregor dealt in their charitable endeavors there. Shortly after his arrival in Detroit, in fact, Thomas had made plans to purchase a large mansion on Fort Street and Swayne Avenue to provide free lodging and meals for needy women who have "become outcasts from Society."[35] This four-story house, known as the Moore estate, occupied "nearly four acres of lawn, orchard and garden" and could "accommodate over one hundred women." It was here at this home, he announced, that the "Gospel of Jesus Christ will be brought to bear on the hearts and lives of the most degraded and helpless class in this large city."[36]

When Tracy learned of his father's plans to purchase the Moore estate, the first question that came to his mind was how Thomas could ever raise the money not only to finance the home but also to operate it. Thomas's assurance that "the Lord would provide the means to run it" was not enough for Tracy, especially after he had reviewed the costs of operating the Mission for Homeless Men. He immediately canceled the offer to purchase the Moore estate, but he did not completely abandon his father's plans to provide some assistance to the needy women and children of Detroit. As soon as the Cadillac Square facility opened in 1893, he established special programs for women and children. With the aid of his mother, who had moved to Detroit after finding others to take over the operation of the Toledo Helping Hand Mission, they established a "special women's program for mothers and wives" living near the mission, which was located in one of the poorest sections of Detroit in the 1890s.[37]

Meetings were held at the mission every Thursday featuring "religious and economic themes." With the assistance of members of the Methodist Church Deaconess Home as teachers, lectures and workshops were given on "the proper care of children, nutrition and home economic problems." One of the announced objectives was "to help women keep their homes in better shape and take better care of their children." Murray McGregor recalled many years later that his mother and her friends "passed out clothing for women and children" at their Thursday afternoon sessions and taught them how to buy produce at the nearby farmers' market.[38]

On Saturday afternoons, Elizabeth McGregor and her Deaconess Home volunteers held sewing classes for young girls of the neighborhood. In addition, free kindergarten classes were held daily at the mission for local children. The average attendance was forty, and most of the children came from immigrant homes in the nearby Italian section of Detroit.[39]

However, the expansion of the mission programs, the steady increase in the number of men lodging and eating at the mission, especially after the severe national economic depression in 1893–94, and the constant pressure on McGregor to raise funds were taking their toll. The arrival of his mother to devote her energies to "women and children work," the aid of volunteers from local churches, and even the fourteen- to sixteen-hour days worked by McGregor were not enough. He recognized that he must have a paid, full-time staff to assist him. At that time, Tracy received a salary of $12.50 a week, which he promptly turned over to his mother for her family expenses. He ate his meals at the mission and obtained his clothes from the "cast off pile, sent to the Mission."[40]

Edward W. Pendleton was the first appointee to the mission staff who had not been a resident. As an experienced attorney, financier, and estate planner, he was hired to supervise the financial operations of the mission and later served as treasurer. McGregor had hired Pendleton to assure local business, community, and church leaders, whose support was essential, that their financial contributions were properly applied.[41]

Edward Carrabin was the mission's second major appointee, and, unlike Pendleton who was a prominent and respected Detroiter, Carrabin was a product of the mission and served it admirably during his thirty-six-year tenure. He was one of Tracy's most successful converts. He was born in Glasgow, Scotland, on January 1, 1857, one of four children of "humble Scottish parents." At the age of eleven, with limited schooling, he secured a job in a local pottery, running molds. "Whiskey and card playing," he later recalled, became his hobbies and caused a split with his parents. At the age of twenty-five he left home and immigrated to America. For several years he "drifted around the country," unable to hold a job for long and continuing "the downward path of alcoholism."[42]

Early in 1892 Carrabin arrived by rail in Detroit and joined the growing army of homeless men who lived on the streets of the central downtown district. On February 27, 1892, he attended a religious service at the mission and listened to a sermon by McGregor on the "Gospel of Jesus." He was so impressed with the sermon, the response of those in attendance, and McGregor's sincerity that he knelt and prayed, "O God, if there be a God, and you will save me from the miserable life I am leading, I will promise to serve you as long as you permit me to draw breath."[43] A year later, after living at the mission and performing a variety of tasks, McGregor hired him to work full time. His first major assignment was supervising the kindling wood business, then later was appointed assistant manager for religious work. Several years later, Tracy appointed him assistant superintendent of the mission, a position he held for the remainder of his long tenure there.

Despite the addition of a full-time staff to operate the mission, fundraising continued to be the major challenge that faced McGregor. The severe economic depression of 1893 and the periodic business downturns that swept through the United States, and especially urban cities like Detroit, made it clear that the mission must find a way to get continuous, permanent financial support.

McGregor came up with a plan to establish a board of trustees made up of prominent community, church, and business leaders. Such a governing group would not only give counsel in operating the mission but could also provide valuable contacts in Detroit's financial community. His first choice to serve on the board of trustees was Joseph Lowthian Hudson, who by 1892 ran the leading retail establishment in Detroit. He was an ideal choice. Born in England on October 17, 1846, he had come to Hamilton, Ontario, in 1855 with his family. One of six children in a family of "very modest means," he knew firsthand the problems of the poor. At thirteen years old he got a job delivering groceries. After his family moved to Michigan, Hudson got jobs in various clothing stores in Ionia and Pontiac, and by 1881, he had opened his own clothing store in the Detroit Opera House on Campus Martius in Detroit. He was extremely successful in this venture and soon won acclaim as a "merchandising genius." He also was recognized as a "fair, honest and concerned merchant and employer." Deeply involved in various Detroit charities and a leader in the Associated Charities of Detroit, Joseph L. Hudson was an obvious choice for the mission's board of trustees.[44]

McGregor never forgot the first meeting he had with Hudson at his new store on Woodward Avenue. He explained to Hudson the important work of the mission and how it had helped hundreds of indigent and homeless men to lead useful and Christian lives, as well as its role in reducing the number of beggars on Woodward Avenue and other main streets in the downtown business section of Detroit. After this introduction to the mission, McGregor asked Hudson to serve on the newly created board of management. Hudson's initial sharp negative response, which McGregor later explained was because "he wasn't feeling good that day," prompted McGregor to change the subject so that he could gracefully leave Hudson's office. As he rose to depart, he was surprised to hear Mr. Hudson say, "Well, young man, if I've got to go on your Board, I suppose I've got to go. You can put me down for $100 a month and keep it up until I cancel it."[45] A warm friendship between the two men was kindled that day, and the mission gained one of its strongest supporters: Hudson remained on the board of trustees until his death in 1912, serving for most of that time as chairman.

McGregor's second choice for the board was Clarence A. Black, one of Detroit's most popular and influential community leaders. He held several positions in Detroit city government as controller, member of the Board of Aldermen, and member of the Detroit Library Commission. On two occasions he was candidate for mayor of Detroit. He was one of the original organizers and later vice president of the Cadillac Motor Company and director of the Old Detroit National Bank.[46]

Other members of the mission's first board were Alexis Angell, a prominent Detroit attorney and later U.S. district judge, and Thomas T. Leete, assistant corporation council of Detroit, member of the Detroit Board of Education, and active member in numerous charities, including the boards of directors of the Young Men's and Young Women's Christian Associations. Edward Pendleton, the prominent Detroit financier and attorney, served as auditor for the mission. In 1892, he was elected treasurer of the board.[47]

In 1897, several new members were added, including Lem W. Bowen, who held key positions in the business life of Detroit, serving as treasurer of the D. M. Ferry Seed Company, vice president of the Security Trust Company, director of the Michigan Fire and Marine Insurance Company, and president of the Cadillac Motor Company.[48] He also served on the governing board of several Detroit financial and insurance companies and as president of the Detroit Board of Commerce.

Sidney Trowbridge Miller was another important addition to the board. Not only a highly respected member of the legal profession in Detroit, serving as president of the Detroit Bar Association for three terms and vice president for Michigan of the American Bar Association, he was also active in Detroit's charitable endeavors. For many years he was president of the Detroit chapter of the Red Cross. He also served as director and general counsel of the Detroit Savings Bank, the Detroit Trust Company, and the Wyandotte Savings Bank and, for many years, as president of the Detroit College of Medicine.[49]

The appointment of such a distinguished group of Detroit business and community leaders to serve on the board of trustees reflected not only the successful program of the Mission for Homeless Men but also the high regard in which these men held McGregor. Although still only in his twenties, he had won their respect.

It was soon evident to board members that they would be expected to play an active role in the various activities of the mission. They not only helped set policy but also participated in mission programs, including lectures and other events. McGregor also frequently sought board members' advice, especially that of J. L. Hudson, Clarence Black, and Alexis Angell.

The occupancy of the Cadillac Square headquarters lasted only a few years before McGregor, his staff, and the board of trustees recognized that the facility was no longer large enough for the mission and its programs. The increased number of homeless and indigent men taxed the sleeping and dining accommodations of the mission, and the successful operation of its employment bureau resulted in a steady increase in the number of men who could pay for private rooms there. Furthermore, the success of the mission's wood and kindling business resulted in a demand for more space.

Of special concern to McGregor was the limited seating space in the chapel where evening services were held. On many evenings as well as on Sundays, mission men and community visitors were turned away because of a lack of seating space. In addition, programs for women and children had to be curtailed because of space limitations. Furthermore, the location of the mission on Cadillac Square posed serious problems for security, and disruption in services by local street dwellers was common. Surrounded by bars and taverns, the mission became the target of drunkards, especially during winter months when it was too cold to sleep in alleys and storefront entrances.[50]

Since its opening in April 1891, McGregor had encouraged homeless men to come to the mission for food and lodging and religious assistance. Alcoholics were also welcomed if they promised to abstain from drinking, but the lack of facilities and the need to turn away those who requested assistance caused other serious problems. Drunken rowdies often disturbed the sleep of other mission men, and fights erupted frequently, resulting in police response. The situation became so serious that McGregor assigned some of the larger and stronger men to act as "bouncers" at the mission entrance. If drunken newcomers had difficulty climbing the stairs at the entrance of the mission, they were denied entry.[51] Although additional space and a different location would not solve all such problems, McGregor and the board recognized that a larger facility was necessary and would at least ease them.

In 1899, the board of trustees decided that the time was ripe to undertake a major fund-raising campaign for a new structure. The city had recovered from the severe depression of 1893–94, and several local church and community groups had promised financial support. The board of trustees raised $5,000, matched by a similar grant from David Whitney, a wealthy Detroit industrialist. With these commitments, the board purchased land on Brush Street for $12,250, and a local architect was hired to develop plans for a new facility. A budget of $74,000 was approved by the trustees. Hudson spearheaded the fund-raising campaign. He contacted his business colleagues who operated stores along Woodward Avenue and the adjacent business districts and pressured them to subscribe to the new mission building. He and McGregor emphasized the positive programs of the mission, especially its role in reducing begging in the business areas and harassing of the patrons of local business firms.[52]

Fortunately, by 1899 there was widespread local community support for the mission, especially among local churches, business firms, and charitable institutions. Within a year the needed funds were subscribed, and work on the structure commenced. Completed in late 1900, the building was four stories high, 120 feet wide and 100 feet deep, and divided into two parts. The right side was designed to house the industrial work of the mission, including space for the storage of wood, a buzz saw, and other machinery; a kiln for drying wood; and workspace for the thirty to forty men employed to split and package the wood bundles. In addition, this structure had space and facilities for furniture repair and the storage of clothes given to the mission for distribution to poor families.[53]

The main part of the building was designed for the more traditional work of the mission. The basement area contained a barbershop and a storage area for food and supplies. The first floor had a large assembly hall, large enough to seat seven hundred persons. It was here that the nightly religious services were held, but during the day it could be divided into separate rooms where kindergarten sessions, sewing classes, and other women's meetings were held. McGregor devoted his attention to this facility because he was convinced that the religious services held at the mission had a profound influence upon the men and their conversion to Christianity. In order to make this facility especially attractive, he arranged to have ash wainscoting, five feet high, installed all around the room. The high platform in the front of the room provided space for an organ and piano and a raised area for speakers, singers, and choirs.[54]

McGregor was prepared for the concerns expressed by some donors as to why the meeting room was so large. He presented detailed statistics to document the steadily increasing attendance at the chapel meetings and the number of women's and children's classes held each week. Along with the endorsement of church leaders, he was able to demonstrate that the new "evangelistic, personal and devotional type of religion," rising in popularity at the turn of the century, was attracting large audiences.[55]

The second floor was devoted "to Mission business, gastronomical and living." A library for mission men, 40 feet by 30 feet in size, occupied the front of the building. A lounge and the mission offices, a restaurant and serving room, toilets and work rooms for the permanent boarders, as well as meeting rooms for the several men's clubs sponsored by the mission occupied the remainder of the second floor.

The third floor held a large dormitory with iron beds in tiers plus showers and baths. The top floor contained sixty single rooms, which were available for paying residents. Each room was large enough for a bed, a chair, and a table. A lounge and sitting room allowed residents to congregate in the evenings and weekends.

The Brush Street mission welcomed its first occupants on Thanksgiving Day, 1900, and the formal dedication was held on June 9, 1901. Hudson presided at this ceremony, "his first public appearance since his recent severe illness," the local newspapers reported.[56] Seven hundred Detroiters filled the assembly room on that June day and heard Hudson give a glowing account of the mission and its accomplishments. Hudson took special pride in announcing that the building was "free of debt," due to the generosity of local citizens. McGregor was seated on the dais surrounded by dignitaries that included the Reverend George Elliott, pastor of the Central Methodist Episcopal Church; W. D. Maxon, rector of Christ Episcopal Church; and the Reverend W. B. Jennings, pastor of the First Presbyterian Church. Dr. Maxon addressed the audience "representing the friends of the Mission," followed by Edward Carrabin and Alexander Gunn, who represented "the work of the Mission." McGregor, whom Hudson introduced as "our beloved Superintendent," was the final speaker.[57]

The dedication and opening of the new building in 1901 ended the first decade of McGregor's leadership of a major charitable agency. He considered it one of the most difficult and challenging periods of his life. The loss of his father had devastated McGregor, and the obstacles facing the mission in its early years were enough to discourage even the most experienced leaders of social agencies. Having to drop out of Oberlin had also disappointed him. But during this period he rose to the challenge, finding suitable locations for the mission, developing sound operating rules and regulations, inaugurating new and innovative programs for women and children, and conducting major funding campaigns not only to meet the daily needs of the mission but also to build an expanded facility. As a result of his close association with David Whitney and his marriage to Katherine, the economic condition of the mission now had a much sounder basis. No longer did it have to rely on daily gifts of food and supplies from local restaurants, hotels, and business firms, and in 1900, it was able to inaugurate a successful campaign to establish an endowment fund.[58]

Up to this time many of Detroit's citizens had viewed McGregor as the owner of "a slum mission" and considered his views on aid to the homeless and needy "a bizarre socialized doctrine." After his marriage, he was able to recruit and organize many of these same critics into a "social force" on behalf of the homeless.

McGregor's newfound wealth and his continuing relationship to the men and staff of the mission were scrutinized by colleagues. Prominent local journalist John H. Gruesel wrote in the *Detroit Free Press* in 1905:

> To look at Tracy McGregor you would say to yourself: This man, who takes his daily bath, is on such good terms with his barber, clothes always pressed, orderly to a point just this side of fastidiousness—should find natural environment in a social club house, or, being handsome and stylish, would shine in a ball room. . . . But he lives among the wayfarers. . . . Here is a well-bred, gentle-voiced young man who finds his usefulness among vagabonds,—yes, for years he lived among the drunkards, the rowdies, the course, the unclean, often too, among thieves.[59]

McGregor's "quiet manner" was also admired by the hundreds of mission men with whom he associated. "He has a peculiar pleading way," observed one man, "and there is an inscrutable sympathy, which suggests something strong, beyond analysis but very real."[60] McGregor never lost faith in the troubled, guilt-ridden alcoholic men or in the important work of the mission.

As other community pressures on McGregor increased, and after his marriage to Katherine, he reduced his personal involvement in many of the mission's activities. He hired assistants such as Edward Carrabin as assistant superintendent and William H. Venn as religious director. He continued to lead most of the chapel and religious services but increasingly invited local pastors to participate in the services and counseling of the mission men. In February 1901, the board of trustees approved the hiring of Murray McGregor, Tracy's younger brother, "to take special charge of the financial matters pertaining to the practical work of the Mission." Murray also arranged for medical assistance from the Detroit College of Medicine, which provided a full-time resident physician "to examine all new men, to guard against contagion, to conduct a dispensary for treatment of minor ills and in serious cases to secure necessary outside treatment."[61]

By 1911, during the mission's twentieth year, McGregor proudly recounted its accomplishments. During that year, 15,724 men had registered at the mission, of whom only 4,266 were "repeaters." Most of the men were under the age of thirty, and only 329 were older than sixty. "Colored men" numbered 1,015, which was substantial, given the small population of African Americans in Detroit at that time.[62]

"Most of the Mission men were destitute at first," McGregor reported, "but during 1911 employment was found with so little difficulty that out of an average of the 361 lodged each night, only eighty-four were unable to pay their way." By that year also, a majority paid the cost of "fifteen cents per night for lodging and $1.25 to $1.75 a week for private rooms." Destitute men continued to be sheltered free or assigned to work four hours a day at the mission for their meals and lodging.[63]

McGregor also announced that the budget for the mission during 1911 was $41,577, most of which was met by sales of kindling wood, gifts from donors, and lodging and meal fees. The endowment fund totaled $67,158, which allowed the mission staff to make visits to patients at local hospitals, at homes, and at the county poorhouse in Eloise, Michigan. The mission also sponsored weekly religious services at Eloise and other charitable institutions.[64]

On January 26, 1911, McGregor announced that the board of trustees had officially changed the name of the Mission for Homeless Men to the McGregor Institute. They believed that the new title more accurately represented the overall educational programs of the mission. It also credited the McGregor family with its major role in not only founding the institute but also directing its operations.

McGregor agonized for years over the decision to step down as superintendent but concluded that he could contribute more to aiding the destitute, unemployed, and old and disabled through other avenues. He also realized that such a decision was necessary because of the way he viewed the intense demands of the mission leadership. He now felt that he could make the change and turn his attention and energies to other projects that were already challenging him. Financial affairs at the mission were sound, with an adequate income coming from the mission men who were employed and able to pay for their lodging and meals. An endowment of $65,000 was also available to assist the mission during periodic economic downturns.

In addition, the mission had the support of a superb group of trustees who were also influential business and community leaders. Lem W. Bowen, who replaced Hudson when he died in 1912, served as chairman, and Alexis Angell continued to serve on the board and brought to it not only his commitment to aiding the homeless but also legal counsel. Thomas Leete Jr. also provided legal support, having formerly served as assistant city attorney, as assistant corporation counsel, and as a member of the Detroit Board of Education. Willard Pope contributed his skills as an expert on transportation systems and as president of both the Detroit Bridge and Iron Works and the Canadian Bridge Company. To continue the support of the Hudson family, the McGregor Institute had added Richard Webber to the board in 1912. The son of Hudson's sister Lillian, Richard Webber shared his uncle's enthusiastic support for the work of the institute. Longtime members Edward W. Pendleton and Charles Phelps and the newly appointed James Whitehead rounded out the nine members of the board of trustees.

Tracy persuaded his younger brother to take his place as superintendent. Murray was, of course, very familiar with the institute, its history, and its operation. Although he was only fourteen when his father died, he had been brought into its daily operations by spending his after-school hours at the mission, attending the nightly chapel services, playing the piano, helping with various chores, and later teaching some of the Bible classes. In 1901, at the age of twenty-two, Murray had been employed for a full year at the mission. By 1905, he took a position at the Detroit Savings Bank as a clerk, and within ten years, he rose to the position of chief clerk. Yet he did not hesitate to resign from the bank to return to the institute, which had been his father's inspiration and his mother's life's work, when he was asked by Tracy. By 1916, when he assumed control of the institute, Murray inherited a staff of thirty, many of whom had served between ten and twenty years in some capacity at the mission.[65]

The McGregors were proud of a survey and report by prominent social worker and urbanist Walter Kruesi, who had been brought to Detroit from New York City during the Motor City's depression in 1914–15. Kruesi's report, which will be discussed in more detail later, sharply criticized the city's relief efforts during this crisis, as well as most of the private relief, church, and health agencies. Yet, unlike the criticisms of the McGregor Institute by Detroit police officials for its lenient treatment of the unemployed and needy, Kruesi concluded that the institute not only was excellent in its operation and scope but also compared very favorably with similar missions in Boston, New York, and Buffalo.[66]

In February 1916, a twenty-fifth anniversary celebration of the institute took place as a reunion for hundreds of current and former mission men as well as a testimony to the work of Tracy McGregor. A chapel service commenced the festivities on Sunday, February 6. Following hymns, McGregor recounted the success of the institute in helping thousands of Detroit men find employment and a better life through their conversion to Christianity. Testimonials by several men who had lived at the mission followed, including one by Frank Cleveland, the "oldest living" alumnus, who had arrived at the Larned Street mission on December 31, 1890, even before it was formally opened. In sharp contrast to the conditions of 1915, he told of "the days that tried men's souls," of board beds (hand hewn with an ax) and of singing "accompanied not only by a piano, but by the scampering of a thousand rats." Edward Carrabin described how the mission had helped him convert from a gambler and a "hopeless drunkard" to a "pillar of strength in the Institute work."[67]

That special Sunday evening anniversary chapel service was devoted to music and tributes to Thomas McGregor by several mission men who had worked closely with him during the brief few months he struggled to shape the Larned Street mission into livable space. They emphasized his practical manner of dealing with problems, citing his favorite sayings such as "Take Time by the Forelock" and "When God gets me where he can trust me, I'll have money a foot deep."[68]

An anniversary banquet held the following day at the Elliott-Taylor Wolfenden Cafe welcomed the mission men and workers, many of whom returned to the mission from other parts of Michigan and the United States. Elizabeth McGregor told of her husband's inspiration for the mission and of the spiritual life he had led. Edward Pendleton followed with a reading of a speech given by Hudson to the Mission Brotherhood ten years earlier.

A Tuesday evening chapel service was devoted to "Women's Work in the Institute." Elizabeth gave an account of the children's Sunday school, Mrs. E. W. Kent spoke of the girls' sewing school and the children's meeting, and Mrs. J. W. Fales told of the women's group meetings. Although the mission's programs for women and children had been discontinued several years earlier because of space limitations, it was remembered for the important role it played in the early years of the mission. The Tuesday evening program ended with Mrs. Murray McGregor singing "Lead Kindly Light" and "The Man of Galilee."[69]

The final event of the anniversary celebration took place on Wednesday evening, February 9, and was devoted to a memorial service for deceased mission men, especially those buried in the McGregor mission lot at the Woodmere Cemetery.[70] As the celebration ended, Tracy expressed mixed feelings about retiring as superintendent of the mission. He was immensely satisfied with the program and the public response to it, but sad too that the institute and the mission men would no longer occupy time in his daily life. The pride he had taken in the accomplishments of the mission for twenty-five years and his pleasure that Murray had agreed to assume responsibility for directing its future helped assuage his regret. Now he could devote his energies to other pressing community problems.

5

The Mission Men

After Tracy McGregor stepped down as superintendent of the McGregor Institute at the end of 1915, just as it was celebrating its twenty-fifth anniversary, he maintained a close association with its activities and continued to spearhead mission-funding drives, raised money for the mission endowment, and contributed his own resources when needed. He also participated in many of the evening chapel services and the weekly meetings of the Brotherhood Association when he was in town and available.[1]

McGregor kept in close contact with hundreds of the men who had once resided at the mission and whose lives were influenced positively by their contacts with him and with the staff. He was especially interested in the activities of the "Mission Men," as he called them, who had become involved in church and mission work in other parts of Michigan and the United States. On many occasions he helped these men secure positions, often assisting them with loans and other forms of financial aid.[2]

The subject of the mission men so interested McGregor that while he was still superintendent, he decided to prepare a history of the mission and its residents. He collected biographical information on the men and their careers both before they arrived and after they left in order to evaluate the impact that the institution had upon the community.

One issue that concerned him was the sporadic attacks on the mission by certain segments of the Detroit community. A few of Detroit's downtown business leaders, for example, continuously expressed open hostility toward the mission. They charged that its practices of providing meals and sleeping accommodations for "drunkards and indigents" encouraged and reinforced bad habits. Several church leaders added their voices against sponsoring evening chapel services and Sunday programs, and though the pastors of several Detroit churches often performed services at these sessions, many believed that such services and programs should be the sole function of the church.[3] Detroit police officials added their negative evaluation by charging that the facility had become "a haven for criminals." Even the local Communist Party entered the fray by complaining that the mission paid the men substandard wages, forced them to attend religious sermons and lectures, and was "a cesspool of unsanitary conditions."[4] Some of Detroit's other charitable institutions questioned the policy of allowing the men to get "free" lodging and meals for working only three or four hours a day. For a while, the Associated Charities of Detroit, the agency that represented most of the city's charitable agencies and the forerunner of the Detroit Community Union, expressed some reservations about the mission's policy of not forcing its residents to leave the mission if they could not find a job within a few days. The governing directive of the Associated Charities' "visitors" who investigated the plight of Detroit's poor and needy was to "be on your guard against encouraging idleness, improvidence or gross misconduct, directly or indirectly." The visitors of the Associated Charities of Detroit were also advised that "no person in the work of the Association or representing it shall, under any circumstances, use his or her position for the purpose of proselytism or spiritual instruction." They also believed that Detroit charities should not assist those who came to Detroit from other communities. The McGregor mission, they claimed, violated these directives.[5]

Tracy McGregor was at odds with the Associated Charities' directive. He was never concerned about where needy applicants came from or how long they had lived in Detroit. Nor did he agree that all "chronic beggars should be compelled to return to their home towns for assistance." McGregor had carefully gathered statistics to refute these charges. He disputed the claim that "the Mission was so inviting that the men didn't seek work." "Of the 16,000 men who made their home at the Mission during the past four years," he explained, "less than one in a hundred was here during each of the last four years."[6]

McGregor also disagreed with Henry Ford, who had embraced a different philosophy about charitable aid to the poor and needy. The automobile pioneer's views were reflected in the rules governing worker eligibility for his "five-dollar-a-day" plan, which he announced in 1914. Ford established a special department to investigate workers and determine if their lifestyles met his moral standards. Ford's views were clarified during the severe depression of 1914–15, which left more than eighty thousand Detroiters out of work. He arranged for the Ford Hospital to allocate one hundred beds a night for the unemployed, with the restriction that they could remain there only two consecutive nights. That was ample time, Ford insisted, for the men to find work and more suitable living accommodations.[7]

McGregor responded to the periodic criticisms by using carefully preserved statistics on the mission men. These same detailed records were invaluable to McGregor when he began his historical study. He had always considered the mission a "laboratory" where "the lives of the thousands of aimless men wandering up and down the highways and waterways of America" could be carefully documented. By analyzing these details about the men, McGregor believed he could discover not only the reasons for their plight but also how to turn the men into useful and productive citizens.[8]

McGregor's first detailed study, published in 1910 under the title *The Story of a Man without a Home,* concentrated on a young Norwegian immigrant, Kenneth Ofstendal, whom he considered typical of a large number of young men who were influenced by residence at the mission. After spending his childhood in a "hardworking, honest and deeply religious family" in Bergan, Norway, Ofstendal left his home for a new life in America at the age of seventeen. Arriving in New York City in 1889, he traveled first to southern Minnesota and then to Chicago. Even though he was welcomed in both communities by other Scandinavian families, he could not find permanent employment, especially after the economic depression of 1893. Detroit was the next stop on his itinerary, and he arrived there in 1894, "bitter, broke and without work."[9]

Within a few weeks following his arrival in Detroit, Ofstendal was directed to the Mission for Homeless Men. He was overjoyed to find a "clean and warm bed and good food," after having spent many cold nights on the streets of Detroit. For several weeks he worked for his room and board by chopping wood four hours a day. With the assistance of several of the mission men he found a permanent job with a local roofing company. After learning the carpenter's trade, he married a local young woman and moved with her to New York where he became a successful businessman and a "pillar of his community."[10] McGregor reported that Ofstendal had credited his time at the mission with helping him "turn his life around and his successful business career." McGregor also observed that Ofstendal was typical of a large number of mission men "who are neither hardened nor unhelpable and who need preventive rather than reformative ministry."[11]

In his publication *Twenty Thousand Men,* published in 1916, McGregor described in much more detail profiles of the men who resided at the mission during its first quarter century.[12] During these years, which witnessed three severe economic depressions and the influx of nearly a million new residents, he noted that "more than a quarter of a million different men have come and gone" from the mission. McGregor divided these men into four categories: "The normal, the floater, the unemployable and the parasites."[13]

In describing the "normal," McGregor posited strongly that, contrary to popular belief, "the impression that these men are a low down class must be corrected." The mission records demonstrated "that only a third of the men returned to the Mission; two thirds never returned." Most of the latter group were "as normal in health, mind and morals as the average," but were out of work because of the business depressions and labor strikes." They sought the help of the mission, McGregor explained, only as a last resort when their funds were exhausted, and they left when they found employment.[14]

The "floater," according to McGregor, represented the second class of mission residents, whose basic problem was not due to employment but "to inherited or acquired limitations in themselves." They were described as "restless spirits seeking frequent change, sensitive, eager, easily depressed and without worthy objects of endeavor." It was men of this group, Tracy believed, that "were prone to drink" and corrupted by "John Barleycorn" and drugs. When sober they were dependable workers, but their temperament usually led to a return to alcohol and other bad habits. Unfortunately, he observed, these bad habits "sooner or later results in broken health and a weakened mind."[15]

The third group, the "unemployables," included those physically enfeebled through accident, illness, or age and those that were mentally defective. Although few of these ended up at the mission except during periods of economic depression, McGregor expressed deep concern over their plight and sought to justify the assistance given to them by the mission.[16]

In sharp contrast, McGregor had little hopes or sympathy for the men in his fourth classification, "the parasites." These men were healthy, able to work, but had become dependent on alms, begging, and stealing. Although members of this group sought lodging at the mission, they were not encouraged to remain and when possible were housed separately from the rest of the residents.[17]

Within the framework of these the four main categories, McGregor went on to describe additional characteristics. Of the twenty thousand men who were the first residents at the mission, 10 percent were "mere boys" younger than twenty-one years of age, 50 percent were younger than thirty, and 75 percent younger than forty. He found that two-thirds were American born, and one-third were immigrants from Europe and Canada. Given the ease with which the United States accepted and even encouraged foreign immigration, McGregor observed, "Uncle Sam surely might well assume a foster parents' obligation."[18]

In his studies on mission men, including in *The Story of a Man without a Home* and *Twenty Thousand Men,* McGregor analyzed the reasons why the men were "homeless, destitute and sinful" and had become dependent upon alcohol. He argued strongly that the reform of many of the men was directly related to their residence at the mission and especially to the religious training that they received there. He also concluded from evidence in the files that their "conversion to a better life" was based on the influence of the men themselves in aiding their comrades to find gainful employment and pressuring them to pay a fair share for their lodging and meals. In addition, the mission's employment bureau helped hundreds of men find full- or part-time seasonal positions. Not all of the men, however, lived up to McGregor's high standards and expectations, and he admitted that "of course, there were a few goats around the sheep."[19]

McGregor also cited in his studies the role of mission-sponsored clubs and alumni groups designed to provide a greater sense of loyalty and camaraderie. For example, in 1892, shortly after the mission opened, eighteen men formed the "Rescue Volunteers," which was an informal club organized "to encourage and to assist destitute and needy Detroit men" to take advantage of the mission's services.[20] Later, the Friday Club was organized for men living at the mission. They held weekly meetings each Friday night at 6:30 P.M. "to discuss some interesting topics."[21]

A Fellowship Club was formed in 1908, which continued for several years, comprised "of men who have lived at the McGregor Mission or who have been connected with its work, and who desire to keep in friendly touch with the Mission and each other."[22] This group met monthly at the mission. In December 1908, Professor A. H. Griffith presented a stereopticon lecture to the members on "Ireland and Its People."[23] Other programs addressed such topics as "The Duty of Citizenship," "Prison Reform," and "Health and Sunshine." On February 6, 1911, Joseph L. Hudson, the president of the McGregor Institute Board of Trustees, addressed the club on "The Meaning of Life to Me."[24] The institute's Character Club was established in 1917 and was "founded on the principles that a worthy character can grow only from good habits." The weekly meetings featured programs devoted to personal finances, thought habits, and daily health habits.[25] A Ladies Association, consisting of twelve wives, sisters, and mothers of mission men was also founded in 1917. Among their important activities was the "cutting and hemming of sheets" for the institute.[26]

Of all the organizations affiliated with the mission, the longest lasting was the Mission Brotherhood, founded in May 1898 by McGregor and his staff, which continued until 1935. A special room in both the Cadillac Square and Brush Street facilities was designated as its headquarters for their weekly meetings. The membership of this club was open to those connected with the mission, both those who lived there or those who had left after finding employment or being reunited with their families, and those who "supported its work and forwarded its purposes by their prayers and charitable examples, and by their presence and words at such of the services as they are able to attend." McGregor summed up the main criteria for membership: "Loyalty to God, to the Institute and its work and to one another." Under the approved constitution of the Mission Brotherhood, each meeting opened with the statement of purpose repeated aloud by all members:[27] "We brothers of McGregor Institute, desire to be patient and forgiving to one another and to all men, especially to those who are weak, foolish, or hardened as, in times past, we have been. We desire grace to perform faithfully our daily work as unto God; to live calmly and trustfully; to face hard things with courage; to keep our spirit happy and our focus bright. This is thy Will, O God! Help me so to do."

The Mission Brotherhood met every Sunday evening at 5:45 P.M. and featured musical presentations and speeches by prominent members and guest speakers. They also sponsored social gatherings and in May each year hosted an annual banquet. The spring 1910 event featured music by the Mission Brotherhood choir, an Autoharp solo by Alfred Jolly, and brief speeches by Murray McGregor, Hugh McDougall, and George Brown.[28] In 1911, Joseph L. Hudson, the featured speaker, described his long association with the McGregor Institute.[29]

Another major project of the Mission Brotherhood was the sponsorship of the McGregor mission lot at Woodmere Cemetery in southwest Detroit. This lot was established by Edward Wilson, one of the early residents of the McGregor Mission for Homeless Men. For many years, Wilson, described as "small and weak in body, and broken in will power and moral strength," was "a habitué of ten-cent lodging houses and cheap saloons."[30] In 1893 he entered the McGregor Helping Hand Mission and his life was transformed. Three years later when he died, his savings were sufficient for his own burial expenses and for a plot in the section of the cemetery reserved for mission men.[31] The Mission Brotherhood had purchased additional lots at the Woodmere Cemetery for the thirty-nine mission men who are buried there. The gravestone for the McGregor mission lot lists the names of the men with the following text: "We brothers of the McGregor Institute, desire to be patient and forgiving to one another and to all men, especially to those who are weak, foolish or hardened in times past we have been."

McGregor not only endorsed the establishment of clubs within the mission but also actively supported them. In planning the Cadillac Square and Brush Street buildings, he designated a meeting room and facilities for these groups. McGregor also attended many of their meetings, especially those of the Mission Brotherhood, and was always invited to speak at those he attended. Religion was usually the centerpiece of his message. On Sunday, May 12, 1912, McGregor elaborated on the theme "that whosoever would submit to God's leading way was bound to succeed." "Brotherly Love" was the topic of his address on November 4, 1912.[32]

The weekly meetings also featured remarks by members, often describing their lives, especially the circumstances that prompted them to enter the McGregor mission and the impact of that experience. The Mission Brotherhood also sponsored annual banquets and other special events for members and their families. On September 12, 1912, sixty-one "brothers and their wives and children held a picnic at Sugar Island." The secretary noted, "The trip down the River was enjoyed by everyone present, from the youngest to the eldest" as well as "the sweets provided by the Ladys."[33] The minutes of the Mission Brotherhood meetings reflect how much McGregor was revered by the members. In them, members all recalled the meeting they had with him when they first entered the mission as well as the kind, gentle way in which he received them.

6

The McGregor Institute

Tracy McGregor's resignation as superintendent of the mission, which, as noted, had changed its name to the McGregor Institute in 1911, was a difficult decision for him to make, but it was made more palatable after he had persuaded his brother, Murray, to take over. Although Murray had worked at the institute for only a year, fifteen years earlier he had become intimately familiar with the mission and its operation. As a teenager he had participated in the nightly religious sessions by singing and playing the piano. Even after he gained employment as clerk at the Detroit Savings Bank, he continued his close association with the mission. He attended meetings, participated in chapel services, and met frequently with his brother to discuss the work of the mission. Although he had risen to the position of chief clerk at the bank by 1915, he did not hesitate to accept his brother's offer of a new, challenging position at the institute. He recognized that the institute was in sound financial condition with a respectable endowment fund, a paid staff of "about thirty individuals," and an active group of volunteers. Edward Carrabin, the assistant superintendent, was in charge of institute operations, and David Scott served as the director of religious work. Both of these dedicated colleagues had been there since the early 1890s, and both had successfully overcome alcoholism while they were "guests" of the McGregor Mission for Homeless Men.[1]

In 1915 the McGregor Institute was governed by a respected and influential board of trustees, which consisted of Lem W. Bowen, Edward W. Pendleton, Alexis C. Angell, Thomas T. Leete Jr., Charles B. Phelps, Willard Pope,

Richard H. Webber, and James T. Whitehead. Tracy McGregor continued his active association with the institute as "managing trustee," where "he will plan and advise as heretofore" and "will not in any sense drop out" of its work.[2]

For the next twenty years, Tracy McGregor served in this capacity and worked closely with Murray and the staff in its operation. Whenever he was in town, he attended meetings of the trustees, gave speeches and sermons at chapel services, and gave financial assistance when needed. He also used the institute as the headquarters for his work with the Associated Charities of Detroit, the Detroit Community Union, the Merrill-Palmer Institute, and the Thursday Noon Group. This gave him daily contact with Murray and the staff of the mission.

By 1915 the McGregor Institute had become an established and respected organization in downtown Detroit. Community and business leaders supported its programs, and many gave it special attention by purchasing tickets providing a day's lodging and meals to beggars who frequented their local business establishments.[3] The Detroit Welfare Department had officially recognized and endorsed the institute and its programs. The mayor and members of the city council as well as officials of local charities and most local churches were supporters of the institute. The only local detractors continued to be the Detroit police officials, who believed that the institute was a "Tramp Paradise" and a haven for "lazy and shiftless" transients who flocked to Detroit for handouts. The local Communist Party also led a vicious attack on the institute, largely because of the pressure placed on the mission men to attend chapel and religious services.[4]

From 1915 to 1935, the McGregor Institute continued to provide a needed service for the city of Detroit. World War I, however, had a serious impact on its programs and operations. With its automobile factories, tool and die shops, foundries, boiler works, pharmaceutical manufacturers, and shipbuilding operations, Detroit became one of the nation's war production centers and earned the reputation of "Arsenal for Democracy." Tens of thousands of Detroiters joined the army once the United States entered the European conflict in April 1917. Included among the Detroit contingent were a number of men from the McGregor Institute. By March 1918, thirty-seven current or former "guests" of the institute had enlisted and were serving at the front in France. They kept in touch with the institute by writing letters to Tracy and the staff, and especially to members of the Mission Brotherhood, the most active of the organizations within the institute.[5]

The war triggered serious challenges for Detroit, especially as the enlistments and sharp decline in new immigrants from Europe and other parts of the United States resulted in a severe shortage of workers. This problem was resolved in part by the active recruitment of African Americans from the South and the use of women workers. The enhanced employment opportunities in all sectors of the city also resulted in a decrease in the number of homeless and destitute men.

The impact of the war can be clearly seen in the detailed records kept by the institute staff for 1917. The largest volume of business ever transacted by the institute occurred during the first half of the year, and the smallest occurred during the last half.[6]

	First Half	*Second Half*
Average lodged per night	570	227
Average meals per day	1,151	644
Odd jobs per day	67	34
Daily chapel attendance	143	90
Percentage under 40 years old	76	67

A comparison of activities in the various departments between 1917 and the previous year also reveals the impact of the war on the institute.[7]

	1917	*1916*
Total lodgers and roomers	159,685	202,468
Average meals per day	329,963	246,483
Odd jobs per day	42,603	46,378
Daily chapel attendance	18,358	20,502
Percentage under 40 years old	7,598	8,027

Additional statistics maintained by the institute staff reveal other interesting insights relating to its programs. The average age of the mission men, or "guests" as they were often called, was higher for 1917 than for 1916, and the number of men younger than twenty-one years of age and older than thirty was larger. Thirteen percent of the arrivals at the institute were African Americans, as compared with 6 percent in 1916. Odd jobs filled by the institute's employment bureau in 1917 decreased by 3,146 from a year earlier. There were more requests for clothing in 1917, and a smaller percentage of men took advantage of the mission's practice of depositing money for safekeeping. Attendance at chapel meetings was smaller in actual numbers during 1917, but the percentage of the "men in the house who attended meetings was larger than for the preceding year." The statistical records as well as other data kept by the staff also reveal that a significant number of men who were "guests" at the institute during the war had health and related problems, which prevented them from qualifying for the well-paid wartime jobs.[8]

The wartime adjustments had some unexpected benefits for the institute. The decline in overnight or short-term guests allowed the institute to convert the fourth floor, which had remained empty for eighteen months, from a dormitory with sixty-six beds to thirteen individual rooms and five rooms that accommodated from five to seven beds each. These individual and larger rooms attracted a number of lodgers who were seeking longer-term accommodations and had the financial resources to pay the larger fee. With the surplus resulting from more permanent paying lodgers, the institute renovated several other sections of the building in the spring of 1919. In addition to the fourth-floor alterations, it substituted an "open counter for the office after the usual hotel style" providing a "quicker and more complete service to guests."[9]

Shortly after the war's end, the situation at the institute again changed. First, the number of men seeking lodging, meals, and assistance in finding employment increased steadily. During the first two months of 1919, for example, the institute registered 15,650 men for lodging and 16,737 for meals. A year later, during the same two months, it jumped to 38,017 and 37,141, respectively. The number of younger men increased also, with 72 percent of the new arrivals in January and February 1920 under thirty years of age, as compared with 42 percent a year earlier. The new arrivals were also better off financially. Only 9 percent of the arrivals in January and February 1920 were unable to pay for room and board, and the average deposit for safekeeping increased from $14 to $26. The total amount deposited during the two-month period increased from $3,259.34 to $9,750.94. The attending physician at the institute also reported that the men in 1919 were in better physical condition than in previous years.[10]

Another event that had a profound impact upon the work of the institute was the passage of legislation in November 1916 that mandated the statewide Prohibition of the manufacture and sale of alcoholic beverages, effective May 1, 1918. Since his arrival in Detroit in 1891, McGregor had viewed alcoholism as the most serious social problem facing the young men of Detroit. It was the cause, he firmly believed, of broken families, unemployment, crime, and a host of other social problems. During his twenty-five years as superintendent of the institute, he had devoted special attention to the evils of alcohol in his nightly sermons and in his personal contacts with the men of the institute. His active support of J. L. Hudson's Detroit Municipal League was based in large part on its active campaign against the evil influence of saloonkeepers, brewers, and liquor interests, which, the league maintained, controlled the political life of Detroit. As head of the Associated Charities, McGregor gave personal attention to the needs of Detroit's charitable agencies, which dealt with the problems caused by alcoholism. He and Katherine McGregor also gave substantial financial support to national, state, and local prohibition organizations.[11]

During the fall 1916 election campaign, Tracy McGregor, the staff of the institute, and many of the mission men took an active role in supporting the prohibition amendment. They wore "Michigan Day" buttons and distributed thousands of prohibition leaflets on the streets of Detroit. They described themselves as "'former booze fighters' who were fighting the booze, this time to kill it!"[12]

The institute's monthly newsletter, distributed in May 1918, after statewide Prohibition went into effect, reflected Tracy McGregor's and his staff's views on Prohibition. In words that sounded more like an evangelistic speech by Billy Sunday, McGregor described the impact of the closing of local saloons and taverns in Detroit. "John Barleycorn is now an outcast . . . at night streets are quiet where hilarity and confusion reigned before. Policemen are in a strange atmosphere of peace."[13] The newsletter also described the impact of the May event upon the conditions at the institute. "Bleared eyes are cleared up, red noses and beards of several days['] growth began to disappear." Institute watchmen on duty in the evenings noticed "the new atmosphere of orderly quiet" and more "attentiveness" during the chapel services.[14]

It is difficult to assess the impact of Prohibition on the institute because it coincided with demobilization from the war. Some had predicted that "a closed saloon would mean an empty Institute," but this did not occur. During the months between May and November 1918, there was "an increase of 42 percent over the first few months of 1918, as compared to an increase of only 18 percent for the same period of 1917." The institute also recorded that lodgings increased by 20 percent and breakfasts by 50 percent immediately after Prohibition went into effect. Furthermore, it was noted by the institute restaurant staff that the "men were ordering small steaks and pork chops instead of the less expensive liver."[15]

The institute's carefully maintained records also reveal that requests for free beds decreased, money deposited by the men for safekeeping increased by 300 percent, and requests for cast-off clothing declined. Prohibition resulted in "an increase of suitcases and a decrease in small clothing packages checked at the office."[16] Murray McGregor later recalled that, after the statewide law on prohibition went into effect in May 1918, the "Mission no longer needed a bouncer to keep 'plastered drunkards' out."[17]

Despite the positive results of the closing of Detroit's saloons and taverns, Tracy McGregor and the staff were fully aware that the McGregor Institute would continue to serve an important role in the life of Detroiters. They recognized that the general economic conditions of the city would continue to produce "the lodging house type of men."[18] From his years of contact with the men, which involved not only the entrance interviews at the institute but also lifelong friendships with many, as well as his study of the economic patterns of Detroit, McGregor observed that many of the thousands of men who worked on the Great Lakes, building railroads and skyscrapers and working on farms during the summer season, crowded into Detroit during the winter. "These men" he observed, "are restless and seldom stay long on one plan."[19] Although Prohibition was an influential factor "in developing the homeless man," it would not eliminate them from the scene. "But it will," he believed, "make the transient worker a more reliable and independent man."[20]

The consumption of alcoholic beverages did not disappear altogether in Detroit with the passage of the prohibition legislation in 1916, which outlawed the manufacture and sale of alcoholic beverages in Michigan effective May 1918, and with the passage of the Eighteenth Amendment providing for nationwide prohibition. Hundreds of families produced beer, wine, and distilled liquor with home recipes accompanied by scores of more extensive local business operations. Canada was the main source of liquor smuggling after 1920, when nationwide Prohibition went into effect. Although the province of Ontario and all other Canadian states except Quebec also adopted Prohibition in 1920, the Canadian government continued to license distilleries and breweries to produce alcoholic beverages for export to foreign countries.

Detroit became the focal point of distribution for Canadian liquor, enhanced by the Canadian government's decision to establish a series of official government-operated export docks along the Detroit River from Amherstburg to Windsor. This opened the way for Detroiters to cross the narrow river, purchase liquor from the official Canadian export stores, and return to the Michigan shore while striving to be undetected by the U.S. Coast Guard, the "Prohibition Navy," or by state or local police. Trains, planes, and the numerous ferries that operated on the Detroit River prior to the opening of the Ambassador Bridge in 1929 and the Detroit-Windsor Tunnel in 1930 also provided a means to smuggle liquor into the Detroit area. In fact, it is estimated that approximately 75 percent of liquor smuggled into the United States during Prohibition from 1920 to 1933 came across the Detroit River and the waterway separating Ontario and Michigan.[21]

Once it arrived on U.S. shores, the contraband alcohol found its way into the homes and warehouses of smugglers, where it was stored until shipped by caravans to other cities in Michigan and the Midwest and into the thousands of blind pigs and speakeasies that operated in the Detroit area. By 1925 the common expression heard throughout the city was "If you can't get a drink you aren't trying."[22]

By the mid-1920s an anti-Prohibition movement began to organize in Michigan and nationwide. Many business leaders who had led the Prohibition campaign began to have doubts about its effectiveness and expressed deep concern about the violence, murder, and crimes associated with it. U.S. senator James Couzens, for example, one of the Prohibition leaders in the formative stages of the campaign in 1916, had by 1923 altered his position and urged the legalization of the manufacture, sale, and consumption of beer "containing less than 5 percent alcohol." The Eighteenth Amendment and the Volstead Act, he announced, were "not working and [were] unenforceable."[23] Tracy McGregor, the staff of the institute, and local church leaders also recognized the difficulties of enforcing Prohibition, but they steadfastly opposed any attempts to repeal it.

In October 1932, Tracy McGregor, in a major radio address under the auspices of the United Dry Campaign of Michigan, presented his views on "The Effects of Prohibition on Homeless Men."[24] He based his analysis on his experience at the McGregor Institute and in typical fashion carefully utilized the extensive records kept by the institute as well as his personal contacts with hundreds of mission men. He drew several conclusions "regarding the effect of both the wet and dry periods upon Homeless Men."[25]

First, he concluded, "there is less destitution and consequently more prosperity among Homeless Men under conditions of closed saloons and outlawed liquor than under saloons and legalized liquor." To support this conclusion, he compared the McGregor Institute's experience between two periods, the "five year wet period, 1913–1917" and the "five year dry period, 1919–1923." This comparison showed that during the dry period there was a decrease of 27 percent in the number of men "unable to pay anything for food, lodgings and other services," a decrease of 61 percent in the number of men requesting clothing, and an increase of 25 percent "in the average amount of surplus money left with the Institute for safe keeping."[26]

Next, McGregor maintained that the homeless men of the institute were "in better health when the sale of liquor is forbidden." Based on the records maintained by the institute's physicians, he observed that there was "less venereal disease, less gastro intestinal troubles and much better skin conditions" between 1917 and 1923 than the earlier five-year period. Furthermore, he reported, "they are also living cleaner and manlier lives."[27]

McGregor also devoted attention to the impact of the Eighteenth Amendment on professionals. "It was not uncommon" McGregor noted, "to see in the free line of applicants for help . . . doctors, lawyers, teachers and even preachers," and it was "not unusual for McGregor Institute to find a capable physician for its own work in the Bread line." Except during the years of "unusually severe business depression," this trend changed after 1918, when men with such professional training "were not so plentiful."[28]

The experiences of the institute's "day watchman" also proved his point. Prior to May 1, 1918, this employee stood outside the men's reading room and turned away "those men too intoxicated to be allowed in the sitting room with other men." It was not uncommon, McGregor noted, for the watchman "to turn away as many as 50 drunks in one evening." After 1918, he reported that few drunks visited the institute and that the watchman was assigned to other duties. McGregor acknowledged that liquor was readily available in Detroit after 1918 but was not as widespread as it was prior to that year. He pointed out that after 1918 to see a "staggering drunk man rolling down the street is sensational and draws a good deal of comment even in the vicinity of Brush and Gratiot Avenue," but prior to Prohibition such behavior "attracted little special attention."[29] Finally, McGregor concluded that Prohibition reduced the "temptation to drink." Though he noted that "there are places where liquor can be bought, . . . they are hidden away in dark corners" and "conscience must be stifled when they are visited."[30]

Besides Prohibition, the "return to normalcy" after the end of World War I brought many challenges to the institute and its staff. The second influenza epidemic, which impacted Detroit from 1918 to 1920, devastated the community. Schools, churches, stores, and other facilities that held public meetings were closed, and Detroiters wore gauze masks to prevent the spread of the deadly disease. Many of the men boarding at the institute became ill and were confined to their beds. By March 1920, a section of the institute was turned over to the Detroit Board of Health to treat not only those who roomed there but also others who were transferred from nearby rooming houses.[31]

The severe recession of 1921 followed on the heels of the influenza epidemic, throwing more than 4 million people out of work throughout the country, including tens of thousands in Detroit. Street begging again became a common sight in the city, and attendance at the institute increased sharply. In 1921, 82,095 lodgings at the institute were supplied "without cost to needy men, an increase of 71,112 over the previous year."[32]

Despite the end of the recession in 1925 and a return to "prosperity," the number of families seeking relief in Detroit and in the rest of the country increased steadily. According to a Russell Sage Foundation national survey of ninety-six public and private charitable relief agencies in thirty-six cities, "the number of families seeking relief increased sixty-three percent between 1916 and 1926," and the year of the greatest relief expenditure "was the year of the great prosperity, 1925."[33]

Detroit's experience reflected this pattern. Although the automobile industry, which now dominated Detroit and reflected that city's reputation as the "automobile capital of the world," flourished, there was less need for unskilled workers. "Inefficient workers are soon discarded and weeded out," throwing thousands into the ranks of unemployment, Murray McGregor observed.[34] But despite this trend, Detroit attracted tens of thousands of new workers every year. A survey conducted by the McGregor Institute, "Why Men Leave Home," based on a survey of the men applying for assistance, cited three reasons for this.

The main reason was the need for employment or "the desire to better one's working condition." Detroit was a magnet for such workers, encouraged by the well-advertised statements of the automobile companies announcing attractive jobs for new workers. In response, they arrived from abroad, from rural America, from smaller towns and villages, and from other cities to start new lives in Detroit.[35]

The second reason was "adventure." An estimated 20 percent, mostly "young, strong, restless fellows scarcely of voting age," were attracted to Detroit in the 1920s. They had read about Detroit in newspapers and magazine articles that gave a glowing picture of life in the city, where "work was plentiful, money abundant, entertainment varied and satisfying and opportunities unlimited."

The third reason cited was the "serious rupture in home life," caused by the death of parents, remarriage of a mother, or other family disruption. This group was mostly younger than twenty-one years of age and represented nearly 25 percent of the total number of newcomers.[36]

The impact of these trends on the institute was profound. Despite the positive influence of national Prohibition, the decrease of alcoholics, and the recovery from the 1921 recession, the number of men who sought assistance at the institute rose steadily. Between 1900 and 1927, the number of "destitute" men who came to the institute for assistance increased from 10,983 to 74,505. The total number lodging at the institute in 1927 had reached two hundred thousand, and those attending chapel services also increased. By 1928 the institute was holding sixteen religious services each week, including Bible classes of ten members each and gospel meetings attended by an average of two hundred persons. Attendance at these religious meetings was voluntary, although Murray reported that "good speakers and attractive music insured a keen interest."[37]

In 1930, Murray summarized the work of the institute during its forty years of operation. He gave a touching account of the founding of the Helping Hand Mission by his father and "the same spirit and unselfish sacrifice" of his brother, Tracy, and his mother. He told of the innovative programs developed by the institute to meet the needs of the men, such as the sale of kindling wood; the repair of furniture, clothing, and shoes; the 140-acre farm on the outskirts of Detroit; and the development of an employment bureau to aid the men in getting jobs. With great pride he reported that "five hundred thousand different men have found in the McGregor Institute a home and a friend in need." He ended his report with a list of the five aims followed by the board of trustees and directors, "to preserve the Founder's spirit of kindly helpfulness expressed in practical ways":[38]

To extend a friendly hand of sympathy and service

To give material aid without pauperizing or diminishing self-respect

To provide a temporary home with surroundings clean and of a good moral tone

To assist men in finding jobs and in supporting them until able to support themselves

To raise the ideals and strengthen the spiritual life by the inspiration of Gospel meetings, study of the Bible and in counsel and contact with good men

Murray's account of the institute's forty-year history had been circulated only a few months when another report on the institute was featured on the front page of the *Detroit Daily,* a recently established local paper. "Men's Mission Den of Filth: Charity House as Horror Pit" read the headlines. The account was written by Ray Harvey, a *Detroit Daily* reporter, who dressed as a "down and outer," applied at the institute for food and lodging. Based on his two days at the facility he described it as the "vilest charity flop house," a "fire trap," a "stench infested, garbage-purgatory swill house" where he was treated "worse than meanest carrion-fed dogs." In addition to his scurrilous attack on the food, he accused the institute staff of mistreating him and described the "filthy un-sanitary lavatories and the odorous, damp sleeping quarters."[39]

It didn't take the institute long to respond to the *Daily*'s attacks. Alexis Angell, the president of the institute's board of trustees, requested an immediate investigation by the mayor, the Detroit City Council, and the Detroit Welfare Department. Mayor Frank Murphy responded by appointing a special committee to investigate the institute, and before the week ended, members of the city council, the Detroit Board of Health, and the Detroit Health Department visited the institute for a hands-on review. Nothing but praise for the institute and its program and facilities resulted. John C. Nagel, president of the city council announced, "The criticism of the Institute is unjust," and he concluded that the "conditions there are most commendable. I think they are doing extraordinarily well under the present deluge of applications for meals and beds."[40] Dr. Harry Vaughan, the Detroit commissioner of health, reported that he could find "no condition . . . that would warrant criticism by the Health Department." He also "approved the facilities for beds, lavatories, toilet facilities, the dining room area and food."[41] Several staff members of the Health Department, including F. G. Legg, sanitary engineer, and E. Shultz, chief of the food, meat, and milk division, conducted intensive investigations of all aspects of the institute's program, including the structure of the building, food services, and sleeping accommodations. They also interviewed a "half dozen patrons selected at random" who revealed, "they had no fault to find with the service or with the cooking of the food."[42] The Vaughan report is especially valuable because it provides details about the institute building, its sleeping facilities, toilets, washrooms and baths, fumigation facilities, food storage and preparation facilities, and meeting rooms.

H. W. Zahrn of the Detroit Department of Welfare also expressed his strong criticism of the *Detroit Daily* report and challenged the accuracy of Harvey's charges. The McGregor Institute was not, he charged, financed largely by public tax dollars. The city, he pointed out, was only paying the cost of food; the institute was bearing the expenses of "registering the men, cooking and serving the free meals, now amounting to 4000 a day." But, he added, "not a cent has been paid so far [by the city of Detroit]."[43]

City council member John S. Hall, who "had a close acquaintanship with the Institute over a period of many years," summed up the views of other council members when he stated: "I know the place has been conducted on the highest plane. I have known Tracy McGregor for many years and I have the highest opinion of his honesty, ability and humanitarian instincts." He added, "He is one of the best practical Christians Detroit has."[44]

Reverend Roger Eddy Treat, pastor of the Bushnell Congregational Church, who had investigated the institute on behalf of a subcommittee on homeless men for the Welfare Department, added his endorsement: "I have stated and still insist that of all the Detroit institutions making serious efforts to feed and lodge homeless men, the McGregor Institute is doing the task least objectionably," and the *Detroit Daily* charges represent "a grave injustice to the management of the McGregor Institute."[45]

The McGregor family as well as the staff and trustees of the institute were startled and upset by the *Detroit Daily*'s allegations, but they felt vindicated by the prompt actions and findings of Dr. Vaughan, the officials of the Detroit Health and Welfare departments, as well as the members of the Detroit City Council. It was not the first time that the McGregor Institute had been a target of those who disapproved of their program. For forty years it had been characterized by segments of the press and the Detroit Police Department as a "haven for criminals, the lazy and shiftless." But the *Detroit Daily* expose was the first time that the facilities at the institute—the food, the lodging conditions, and the staff treatment of its guests—became the target of such allegations.

As serious as this criticism was, it was not the only crisis facing the McGregor Institute at this time. By the close of 1930, the country and especially Detroit faced its most severe economic crisis in its history. It was, of course, not the first time that economic conditions had affected the institute and its programs. Indeed, it had faced major recessions in 1893, 1907, 1914, and again in 1921. But what made this one different and much more serious was its depth. Before it ended, millions of workers had lost their jobs, and in Detroit an estimated 46 percent of the work force was without employment. By 1930 the situation in Detroit had become especially critical. Bread lines were found on city streets, apples were sold on every corner for five cents, begging throughout the city was commonplace, and petty crimes were increasing. In March 1932 many city workers were paid in scrip, and a hunger march led by unemployed factory workers resulted in the shooting deaths of five workers near the Ford Rouge Plant. Another characteristic of these economic crises was the depth of despair and hopelessness that descended on all segments of the Detroit community, including not only unskilled and skilled factory workers but also automotive officials, bankers, and leaders of industry. Unlike the previous recessions, few expected a quick recovery from this depression.

The McGregor Institute felt the impact immediately. The three years between 1930 and 1933 set new attendance records. In 1930 the institute served 239,142 lodgers and 572,364 meals, more than during any period in its forty-year history.[46]

The opening of city-operated lodging houses eased the burden on the McGregor Institute, but the popularity of the meals forced it to adopt a new policy in 1932 "of feeding only men who slept in the Institute building."[47] In 1930 the number of "free" lodgers represented 75 percent; in 1931, 83 percent; and in 1932, 67 percent. The 1932 decrease resulted from the policy of the institute asking boarders "to do more for themselves."[48]

A breakdown of new arrivals in 1932 revealed that of the 15,849 registered in 1932, 745 "were boys between 16 and 20 years of age," although the relative number of such youthful newcomers did not match their counterparts who traveled to the West and Southwest, "riding on freight trains . . . and living with groups of older men in jungle camps and other places." Detroit city officials were concerned enough to establish a committee "to study the Homeless Boy problems and devise means for reducing its dangers to the city and to the boys."[49] Two-thirds of the institute men were younger than forty years of age, with the largest between thirty-one and forty-nine, and only 12 percent were older than fifty. Also, the institute's statistics show that about 30 percent of the total were African American in 1932, reflecting the recent migration of substantial numbers of this group from the South.

The most pronounced change in 1932 was the response to the institute's programs related to chapel services. "Every third man lodging at the Institute attended some religious service," and "the number of men who openly showed a desire to follow Christ and accept him as a personal Savior has not been equaled since 1913."[50]

The availability of other facilities for homeless and needy men during the Great Depression also impacted the situation at the McGregor Institute. In addition to the institute, two privately run missions were available, the Detroit City Rescue Mission and the Howard Street Rescue Mission. The former, located at 166 Randolph, opened on February 14, 1908, and was run by David Stucky.[51] Tracy McGregor was on the incorporating board of the Detroit City Rescue Mission and also one of its financial supporters. The Howard Street Rescue Mission, located at Third and Howard before moving in October 1930 to 435 Rivard, opened on November 13, 1929. This four-story building, which catered to African American men, provided free meals, lodgings, and religious services.

The three missions were adequate for Detroit's homeless during normal economic downturns, but they could not meet the needs of the skyrocketing number of men who sought food and lodging in the 1930s. Political feuding between the mayor, city council, and various city departments prevented any concerted action until late in 1930 when a Homeless Men's Bureau was established by the mayor. By early 1931 it had opened two municipal lodges, housing nearly eight thousand men each night. The first of these facilities was made possible by a gift from the Fisher Body division of General Motors of its vacant plant at West Fort and 23rd Street. Opening on December 31, 1930, and known locally as Detroit Emergency Lodge or the "Fisher Lodge," it was operated and supervised by the Salvation Army, which provided evening musicals and other programs. A month later a similar municipal lodging house was opened in the vacant auto plant at Piquette and Beaubien, a gift from the Studebaker Automobile Company. The city also opened several "feeding stations for homeless men."[52]

These municipal lodges supplied benefits to hundreds of homeless men, but they also had their critics. The operator of local flophouses and rooming establishments attacked the city for competing with private enterprise; others claimed that such lodges only encouraged men to loaf rather than find work. Still other critics charged that the lodges were "hot beds of Communist activity."[53]

By June 1931, the growing public opposition to public tax support of homeless lodges led the city council and Welfare Department to close the Fisher and Studebaker facilities and send the indigent homeless to the Wayne

County Infirmary at Eloise, located fifteen miles west of Detroit. Known as the "finest poorhouse in the World," it housed several thousand of the aged and infirm, physically handicapped and feebleminded, and after the closure of the local lodges, hundreds of Detroit's homeless.[54]

By 1931, Tracy, Murray, and the McGregor Institute trustees became increasingly concerned about the depth of the Depression and its impact on the programs of the institute. They began to entertain serious doubts as to whether the institute could continue to function effectively and still pursue its goals. They were, of course, fully aware of the demographic changes in Detroit during the forty years since the mission had been established, especially its burgeoning population. Detroit's international reputation as the automobile center of the world had served as a magnet for thousands of young men who came to the city in search of "a well-paying job." During normal times and especially during periods of prosperity, the institute was able to handle the homeless men who needed food and lodging. Even during the periodic recessions it had been able to expand its facilities to provide needed help. But because of the severity of the economic downturns in the 1930s, Tracy McGregor and the trustees found it necessary to review the future of the institute.

There were several major concerns. First, the institute building was "no longer large enough for the number of men requiring shelter."[55] The food services became hopelessly inadequate as the depression worsened. On one day alone in 1930 the institute struggled to feed more than a thousand meals "free to every man who could not pay."[56] Also, relief aid to the unemployed, needy, and homeless was perceived by the public as a "governmental function," especially after the Federal Emergency Relief Act was passed by Congress in May 1933. Tracy and Murray and the staff also recognized that the men registered at the institute did not need temporary assistance; they needed food and lodging for long periods of time, and many needed extensive medical treatment.

Another factor, which greatly influenced their deliberations, was the loss of several of the most loyal and trusted leader members of the institute. On December 24, 1932, Alexis C. Angell died. He had been on the board of trustees for forty years and since 1924 had served as its chairman. A former U.S. district court judge, a respected legal scholar, and a highly regarded community leader, he was an "incredible member of the Board of Trustees" during some of its most difficult years.[57] The death of Edward Carrabin on April 8, 1932, had dealt another serious blow. He had been associated with the mission since 1890 and had served as its religious director for most of his tenure and later as assistant manager of the McGregor Institute. McGregor's permanent move to Washington, D.C., in 1931 was also a factor in determining the future of the institute.[58] Although he had resigned as superintendent in 1916, he had remained on the board of trustees as a "managing trustee" and continued to be involved in the operation of the institute, but by 1931, Katherine's declining health made him decide to locate permanently to Washington.

In 1933 Tracy and Murray and the trustees concluded that they had to consider other alternatives for the institute. They first contacted John Ballanger, head of the Detroit Homeless Men's Bureau, to offer the institute building to the city either permanently or "for the time being as a sort of supplement to municipal activity."[59] When this offer was turned down by the Detroit Public Welfare Department, the institute contacted the Michigan state relief administrator, William Haber. They proposed that the facilities at 453 Brush Street be turned over to the state "for a year as an experiment."[60] When these alternatives failed, Tracy McGregor considered whether the institute might operate as a mission "carrying on little else but strictly religious activity."[61] The McGregors and the trustees were in agreement that such a course of action was not practical. Other alternatives had to be considered. They met with leaders of other charitable organizations affiliated with the Detroit Community Fund and reviewed their programs dealing with the homeless men of the community. They were most impressed with the work of the Goodwill Industries of Detroit. Founded in Delray in 1921 and later operating from a small garage in downtown Detroit, it had expanded by the 1930s into an active citywide organization, assisting scores of disabled and handicapped men and women who renovated or repaired donated furniture, appliances, and clothing for resale to needy Detroit families. Much of this work was similar to that performed at the McGregor Institute since its founding in the late nineteenth century. Furthermore, the McGregor family was closely associated with the Goodwill organization. Murray McGregor was one of the original members of the Goodwill Board of Directors when it was founded, and he later served as secretary of its board. Tracy had supported Goodwill with generous financial gifts for a number of years and assisted the organization annually with support from the Community Fund. In June 1935 the McGregors decided that they would close the institute and on July 15 turn the building over to Goodwill for five years "under a virtually rent-free lease" with the tacit understanding that the "lease may develop later into a rent-free gift."[62]

The directors of Goodwill immediately accepted the generous offer, and on September 27, 1935, the official dedication of the building took place.[63]

Within weeks it was converted to the needs of the Goodwill program. A new freight elevator was installed, and the dormitories were closed and converted into departments for shoe repair, dressmaking, cabinetmaking, upholstery and electric repair, and a sorting area for the "bags given to Goodwill."

Tracy McGregor was heartbroken by the decision to close the institute. He wrote that he felt "a wrench and deep regret that an enterprise, in which we have taken such interest and satisfaction over so long a period, must now be closed." He added, "Whatever regret we may feel, however, can be offset by recalling the service rendered and the good done to many thousands of men during more than forty years." The closing of the institute was "natural" he believed "in view of the changes which have taken place in Detroit. . . . Our beloved Institute has lived its life and fulfilled its purpose."[64]

Tracy McGregor and his family were not the only ones saddened by the closure of the institute. Hundreds of former residents wrote to express their regrets and their appreciation for the work done at the institute over the years. The Detroit City Council passed a long resolution praising the work of the institute, and its president, John C. Lodge, summed up the sentiments of his colleagues: "The McGregors rate among Detroit's first citizens because of the great work they have done so modestly. I don't know what the City would have done without their help."[65] In its lead editorial, "The End of an Era," the *Detroit Times* announced, "The Institute itself may go out of existence, but it will leave behind it kindly memories of its humanitarian services to Detroit's unfortunate during nearly half a century."[66]

Murray McGregor added his feelings when he reminisced about the "more than 7,000,000 men [who had] found food and lodging at the Institute, many of them bums, were changed from ways of useless wanderers into useful citizens . . . many a drunk and many a tramp of yesterday today have families and homes of their own after getting a fresh start in a hostile world through the helping hand of the Institute."[67]

Before the five-year lease expired, tragedy struck the new headquarters of Goodwill Industries. On a cold March day in 1938, the six-story McGregor Institute building caught fire, and despite the help of all available fire equipment called in by five alarms, the structure was ruined.[68] Fortunately, the McGregor Institute trustees carried insurance on the building, which provided $101,802. In September 1938 the trustees of the institute gave Goodwill Industries $90,000 to buy the Boyer Building at 356 East Congress and an auxiliary building at 1024 Holbrook.[69] Following Tracy McGregor's directive, the remaining funds of the institute were to be distributed to other charitable organizations, including the Detroit City Rescue Mission, which received a gift of $5,000. In addition, Murray McGregor, who served as secretary on the board of trustees of the Goodwill Industries, distributed small grants to "143 needy boys and men" from a fund made available from the McGregor Institute.[70]

The McGregor Institute was dissolved by the Michigan Corporation and Securities Commission on March 11, 1940, ending one of the most remarkable social endeavors in Detroit's history.[71]

The McGregor family, 1880. Thomas (standing), Tracy, Elizabeth, and Murray. Courtesy McGregor Fund.

Tracy McGregor in 1901, the year of his marriage to Katherine Whitney. Courtesy McGregor Fund.

One of the few surviving photographs of Katherine Whitney McGregor, 1901. Courtesy McGregor Fund.

Beginning in 1893 the sale and home delivery of wood provided funds for the mission. The McGregor Mission wood delivery wagons were a common sight on Detroit streets in the 1890s and the early years of the twentieth century. Courtesy McGregor Fund.

The mission had facilities for cutting the kindling wood. Courtesy McGregor Collection, Walter P. Reuther Library, Wayne State University.

The Mission Brotherhood, ca. 1920 (Tracy McGregor is standing, second from the left). Courtesy McGregor Collection, Walter P. Reuther Library, Wayne State University.

Evening chapel services were held at the McGregor Institute several evenings a week. Courtesy McGregor Collection, Walter P. Reuther Library, Wayne State University.

Thanksgiving Day Evening

at McGregor Mission,

239 Brush Street.

A SPECIAL PROGRAM HAS BEEN PREPARED AND WE CAN PROMISE THAT ITS EXERCISES WILL BE EVEN MORE SATISFYING THAN THE FEAST FOR THE BODY, SERVED EARLIER IN THE DAY.

Bring Your Family and Friends.

COME AT 7.30 O'CLOCK.

McGregor Institute Brotherhood

Season 1911-12

October 2—Fall Rally and Supper

November 6—"How to Get a Job and Keep It"—Short Talks

December 4—Mr. J. L. Hudson

January 1—"The New Year"

February 5—"Washington" Rev. J. D. MacDonald

March 4—"The Cultivation of the Mind"—Short Talks

April 1—"Our Socialist Brothers" Mr. Wm. H. [illegible]

May 6—Banquet

W. D. MONTGOMERIE, CHAIRMAN
GEO. BATCHELDOR, SECRETARY

Weekly Brotherhood Meeting Sunday at [illegible] in Mr. McGregor's Room.

Sunday Night at McGregor Mission

Stereopticon Views illustrating Mission Work in the Interior of Africa, with an Address by Mr. James H. McConkey

YOU WILL BE WELCOME

Friday Club

Each Friday night at 6:30 a group of men, who call themselves the Friday Club, meet around the table on the upper floor to discuss some interesting topic.

If you can attend either regularly or occasionally, they will be much pleased.

(over)

Mission men joined the Brotherhood, Fellowship, and Friday clubs, which sponsored a variety of weekly and monthly meetings. Courtesy McGregor Collection, Walter P. Reuther Library, Wayne State University.

Murray McGregor was closely associated with the McGregor mission from its founding in 1890 to its closure in 1935. He later served as secretary of Goodwill Industries. Courtesy Goodwill Industries.

McGregor provided a library in each of the missions with newspapers, journals, and books. Courtesy McGregor Collection, Walter P. Reuther Library, Wayne State University.

Edward Carrabin shown with his wife served on the mission staff for more than thirty years. Courtesy McGregor Collection, Walter P. Reuther Library, Wayne State University.

Fred M. Butzel, head of Jewish Charities, longtime friend of Tracy McGregor. Courtesy Walter P. Reuther Library, Wayne State University.

PART 3

Philanthropy and Detroit's Public Policy

7

Tracy and Katherine McGregor's Partnership in Charity

AFTER TRACY MCGREGOR ARRIVED in Detroit following his father's sudden death in 1891, he devoted his energies largely to the Mission for Homeless Men until he resigned as superintendent in 1915. During those twenty-five years, though, he also became increasingly involved with a number of charitable agencies in Detroit that were dedicated to aiding the ill, homeless, and destitute. He developed close working relationships with the leaders of local agencies, clinics, and hospitals who referred men to the mission and also with the charities to which the mission referred residents who needed specialized assistance or medical treatment.

The Associated Charities of Detroit (ACD) was an organization with which McGregor and the mission staff worked closely, even though at times the two agencies were at odds over some of the policies and practices of the mission. Founded in 1878 with the major objective of "preventing street begging and assisting the deserving poor," the ACD was operated by a group of volunteers, mostly female, who were committed to aiding Detroit's burgeoning population of destitute and needy citizens. These "visitors," as the staff members of most charities were called, were the wives and daughters of Detroit's community and business leaders who believed that it was their religious and moral duty to help the less fortunate members of the community. They visited families or individuals who applied for aid or who were referred to the ACD by other private or public agencies. Contacts with applicants were usually made in their homes so that the visitors could examine and evaluate firsthand their living conditions, their character, their status in the neighborhood, and the treatment and condition of their children. Applicants who passed the "worthiness" test were given direct financial aid or other forms of assistance such as groceries, coal, or wood for stoves. In special cases they were given railroad tickets to return to their homes in other parts of Michigan or the Midwest. Young men in need of lodging, meals, and employment were sent to the Mission for Homeless Men.[1]

After McGregor's marriage to Katherine Whitney in 1901, they both became major financial sponsors of the ACD and other local charitable organizations. Detailed financial records kept by Tracy reflect their generous gifts. In 1909, for example, they were not only the largest contributors to the ACD but also donors of major gifts to the Detroit YMCA, Detroit Rescue Mission, Michigan Audubon Society, Grace Reform Mission, Michigan Child Labor Association, Boy Scouts, Salvation Army, Society of St. Vincent dePaul, Crittenden House, Thompson Home for Homeless Ladies, Visiting Nurses Association, Protestant Orphan Asylum, and the Women's Board of Home Missions.[2]

Katherine continued the Whitney family's long tradition of supporting local charities after her marriage. In 1904, she purchased the Stevens Homestead on Woodward Avenue in Highland Park and converted it into the Home for Orphaned Children. For years she had been financing the care of a group of orphans, but now she provided a special home for them that was ideal for such a purpose. Described as a "roomy, three story structure with walls of field stone and cement" and, with a "gracious sun parlor," it was large enough to accommodate twenty children. Katherine financed the purchase of the home, supervised its renovations, and paid for the staff to operate it.[3]

According to Tracy, Katherine's "aim was to do something more than provide homeless children with a refuge until they could be taken care of elsewhere or reach an age when they could go out into the world and shift for themselves. Instead of being solely objects of charity," he explained, "they are given an education, supplemented by practical training, that will fit them for positions of responsibility in the world."[4] The young children attended nearby local public schools, and the older ones were assigned tasks at the home. The boys did gardening, lawn mowing, tended the furnace, and other "odd jobs that may arise."[5] The girls did the housework, made beds, prepared and served meals, and were "being converted into model housewives." If any of the young children showed a special talent or interest, such as music, they were given lessons.

Katherine McGregor's involvement in assisting young orphans in the community was heartily supported by her husband. In 1905 he poignantly reflected, "We have no little children in our own home but we find great pleasure in caring for nine children whom Mrs. McGregor and I will soon remove to a comfortable home in Highland Park."[6]

She took more interest in the Highland Park home than just underwriting its expenses. She devoted a great deal of personal attention to its daily operation. According to a local newspaper reporter who visited the home in February 1909, "There isn't a detail in connection with the work of the Home with which she is not familiar—not a question of importance on which she does not pass; not a purchase of consequence made without which she supervises it in person or is consulted. . . . [T]he many hours she spends here are busy ones, and all times she is on call, in spite of other matters that require her attention."[7]

Katherine McGregor also took an active interest in other local organizations. On July 1, 1910, she presented to the ACD a large facility in New Baltimore, thirty-eight miles northeast of Detroit on Lake St. Clair. The structure, called Bay Court, built a few years earlier as a hotel, was purchased by Mrs. McGregor to be used as a convalescent home for mothers and children. In order to give the mothers time to recover their health, their children were cared for by a staff of nurses and other professionals. When it opened in 1910, the ACD appointed a committee of distinguished citizens to supervise Bay Court, including Claire M. Sanders, Henry G. Stevens, Louise Webber Jackson, William Ingles, Dr. H. N. Torrey, and Henry Williams. Mrs. Frederick M. Alger was added to represent the Fresh Air Society. Later, Bay Court was placed under the direction of the District Nursing Society, which was also heavily endowed by Katherine McGregor.[8]

Her active interest and involvement in all phases of the work of the orphan home was typical of Katherine's approach to all charities. Although she was extremely wealthy and deeply committed to assisting the poor, she did not give money capriciously. She explained her method to a *Detroit News-Tribune* reporter in 1902:[9]

> Whenever I feel impelled to make a gift of money I always reason with myself until I have brought it down to the lowest possible figure. One's impulse in giving is always to give largely, and the danger is not in giving too little, but too much. It is always possible to give twice, or more than

> twice, and I have discovered it is almost better not to give at all than to give injudiciously. Above all, I want to use money intelligently and not scatter it about in a hap-hazard way.

Katherine McGregor's method of giving differed from many other wealthy benefactors. She did not just give money but also visited the charities, observed their programs, and often volunteered to assist them in their work. "When Mrs. McGregor once became interested in a family," an observer noted, "she sees them through all their troubles, assumes the entire responsibility of the family and shoulders all of the expenses."[10] She did not wait for charities and individuals to ask for her support. She contacted local members of the clergy, reviewed Detroit newspapers, and when she discovered "a sad case of destitution, which was not likely to appeal to anyone else, she at once takes it up."[11] Tracy McGregor heartily approved of her support of the Highland Park orphans home, Bay Court, the Visiting Nurses Association, and the other local charities. On one occasion he confided to a *Detroit Free Press* reporter, "It is an inspiration to me how her heart goes out to the unfortunates."[12]

Tracy and Katherine McGregor's decision to take a more active role in charitable organizations and their related activities was due in part to what was occurring in Detroit at the time. They witnessed dramatic changes in the 1890s when Detroit expanded rapidly to meet the needs of a rising industrial city. But the growth of factories, the rapid expansion of government services, and the beginnings of large-scale immigration to Detroit were minor compared to the impact of the automobile. Detroit's rise as the automobile center of the United States and, by the mid-1920s, the world, had a profound impact. Within a twenty-year period, from 1900 to 1920, the city's population rose sharply, moving it from the thirteenth to the fourth largest city in the United States.[13]

Unlike the previous decades when most of the new residents came from other parts of the United States, the majority of newcomers after 1900 migrated from Canada and Europe. Most were unskilled workers, and a large portion of them could not read, write, or speak English. Furthermore, because many came from rural farming areas of Europe, they were totally unfamiliar with urban life. Nevertheless, after a few weeks of intensive training, they could master the limited skills needed to perform routine functions in the automobile plants.

Language remained one of the major challenges the immigrants faced. This situation caused an immediate crisis in the Detroit school system, which was suddenly required to teach the English language and American life and customs to the children of these immigrants. Not only were there a mere handful of teachers on staff who had the necessary multilingual skills and experiences, but also Detroit was unable to recruit enough qualified persons. The economic downturns and recessions in 1907–8 and 1914–15 exacerbated the condition of teacher shortages and the layoffs of tens of thousands of workers. It came as no surprise that the immigrants who lacked language skills were the first laid off and the last rehired.[14]

The immigrant families, who arrived in Detroit by the thousands each week, faced the daunting challenge of finding adequate housing. With its long-established tradition of single-family dwellings, Detroit did not have the tenements, apartment houses, or multifamily dwellings that most of the East Coast industrial cities had. As a result, newly arrived immigrants to Detroit were forced to live in substandard housing. Often several families lived in one small, single-family house, located long distances from the factories and manufacturing plants. Detroit business leaders immediately mounted a campaign to alleviate the housing shortage problem. Unfortunately, Detroit's government leaders were unable to agree on a concrete plan to provide or even encourage the construction of adequate housing. Thus it became the responsibility of charitable agencies to deal with the social problems that resulted from the crisis.

The sudden and enormous rise in population also created new health problems. Despite the screening procedures of U.S. Customs at entrance ports such as Ellis Island in New York, many immigrants brought communicable diseases with them and passed them on to colleagues in the work places. Immigrant children also fell victim to a series of epidemics that swept through Detroit starting in the 1890s. The most notable and serious of these was the influenza epidemic, locally called the "Spanish Flu," which struck Detroit in 1918 and again in 1919, taking the lives of thousands of local residents. Detroit built several new hospitals—Grace, in 1888, Herman Kiefer in 1893, and the Henry Ford Hospital in 1915—but even they failed to fulfill the needs of Detroit's burgeoning population.[15]

Public services in the Detroit area suffered during these years of rapid expansion. As the city expanded to the east, north, and west, fire, police, water, sewer, and public transportation services became inadequate. The city government was so inefficient and corrupt that it could not respond to these crises, and only after private organizations such as the Citizen's League and the Thursday Noon Group (which is discussed in chapter 9) led reform movements did the situation improve. However, little of substance was accomplished until after World War I.

Tracy McGregor witnessed these crises within the city both as superintendent of the McGregor Institute and through his active involvement in major local charitable organizations. The ACD did a creditable job, given its limited resources, in dealing with these challenges, but the leaders of the major Detroit charities realized the need for new leadership and the establishment of a more powerful central organization. In 1912 Tracy McGregor was asked to head a nomination committee for the ACD to recruit new leadership. With the assistance of several friends and colleagues with whom he had worked at the McGregor Institute, including Richard Webber who was the late Joseph L. Hudson's nephew, Fred Butzel, and Jacob Farrand, he accepted the appointment and created a new slate of candidates for the board of trustees. These new board members recognized that changes in the operation of the ACD must be made immediately in order to more effectively deal with the current crises facing the city.[16]

A majority of these new members of the board of trustees agreed that the ACD "had not closely adjusted itself to the needs of the city, possibly because of Detroit's enormous growth." However, when a controversy erupted between the new and old board members, they agreed that the entire board of trustees should resign. A new committee was then chosen, consisting of Tracy McGregor, Luman Goodenough, Henry G. Stevens, Richard H. Webber, and James T. Whitehead, and given the responsibility and authority not only to "administer the activities of the Associated Charities" but also to develop a full-scale reorganization plan. The select group under Tracy McGregor's leadership developed a new structure and mission plan for the ACD, and in the fall of 1913 a new board of trustees was elected. Tracy declined to serve on the board as a trustee, but he did agree to complete a reorganization plan. Within a year the plan was completed and implemented by the board of trustees.[17]

The reorganization plan's first provision was to establish bureaus that would serve the specific needs of all affiliated charities and would "turn over to individual charities those branches of the work which can be administered through special societies," thus avoiding duplication of effort.[18]

The application bureau was formed to direct "any person to the individual charity suitable for handling the situation." This bureau did not want to get involved in "how such a case so referred should be handled, unless asked for advice." The investigation bureau was directed to study and evaluate the activities of the various charities and determine which charitable organization was best suited to handle a specific case.[19] The registration bureau was "established to assist organizations and individuals in their efforts to prevent duplication of unwise aid." Finally, the new plan called for a finance bureau to raise funds for the work of the ACD. By clearly defining the fund-raising responsibilities to a designated bureau, the board of trustees could devote their major efforts to developing policies for the ACD, giving special attention to a plan "preventive in nature" that dealt with the charitable needs of the city.[20]

Tracy McGregor's reorganization of the ACD also called for a full-time professional staff to administer the program, rather than relying on volunteers. The board decided to proceed slowly in their hiring agenda until they could locate competent persons for each position. The office supervisor position was filled on February 1, 1914, with the appointment of Miss Ada Freeman. Her success in "systematizing the office work" was rewarded on January 20, 1915, when she was promoted to the position of general secretary of the ACD. Unfortunately, ill health forced her to resign a few weeks later, and her functions were assigned to three board members and the secretaries of the application, investigation, and finance bureaus.[21]

McGregor devoted considerable time to the reorganization of the ACD during these formative years, but his interests extended beyond both this charitable organization and the McGregor Institute. He and Katherine also played a key role in the establishment of the Visiting Housekeepers Association, which was founded on December 1, 1912.[22] Based on their experience in dealing with Detroit's poor and needy at the institute and with other charitable endeavors, the McGregors helped finance this new organization on an experimental basis. Its prime objective was to assist the poor in buying groceries and dealing with household problems. It met with immediate success, especially for the families of foreign immigrants who knew little about urban life and its challenges. Classes were established for older girls to be taught cookery adapted to the unique needs of these immigrant families. This program was such a signal success that it led to an expanded program developed to teach women of all ages "how to plan nourishing meals, buy to good advantage, prepare pleasing dishes, make new garments and make over old ones, prepare food for invalids and take proper care of children and house."[23] By October 1912, the work of this experimental program was so successful that a permanent Visiting Housekeepers Association, funded by the finance bureau of ACD, was established.[24]

Tracy and Katherine McGregor followed the work of the Visiting Housekeepers Association with great interest and continued to support it financially. Tracy believed this program effectively dealt in a "preventive" way with the problems of Detroit's poor and needy. In 1914, with his support, the association expanded its activities to aid the Detroit Poor Commission and the Babies Milk Fund. A year later, in 1915, the association purchased and renovated a home on Livernois and sponsored cooking and sewing classes there. The success of these classes soon led to the formation of a "Mothers Club" with headquarters at the Livernois site. Judge Henry S. Hulbert of the Juvenile Court, and a close friend of Tracy McGregor, was so impressed with their program that he secured their services to supervise delinquent mothers "in order to eliminate the necessity of disciplining them by revoking their pensions."[25]

Tracy McGregor also saw the crisis of health issues among Detroit's poor, and he made it another high priority on the agenda of the Associated Charities. As a major benefactor of several Detroit hospitals and clinics, he soon learned of the inefficient and biased system of treating the needy poor. Most local hospitals set aside a few rooms and wards for the poor, but they could not handle the huge number of people in need of medical attention, especially during the periodic epidemics that struck Detroit. McGregor used his prior experiences at the Mission for Homeless Men to develop a plan for the ACD to sponsor the "Detroit Federated Clinics to give free medical services to the needy" and to solicit the aid of the "philanthropic physicians" of the city.[26]

By 1916, under Tracy McGregor's leadership, the ACD had not only greatly expanded its scope of programs but also become much more efficient in handling its normal cases. But the number of applications for assistance increased, and during 1915–16, for example, an average of 2,500 new cases were registered each month. Health-related registrations and those connected with "industrial welfare and unemployment problems" were largely responsible for these increases. Also, for the first time "trouble cases" and the so-called subnormals were given special attention.[27] As the housing shortage in the Detroit area reached a critical stage in 1915, the ACD responded to the urgent needs of Detroit families who had lost their homes due to sharply increased rental fees.

The Visiting Housekeepers Association; the Detroit League on Urban Conditions among Negroes, which had been established in 1915 "to act as a clearinghouse for social work among Negroes and as an agency for improving every phase of the living and working side of the Negro's life"; the Federated Clinics; and the Bay Court home all contributed to the expanding role and widening influence of the ACD.[28] As 1916 ended, it was obvious to Tracy McGregor and the officers of the ACD that involvement in the war in Europe placed another burden upon charitable activities in Detroit. The American Red Cross, already actively involved in the war effort, was joined by new charitable groups founded to aid the victims of the war abroad as well as local citizens who were seriously affected by the shortages of coal, heating supplies, and other consumer goods. Detroiters responded promptly and enthusiastically to the Allied war effort. New war bonds and war-related fund-raising efforts were, as one reporter noted, "burgeoning every hour on the hour," causing community leaders to become concerned as to "where this trend would lead." The Detroit Chamber of Commerce had tried "to establish federated fundraising," but many of Detroit's charities were concerned that such a centralized effort would be dominated by business groups, often overlooking the legitimate needs of their organizations. Tracy McGregor and his colleagues shared this concern. They feared that such a centralized fund-raising effort would be more interested in the raising of funds rather than in *how* the funds would be used.[29]

In order to resolve a deadlock that ensued between the Board of Commerce and the Associated Charities, Tracy McGregor met with officials of the former and worked out a compromise. They agreed to hire a nationally recognized social worker to develop a carefully coordinated war fund campaign and to take over the leadership of the ACD.

McGregor spent several weeks of careful consideration and contact with social agencies all over the country, after which he named his top choice, William J. Norton, director of the Cincinnati Council of Social Services. The records do not reveal whether McGregor or any of his Detroit colleagues had ever met Norton, but they were certainly aware of his accomplishments. Tracy had often been to Cincinnati to investigate the Council of Social Services' program for the homeless. Furthermore, Norton had received national acclaim for establishing in Cincinnati a single fund-raising campaign representing all social agencies in that city.[30]

Although a relatively young man, thirty-four years old in 1917, he had already established a national reputation in the social work field. Born in 1883 in White Head, Maine, he received his education at Bowdoin College and subsequently entered the social work field. From 1905 to 1909 he served as assistant director of the Goodrich House Social Settlement in Brooklyn, New York, followed by a two-year stint with the Department of Charities and Corrections in Cleveland, Ohio, and then in 1911 he relocated to Cincinnati.[31]

After contacting social work leaders and those public officials in Brooklyn, Cleveland, and Cincinnati who knew the candidate, Tracy invited Norton to Detroit to review and evaluate the program of the ACD and to present his findings to the board of trustees. This gave McGregor the opportunity to not only meet Norton but also to observe the manner in which he conducted his review and how he handled his meetings with city officials and business leaders. On March 28, 1917, Tracy recommended that the Detroit Board of Commerce sponsor Norton at a major public meeting in Detroit. The topic of his presentation was "Cooperation and Community Services."[32]

Norton made a favorable impression. His speech to the Board of Commerce and his meetings with the officers were well received, and social agency leaders endorsed his candidacy. In May 1917, he was offered and immediately accepted the position of director and secretary of the ACD. This opportunity propelled Norton on a lifelong social work career in Detroit and a lasting and close friendship with Tracy McGregor.[33]

Norton did not waste any time in taking over his new position. He spent the summer months of 1917 meeting with the leaders of Detroit's charitable agencies and their staffs. McGregor often accompanied him to make sure that he received the proper reception and cooperation. These visits coincided with Norton's assignment to draft a reorganization plan for the ACD and his endeavor to develop a "federated giving" program for Detroit.

After a series of meetings with Tracy McGregor and other ACD leaders, William Norton presented his ideas and recommendations for the formation of a Detroit Community Federation of Social Agencies on October 17, 1917. He suggested two plans.

One would essentially continue the ACD in its current form, "filling vacancies on the Board of Trustees of the Associated Charities, expanding federated activities of the Finance Bureau if possible by securing participation of other agencies, and confining activities to the above programs." The second proposal, which Norton and McGregor preferred, was the establishment of a community union representing "all social agencies, all social departments of government, all civic agencies and each religious denomination."[34] Delegates representing the agencies would constitute the board of trustees, and a special executive committee would be formed representing the major charities. With strong endorsements from McGregor, Fred Butzel, and Richard Webber, the second plan passed unanimously, and arrangements for an organizational meeting were begun.

McGregor, Norton, and key charity leaders selected December 17, 1917, for the organizational meeting, to be held at the Pontchartrain Hotel. One hundred thirty-seven persons, representing fifty-seven local civic and religious organizations, attended the meeting. Allan Templeton, president of the Board of Commerce, opened the session, followed by the mayor of Detroit, Oscar Marx, who pledged the support of the city for the new organization.[35]

After William Norton provided the details of the proposed organization, Fred Butzel, who headed the United Jewish Charities, presented the suggested constitution for the Detroit Community Union, which would be the governing structure of the organization. The proposal was passed unanimously, and the group elected Tracy McGregor as chair; Allan Templeton, Gustavus D. Pope, Clarence Booth, and Mrs. R. B. Jackson, vice-chairs; William Livingston Jr., treasurer; and William J. Norton, secretary. The three-year trustee terms included Henry G. Stevens, John Ballontyne, Judge Henry S. Hulbert, Miss Julie Russel, Fred M. Butzel, and Kirby White Jr. For two-year terms, Claire Sanders, Dr. A. G. Studer, Dr. Lent D. Upson, George R. Bedinger, Dr. Charles Chadsey, and Mrs. James T. Shaw were elected.[36]

The only other major action taken during this meeting was the appointment of a special committee, with Emory W. Clark as chair, "to canvass the feasibility of creating a central organization for the collection of war and local funds."[37] Because of the urgency to meet the needs of the Allied war efforts, the committee began its work immediately. Within a few hours after the Community Union was organized, they requested approval from the Board of Commerce to form a "financial federation," with Tracy McGregor, Lent Upson, Henry G. Stevens, and Clarence Booth in charge.[38] After careful deliberations and meetings with community leaders and the heads of the affiliated charitable agencies and of major corporations, the committee created the Detroit Patriotic Fund. On February 6, 1918, they defined the mission as being "for the purposes of eliminating waste in raising money for patriotic and philanthropic uses, of saving time for those who work in fundraising campaigns and for those who give, and of increasing the number of givers."[39]

The Patriotic Fund invited members of the newly established Detroit Community Union to join with other organizations involved in the war effort. Those member agencies of the Community Union had to submit a uniform budget for review and approval by the Central Budget Committee of the union before any fund requests could be presented to the Patriotic Fund.

Furthermore, in order to join the Patriotic Fund, the agencies had to agree not to raise any money separately.[40]

Tracy McGregor, of course, was actively involved in all phases of the establishment and operation of the Patriotic Fund. He was not only one of its founders but also, as chair and president-elect of the Detroit Community Union, deeply involved with most of the charitable organizations in the greater Detroit area. The high regard in which he was held by the Detroit Board of Commerce, the American Red Cross, and other war-related agencies broadened his influence. His style of leadership and his ability to diplomatically resolve disputes between charities and local governmental departments enhanced his authority. By 1921, when he celebrated his thirtieth year in Detroit, he had become one of the most influential and respected civic leaders in the community.[41]

The employment of William J. Norton as head of the Detroit Community Union relieved McGregor of many of his duties as president of the ACD, but he continued to play a leadership role in Detroit's charitable movement. As president of the Patriotic Fund he coordinated the wartime fund-raising campaign, which was a major task in itself. The American Red Cross and other foreign war relief agencies representing some of Detroit's large ethnic groups were reluctant to turn over the sole responsibility of raising and distributing funds. Under McGregor's leadership and the strong support he received from business and community leaders, he was able to overcome opposition to this new "federated" program. Another crisis erupted when many of the affiliated charities had exhausted their operating budgets and had no resources until the end of the year. Tracy McGregor resolved the impasse by persuading the board of trustees of the Patriotic Fund to borrow $150,000 backed by a promissory note signed by McGregor and several trustees. This action helped eliminate the skepticism of many agency leaders and ensured a successful fund-raising campaign.[42]

Another challenge faced the Detroit Community Union and the Patriotic Fund, which changed its name in March 1920 to the Detroit Community Fund. The competition for funding of the construction of new facilities by affiliated agencies threatened to undermine the authority of the Detroit Community Fund. So, in 1924, the Community Union established the policy that all affiliated agencies must secure prior approval from the Community Fund before embarking on any capital improvements.[43]

In addition, the depression of 1920–21 hit the new federation of Detroit agencies hard. Unemployment rose sharply, and many donors, especially Detroit business firms, curtailed their contributions. At the same time, requests by charities for additional financial assistance increased sharply. As a member of the executive committee of the Community Union and the Community Fund, McGregor faced this crisis and chaired the "Individual Givers" or, as it was commonly called, the "Big Givers" Committee. This required McGregor to persuade wealthy citizens of Detroit to give generously. He was especially effective in this role, not only because he and Katherine were themselves major contributors to the Community Fund but also because he was highly respected by community leaders and by prominent and wealthy Detroiters.[44]

McGregor also used his influence to convince the leaders of the Detroit Community Union to enter "the field of social legislation . . . by throwing [their] weight behind certain legislative measures or administrative actions that affected . . . the well being of the people."[45] These measures dealt with emergency housing, mental health, prison reforms, and better facilities and programs for hospitals. Another initiative, based on McGregor's experience with the Provident Loan and Savings Society, dealt with unscrupulous loan sharks. In 1921 the Detroit Community Union actively and successfully campaigned for legislation to regulate loan companies by placing them under the controls of the state banking commissioner.[46]

McGregor continued to serve on the governing boards of the Detroit Community Union and Community Fund until 1931, when he moved to Washington, D.C., and even in his new residence he took an active role in the work of the Community Fund and the Community Union, which had changed its name to the Detroit Council of Social Agencies in 1932. He was involved with the council during the stock market crash in 1929 and the subsequent Depression.

McGregor's contacts with the mentally incompetent of Michigan during his tenure as head of the Associated Charities of Detroit and the McGregor Institute made him aware of the critical need for new approaches to dealing with these people. He recommended a "new constructive type of education and care for higher-grade feeble-minded children."[47] With such an innovative program, he believed that many such children could be "returned to society as useful citizens."[48] McGregor was joined by Henry Hulbert, Fred Butzel, William J. Norton, and other associates from the Community Union in organizing a countywide campaign for a county-sponsored training school. He persuaded members of the Detroit City Council, county supervisors, and county auditors to join him in setting up a speakers committee to address church and club meetings, parent-teacher associations, and charitable organizations. The campaign met with success. By an overwhelming majority, a bond issue was approved by voters, and the Wayne County Training School became a reality.[49]

Located in the Plymouth-Northville area in northwestern Wayne County, the school opened in 1925. McGregor headed the search committee, along with Henry Hulbert and Frank Cody, to select its superintendent, and for the next eleven years, he served on its administrative board of control.[50] He visited the school several days each month and met with the staff and patients. Later, during 1933, the McGregor Fund paid the salary of Thorleif Hegge, the resident physician, who because of his foreign citizenship could not be paid by the County Board of Supervisors.[51]

McGregor also gave his active attention and support to the Detroit House of Correction. The original facility, located in downtown Detroit, was so overcrowded and poorly managed that the city decided in 1917 to replace it with a facility described as an "old fashioned prison." McGregor and his colleagues in the Thursday Noon Group vehemently opposed this plan and actively led a public campaign against it. As a result, Mayor Oscar Marx forced the Detroit House of Correction board to resign and appointed a new commission under the chairmanship of Tracy McGregor. They immediately rejected the original plan, developed a new design, and acquired property in Plymouth.[52] A new facility was built that was considered a "model of its kind." McGregor also added a personal touch to the program by setting up a revolving fund to be used "to be loaned to misdeaments [*sic*] who do not have enough money to pay their fines . . . to be spared the humiliation of incarceration." This action not only provided a "service to worthy men, but relieved the House of Correction of overcrowding."[53]

McGregor was also concerned about the conditions at state hospitals for the insane, especially overcrowding. When he had difficulty arousing public interest in the problem, he arranged for a survey to be conducted at state hospitals. Completed and published in 1928, the study disclosed that serious overcrowding existed in these hospitals, accompanied by long waiting lists for new patients. In the fall of 1928, McGregor organized a series of meetings with the "newly elected Wayne County Delegation to the State Legislature" and sought their support. His recommendations, backed by careful research, won their support, and they prepared a ten-year plan "to build up the hospital capacity to a point where it met the needs of the state."[54]

Legislators from other sections of the state readily supported the proposal, and a bill was finally passed. It provided for appropriation of $5,700,000 for 1930 and 1931, and $5,900,000 for 1932. As a direct result, a new hospital for the insane was built in Ypsilanti, and the facilities in Lapeer and the Farm Colony for Epileptics at Wahjamega were expanded.[55]

Although McGregor never ran for a major public office, he actively supported candidates for various elective positions, serving on their election committees and contributing to their campaign funds. Prior to 1920, these efforts were channeled and coordinated by McGregor through the Thursday Noon Group; after 1920, when the group temporarily ceased its active work, McGregor gave generous financial assistance directly. Pliny Marsh, Henry Hulbert, Ira Jayne, Allan Campbell, and W. P. Bradley, in their elections to the Detroit Circuit and Probate Courts, were among those who received financial assistance from McGregor. In 1930 McGregor chaired George Engel's campaign for mayor of Detroit—an election won by Frank Murphy.[56]

McGregor also took an active role in supporting social legislation relating to charities, education, and health issues, not only with financial assistance when needed but also by active participation in backing the effort. In 1924 McGregor headed a nonsectarian committee to defeat a parochial school amendment to the state constitution because he believed that such a proposal would weaken the public school system in Michigan. After the racial riots in Detroit in 1925 led by the Ku Klux Klan, McGregor accepted the appointment by Detroit mayor John Smith to head a committee on the "Negro problems of Detroit" to respond to the KKK demonstrations in Detroit.[57]

McGregor also supported national efforts to reform American society. He served actively on the governing boards of the Committee for Transients and Homeless, the National Committee on Mental Health, and several prison reform organizations. He also took an active role in the work of the Good Will Home for Orphaned Children in Hinkley, Maine.[58]

Katherine McGregor had other favorite charities also. Several organizations, which supported "the education of mountain whites and the uplift of the Negro," received generous gifts from Katherine. The Visiting Nurses Association of Detroit and several women's charities were additional recipients. The Bay Court Home for Women and Children on Lake St. Clair continued to receive annual subsidies as well as her special attention. She visited the facility several times a year, assisted in the administration of the program, purchased needed equipment especially for the children, and financed needed building repairs and expanded facilities. In 1927, when the Detroit Community Fund developed a $4,200,000 special building program for "Detroit's Womanhood," Katherine pledged $50,000 and helped in the campaign.[59]

8

Detroit's Political and Civic Upheaval

THE ROUGHLY TWENTY-FIVE YEARS during which Tracy McGregor supervised the McGregor Institute from 1891 to 1915 coincided with changes and developments taking place in the commercial, political, and social life of the city of Detroit. By 1890 Detroit was already emerging as a major industrial center with a diverse economy featuring the manufacture of railroad cars and wheels, marine boilers and engines, stoves, pharmaceuticals, tobacco products, paints, varnishes, and shoes. Shipbuilding plants and dry docks dotted the waterfront of the Detroit River from Zug Island to Lake St. Clair. Its networks of railroads connected the agricultural and manufacturing centers of the central United States with the cities of the eastern United States and Canada, and along with its fleets of sailing vessels and steamships, Detroit had become a major midwestern transportation center.

The rapid rise in population reflected the changes in Detroit's economy. By 1890 the population had risen to 205,876, making Detroit the fifteenth largest city in the nation; by 1900 it had jumped to thirteenth with a population of 285,704. The Germans and Irish continued to be the largest immigrant groups in the city, but soon they would be challenged by an influx of immigrants from Eastern Europe, especially after 1905 when Detroit started to dominate the production of automobiles.[1] The 1890s and early 1900s also witnessed dramatic changes in the demography of Detroit and its suburbs. When the Mission for Homeless Men opened its doors in 1891, the city encompassed an area of 28.13 square miles; by 1930 it had expanded to 139 square miles. The mayor, elected to office every two years on a partisan ballot, controlled the city's government, with assistance from a council of forty-two members representing twenty-one wards. The Board of Education, another powerful governmental agency, consisted of forty-two members.

The political life of Detroit was intensely partisan, with Irish and German groups, along with business leaders, in control of the Republican and Democratic parties.[2] The governmental system for Detroit was unwieldy, inefficient, and thoroughly corrupt. Special interest groups controlled the patronage system involving thousands of positions, and they awarded lucrative contracts for public services including water, gas, electricity, and transportation. Even teaching, administrative, and other positions in the public school system were under the control of partisan officials and were reserved for political allies. The Detroit city treasury was popularly called the "Xmas Grab Bag."[3]

The election process also reeked of corruption and fraud that spanned both political parties. One of the most influential groups represented the saloonkeepers, brewers, and distillery owners who were well organized at election time and, later, as the Prohibition campaign picked up momentum. Even the local newspapers owned by influential Detroit citizens did not escape the control of the partisan political groups and glossed over the widespread corruption in city government.[4]

The first sign of change in this corrupted environment came in 1889 when Hazen Pingree, a prominent Detroit shoe manufacturer, was elected mayor. Born in 1840 in the small village of Denmark, Maine, he was like so many of the new generations of Detroit's business leaders who migrated from the East to find opportunities in the expanding Midwest. Pingree had moved to the Boston area in 1860 and found employment as a leather cutter in a local shoe factory. After serving several years in the Union Army, including five months as a prisoner in the infamous Andersonville prison, he moved to Detroit. He first worked at a local shoe factory there and then founded his own company, which by 1890 had become one of the most successful and profitable business operations in the city.[5]

As a Republican, Pingree was persuaded by Detroit business leaders to run for mayor in 1889, challenging the powerful Democratic machine that had controlled the mayor's office during most of the years since 1861. His election was initially praised by his business friends and Republican colleagues, but they soon regretted their endorsement as he began using the business standards he had developed in operating his shoe factories, carefully reviewing all of the existing policies of Detroit's city government, especially the practice of awarding contracts. He was shocked at the inefficiency and corruption he discovered.

The streetcar companies, which held a monopoly over public transportation, were his first targets. Not only did these companies charge exorbitant prices, but also the service they provided was disgraceful. Many of the city's densely populated areas had no public transportation whatsoever. Pingree turned to the city council to enact legislation forcing the streetcar companies to reduce rates and extend services, but they refused to take action. Instead, they pressured the mayor to use the police to break the workers' strike against these car companies. Pingree rejected this course of action, and when local newspapers refused to explain and publicize his position, he personally published daily reports and promulgated them on public billboards throughout the city.[6]

After he resolved this dispute in his favor, the mayor turned his attention to the private gas companies, which had a monopolistic control over services to Detroit residents and business firms. A prolonged battle ensued in which Pingree marshaled support from small property owners and successfully forced the gas companies to lower rates and expand their services.

Next Pingree took on the electric lighting monopoly. When they refused to lower rates, he introduced municipal ownership of that service. Finally, Mayor Pingree challenged the waterworks monopoly, especially its system of charging only those factories and homes that used water to finance the service. After careful investigation, Pingree successfully introduced public ownership of the waterworks.[7]

Shortly after leaving office in 1897 to become governor of the state, Hazen Pingree discussed his tenure as mayor of the country's eighteenth largest city. He highlighted his bitter but successful struggle with the monopolies and his ongoing feud with members of the city council who were beholden to these business leaders. He characterized these members of the council as "opponents of good government," while at the same time describing them as the "best citizens of the community." He readily acknowledged that some of the "better classes" supported his programs to curb the monopolies, but most of this class "dared not let it be known" that they agreed with him. He credited Detroit's small-property owners with providing the support needed to make the municipal reforms possible.[8]

Despite Hazen Pingree's success in curbing the corrupt practice of Detroit's monopolies, he left the task of reforming city government to others who followed. Joseph L. Hudson rose to the challenge. In addition to operating Detroit's largest department store, Hudson was also well known for his contributions to the religious and cultural life of Detroit and was a leading benefactor of various charitable agencies, including Harper Hospital, the YMCA, the Florence Crittenden Home, and of course, the McGregor Mission for Homeless Men.

In 1902, joined by a group of close friends and business colleagues that included Homer Warren, Oscar Marx, James Scripps, Richard Fyfe, Henry L. Leland, and Tracy McGregor, Hudson founded the Detroit Municipal League. Its major objective was to promote the best interests "of our city in government efficiency and economy and to gather and disseminate the wisest councils of the people for making Detroit the best and fairest city in the world."[9] High among the league's priorities was a campaign to "fight corruption in city government" and especially to curtail the influence of saloonkeepers and liquor interests over the legislative and executive branches of city government. Hudson, Tracy McGregor, and the other league founders were unanimous in their convictions that the misuses of alcohol were one of the major causes of the breakdown of family life, unemployment, and other social ills.

Unfortunately the league's preoccupation with Prohibition weakened its effectiveness as a reform organization and seriously limited public support for its program. The abuse of alcohol was widely recognized as a serious problem, especially by business leaders, social workers, and church officials, but to tens of thousands of the new residents of Detroit, especially those who had migrated from Eastern Europe, Germany, the Mediterranean area, and the British Isles, the consumption of alcoholic beverages such as beer and wine was considered a part of their daily diet, not an evil. In fact, to many foreign-born and unskilled factory workers, the local saloon was viewed as a "poor man's club" and an important part of the social life of the community.[10] As a result, the Municipal League never made much headway as a leader of government reform in Detroit. Indeed, it was constantly ridiculed by the local press as the "City Hall crew and their allies." J. L. Hudson was described as "a visionary whom it would be unsafe for substantial men to follow."[11]

In 1912, after a serious split between Hudson and Anthony Pratt, his top assistant, over the issue of the city control of street railways, the Municipal League collapsed. For ten years it had been vocal in its fight against corruption in Detroit government but had accomplished little. Perhaps its only lasting contribution was its campaign on behalf of Prohibition. Within a few years after the league disbanded, statewide Prohibition was passed in Michigan, and the Eighteenth Amendment to the U.S. Constitution was approved, prohibiting the sale and consumption of alcoholic beverages nationwide. Detroit voters supported the amendment—one of the only urban areas in the United States that voted in its favor.

Fortunately for the cause of good government in Detroit, another well-organized reform group evolved called the Detroit Civic Uplift League. This organization was founded by Henry M. Leland, the automobile pioneer, who like Hazen Pingree, wanted to introduce sound business practices into the operation of city government.

Henry Leland was not a native of Detroit but was another of the hundreds of business leaders who had migrated to that city from New England and the East Coast. After his early years in a small village in Vermont, he moved to Worcester, Massachusetts, and at the age of sixteen found work as a tool and die maker in a local machine shop. He learned the basics of machine manufacture there before moving to Detroit in 1890, where he opened his own machine shop and foundry. A few years later, after a brief association with Ransom Olds, Henry Ford, and the Dodge brothers, Leland helped organize the Cadillac Motor Car Company. Utilizing his experience as a skilled mechanic, he enhanced his reputation as one of Detroit's great automobile pioneers.[12]

Leland did not limit his interests to his automobile enterprises, however. He was also deeply involved in religious and civic affairs in the community, and as he became familiar with the operation of city government in Detroit, he was also appalled at its inefficiency and the depth of fraud and corruption that permeated every level of government. He discovered that local elections were rigged and controlled by a small group of politicians, often under the iron hand of saloonkeepers and distillers, and that the corrupt political system crossed both party lines.

Leland became so concerned about the extent of the corruption that he "arranged a crusade to eradicate it" and replace it with a "well governed and honest city government." The vehicle to achieve these reforms was the Detroit Civic Uplift League, which he founded in May 1912. With the aid of Detroit attorney Pliny Marsh, recruited from the Detroit Anti-Saloon League, Leland organized an active citywide organization made up of representatives from the men's clubs of Detroit's Protestant churches. The league's board of trustees was represented by various denominations. Leland, a Presbyterian, was president; Pliny Marsh, a Baptist, secretary; and Alonzo Ewing, Episcopalian; Herman Ray, Methodist; George S. Hammond, Christian Scientist; and Frank Kennedy, Congregationalist, made up the board. In addition, an advisory committee was established, made up of members from each major Protestant church. No Catholics were included in leadership positions because they were considered too close to the liquor interests of the city and the "Vateswappers League," a powerful political group in Detroit.[13]

The Detroit Civic Uplift League's membership grew slowly but steadily until finally, at its peak, it boasted four thousand members. The expenses of the organization were offset by membership fees plus major contributions from Leland and other wealthy Detroiters. But despite the solid reputation of many of its leaders, it struggled to survive. It, like the Municipal League, concentrated too much on the Prohibition movement, and its critics described it as "self righteousness," with a restrictive membership that left it open to ridicule.

Pliny Marsh, a shrewd politician and organizational genius, recognized the difficulties facing the league in its early years and convinced Leland and other leaders to change its focus. First, it opened its membership to all citizens regardless of religious persuasion. It softened its attacks on the liquor interests and changed its name to the Detroit Citizens League. Finally, in 1912, it began publication of the *Civic Search Light*, which proved to be extremely successful in publicizing its program and winning the support of an increasing number of Detroit voters.[14]

The league's most significant achievement was making improvements to the election process in Detroit. Under the leadership of Pliny Marsh, who had become familiar with the complicated techniques used in election fraud, the league led a campaign to reform the voting system. Marsh organized a campaign against the infamous "Vateswappers League," a group dominated by saloonkeepers and liquor dealers, which had successfully infiltrated and influenced the controlling sixty of the three hundred voting precincts. In the *Civic Search Light* and at public meetings, Marsh exposed the techniques used to rig elections.[15]

In addition, Marsh turned to the Michigan state legislature for help. With the aid of representatives George Scott and Charles Flowers, an "Honest Election Law" was passed in 1915, which "guaranteed the right of non partisan challenges at the polls, restricted the access of office holders to voters' ballots and prevented them from serving on election boards and finally provided penalties for violations." This legislation not only was a victory for the league but also gave them widespread public support for other reforms.[16]

In 1916 the league led a campaign to change Detroit's city charter, followed two years later by legislation strengthening the power of the mayor, reducing memberships on the city council from forty-two to nine and providing for nonpartisan elections.[17] Finally, in 1919, the league championed the consolidation of the city's criminal courts into a single Recorders Court.[18] The appointment of Pliny Marsh to that newly created court reflected the growing influence of the Detroit Citizens League.

During these years of progressive reforms, Tracy McGregor was busy establishing the Detroit Mission for Homeless Men on a sound operating and financial basis, but he was aware of the political upheavals occurring in the city. The mission benefited from Mayor Pingree's campaign against the public service monopolies that resulted in lower rates and increased services, but there is no evidence that McGregor was actively involved in Pingree's reform initiatives. Although Pingree was a successful and wealthy business leader, he was not among the benefactors of the mission. Nor is there any evidence in McGregor's voluminous papers that he had any personal contact with Pingree or the reforms the mayor championed at this time. Given his daily exhausting schedule, it is not surprising that he had little time for political activities.

McGregor and the mission's staff and supporters did, however, have frequent contact during the 1890s with one branch of city government—the Detroit Police Department. From the day the mission began its operation in December 1890, it was the target of local police officials who charged that it was a "haven for criminals" and called it a "Tramp Paradise." Mission men were constantly harassed by the police as they sought employment at local business establishments. Despite McGregor's frequent meetings with police officials and his invitations to them to visit the mission and review its programs, the police continued their attacks as long as the mission remained in operation. This situation rankled McGregor because it brought into focus the prevailing public attitudes toward the plight of the unemployed, homeless, and destitute. His frequent trips to the police stations and local police courts on behalf of mission men who ran afoul of the law opened his eyes to the need for reforming the legal system as well as the policies and practices of jails and prisons.[19]

McGregor's close association with business leaders, as well as his marriage to Katherine in 1901, aided his progress with the mission, and by the turn of the century he had more time to become involved in the political and cultural life of Detroit. In 1900, he accepted an appointment by the governor to serve as the Wayne County agent on the State Board of Corrections and Charities.[20]

His experience on this board, as well as his work with the mission, made him acutely aware of one of the major problems facing thousands of Detroit citizens who needed money to purchase homes and automobiles and to meet other pressing financial obligations. They could, of course, obtain small loans from local lending companies, but the usurious rates charged—often as high as 20 percent—were only causing greater financial hardships. To combat this serious crisis, McGregor turned to his friends, J. L. Hudson, James Ingles, and Dexter M. Ferry Jr., to create a capital fund and organize the Provident Loan and Savings Society in 1906. The new company, with J. L. Hudson as its first president, made loans on chattel mortgages to families at a 3–5 percent interest rate, creating such intense competition that local lending companies were forced to cut their rates. During its first year of operation, the society approved four thousand loans, and within a few years it had become so successful that it was able to open additional offices in Wyandotte and Pontiac.[21]

The success of the Provident Loan and Savings Society and the widespread support it received from low-income Detroit families led McGregor and Hudson to mount a successful statewide campaign for a uniform small loan statute limiting, by law, interest rates and service charges. For the rest of his life, Tracy McGregor directed the Provident Loan and Savings Society, which provided indispensable services to tens of thousands of Detroit area families.[22]

The Detroit Municipal League also interested him. Although the league embraced a widespread program to reform Detroit city government, McGregor was primarily interested in one of its main objectives: curbing the power and political influence of distillers, brewers, and saloonkeepers. His experience at the mission and his strong conviction that alcohol was one of the main causes of unemployment and destitution led him to take an active role in all groups supporting Prohibition.

By 1910 Tracy McGregor was no longer regarded as only a leader of a renegade homeless mission. His "common sense, humanitarian service" at the McGregor Institute, his active role in the Provident Loan and Savings Society, and his growing leadership of charitable programs "attracted the admiration of a number of strong professional and business Detroiters."[23] Leaders of local charities sought not only his financial support, which was usually forthcoming, but also his advice on the management of their programs. According to William J. Norton, McGregor "towered head and shoulders above all other devoted citizens in the charitable world of Detroit."[24]

McGregor's work with the homeless and unemployed of Detroit and his successful programs to find them jobs, as well as his knowledge and concerns about the conditions of jails and prisons, led the Detroit Board of Commerce to appoint McGregor in 1911 to represent it on a state senate and House committee to investigate the state prison in Jackson, Michigan. He not only accepted the assignment promptly but also immediately went to the prison on his own to conduct an onsite investigation. He also sought the advice and counsel of prison experts throughout the country. He was already well informed when the committee visited the prison in March 1911, and he was able to influence their deliberations. The committee approved of the general conditions of the prison and its programs to rehabilitate the inmates, but they joined McGregor in his sharp criticism of the "Cell Block."[25] He reported to the Detroit Board of Commerce that he was "thunderstruck" with the cell-block, which had been built forty years earlier, and that "in an enlightened civilized society" men could be put in such a place. McGregor presented his sharp criticisms not only to the Board of Commerce but also directly to the House and senate. His impassioned speech to the Joint Legislative Committee was credited with winning their approval for legislation to reform the Jackson Prison program.[26]

9

The Thursday Noon Group

THE JACKSON PRISON INVESTIGATION and Tracy McGregor's successful campaign for reform of prison policies and procedures encouraged him to take a more active role in political and community affairs. He had also studied the economic conditions and trends in Detroit and other industrial centers in the United States and recognized that the causes of chronic unemployment were more complicated than seasonal layoffs in business and agriculture. He witnessed firsthand the sharp rise in bankruptcies among employers and the influx of tens of thousands of immigrants from Europe who often competed with native-born citizens for jobs. McGregor was aware also that the federal and state governments had done practically nothing to alleviate the hardships faced by the unemployed and unemployable. The municipal and county relief agencies and the limited number of Detroit's private charities were ill-prepared to assist all of those in need, especially during periods of economic crisis.

In the spring of 1912 McGregor decided that a more organized effort must be undertaken to solve these problems facing Detroit and its citizens. He called together a group of professional and business leaders into an informal organization to discuss the serious problems facing Detroit. In his letter of invitation he wrote: "Why not let one's friendships and closer associations develop around the purpose to do good? To this end let us get together a group of congenial men with serious aims, and without expecting overmuch at first or at any time, let us go in for a long pull together. We will put in our brains and hearts, and, when needed, our money, and will stand together for any good thing that seems possible and advisable to do." [1]

At the well-attended initial luncheon meeting, held at the Pontchartrain Hotel, McGregor presented his views on the crisis facing the city of Detroit. The commercial interests of the city, he noted, were being "adequately covered by the Board of Commerce, the Employer's Association and kindred leaders." The recently formed Detroit Civic League was addressing the issue of "better municipal government," and the Associated Charities of Detroit was responding to the needs of the local social agencies. What was urgently needed, McGregor concluded, was special attention to the "social needs of the rising population, especially in the areas of city planning, sanitary housing, playgrounds for children, industrial education, child labor and workmen's compensation laws." He spoke eloquently and with great feeling about the plight of the young unemployed workers and the destitute, the so-called mission men.[2]

Although some of McGregor's proposals were quite progressive, the men at this meeting immediately agreed upon creating a formal organization to deal with these issues. They chose the name the "Thursday Noon Group" and decided to meet each week for a luncheon at the Pontchartrain Hotel. Additional members were added until the group reached a total of about twenty-five. According to William Lovett, the executive secretary of the Detroit Citizens League from 1916 to 1947 and author of *Detroit Rules Itself*, the Thursday Noon Group was made up of "young business and professional men, intellectual types, above average in financial means and interested in social questions of the day."[3]

Most of these men were born between 1870 and 1882; the oldest member was John R. Russel, who was born in 1857, the youngest was Dr. A. W. McGraw, born in 1893 and who joined the group in 1919. Many members had close connections with Detroit's influential organizations, including the Board of Commerce, the Employer's Association, the Citizens League, the Detroit Club, and the Detroit Medical Society. Several were officers in prominent Detroit charitable agencies, and others served with McGregor on the board of trustees of the McGregor Institute.[4] The majority had college degrees, and at least half practiced law. Several were associated with local banking institutions, and most of them were connected with business establishments in the city. Several held appointments on government boards and commissions.[5]

Tracy McGregor selected the members, set the agenda for the weekly meetings, and chaired the sessions, unless he was out of town. James Ingles, one of the most active members of the group, later commented on the leadership of the group during its early history. "If there was a dominant figure, it would have been Tracy McGregor, but that gentle soul never forced his personality on any crowd. He just naturally won them over. He was a great man."[6]

McGregor relied heavily upon several friends in the operation of the group. His most trusted colleague was Henry Schoolcraft Hulbert, who in 1912 was a judge in the juvenile division of the Wayne County Probate Court. Hulbert was born in Utica, New York, in 1869, and after the death of his father, his family moved to Detroit. He was enrolled in public high school in Detroit but had to drop out before graduation in order to help support his family. From 1882 to 1889, he served as clerk in the office of the Michigan secretary of state in Lansing, and in 1889 he returned to Detroit to accept a clerkship in the Wayne County Probate Court. He rose steadily in the ranks and in 1909 was appointed judge in charge of the juvenile division. He held this influential position until 1927 when he became presiding probate judge. He retired from the court in 1934 to become director of the Trust Department of the National Bank of Detroit. Hulbert won national recognition for his pioneering work in the probate court system, even though he never studied law or was admitted to the bar.[7]

Fred M. Butzel was another influential founding member of the Thursday Noon Group. McGregor and he became close friends and colleagues in their work with the Associated Charities of Detroit. Born in 1877, Butzel received his legal training at the University of Michigan and returned to Detroit to practice law. He was active in several local charitable institutions, including the Ford Republic, the Boy Scouts, and the Jewish Charities of Detroit. Along with Tracy McGregor he led the campaign to organize the Detroit Community Union and the Detroit Patriotic Fund. His interest in the Thursday Noon Group continued into the 1940s.[8]

Dexter M. Ferry Jr. joined the group shortly after it was founded and remained an active member for years. Born in 1873, the son of the founder of the Ferry Seed Company, he was active in the business and political life of Detroit. From 1901 to 1904, he served as a representative in the Michigan state legislature, and in January 1906 he was appointed to the state Board of Education, a position he held until 1912, including four years as its president. In addition to serving as treasurer of the Ferry Seed Company, he was also treasurer of the American Harrow Company and the National Pin Company and director of the First National Bank of Detroit. Ferry had a close working association with McGregor as a fellow board member of the YMCA and the Merrill-Palmer Institute. Ferry's influential role in the Republican Party and his close contacts with members of the state legislature were invaluable to the Thursday Noon Group in promoting their legislative agenda.[9]

In any account of the Thursday Noon Group during its long history, James Ingles must be given special attention. Not only was he one of the founders of the organization and a close friend of McGregor, but also he kept the organization active when McGregor moved to Washington, D.C., in 1931. A Detroiter by birth, he was one of seven children and was of Scottish descent. In 1890, at the age of twenty-six, he organized a company that manufactured exhaust fans used for carrying off shavings in woodworking shops. Named the American Blower Company in 1895, Ingles ran the company until 1933. He also served on the boards of other Detroit business and banking firms. Ingles's first contact with Tracy McGregor took place in 1892 when he joined the board of trustees of the Mission for Homeless Men. He was a tireless worker on behalf of the mission, raising funds for its operating expenses and its buildings and helping McGregor establish contacts with Detroit's business community.[10]

Another member, Gustavus Pope, born in Detroit 1873, was a field engineer for the Canadian Bridge Company headquartered in Walkerville, Ontario, and later became active in the pharmaceutical business in Detroit. He held leadership positions in several charitable organizations, most notably the American Red Cross. In 1917, at the height of World War I, he resigned his business positions to take over the Detroit branch of the Red Cross and was director, along with Tracy McGregor, of the Detroit Patriotic Fund, the fund-raising arm of the Detroit Community Union.[11]

Richard Webber, the nephew of Joseph L. Hudson, carried on his uncle's interests in charitable and community work in Detroit and in 1912 became president of J. L. Hudson's department store and joined the board of trustees of the McGregor Institute. He also served on the governing boards of Harper Hospital and other Detroit charities.[12] Other members of the Thursday Noon Group included Francis McMath, the bridge engineer; Edwin Denby, a prominent Detroit attorney, member of the state legislature and United States Congress, and secretary of the U.S. Navy; Clarence Lightener, a prominent Detroit attorney; James Holden, a real estate entrepreneur; and Joseph Schlotman, a highly respected Detroit business leader.[13]

At first, the weekly meetings of the Thursday Noon Group were devoted to general discussions about the serious problems facing Detroit. Led by Tracy McGregor and James Ingles, every member was encouraged to participate in the discussions and present their own observations and recommendations. McGregor avoided controversial political issues, choosing instead to leave these issues in the hands of Henry Leland and Pliny Marsh and the Detroit Citizens League. He was aware also that several members of the Thursday Noon Group were active members of the Citizens League, and he wanted to avoid any overlapping of programs.[14]

McGregor was particularly concerned about the potential of disputes between the two organizations. Although he was a major financial benefactor of the league and met often with Leland and Marsh regarding fund-raising, McGregor differed with them on a number of issues. Leland and Marsh, for example, wanted the membership of the league limited to Detroit's most influential and wealthy Protestant business leaders; McGregor did not support the religious exclusion of Catholics and believed strongly that membership in the league should also be opened to "the humble workers" of the city.[15]

Although McGregor did not unilaterally control the agenda of the Thursday Noon Group, he did make sure that the group gave special attention to the problems facing the sharply rising population of unskilled immigrants. Based on his experiences at the McGregor Institute and the Associated Charities of Detroit, he presented his views on such issues as "housing, pauperism, sickness, the mentally ill and the treatment of prisoners in jails, prisons and mental hospitals, critical problems which are inter-related in the fabric of social services."[16]

At the Thursday meetings in the spring of 1913, with the strong support of Judge Hulbert and Fred Butzel, McGregor placed high on the agenda the critical problems facing juvenile delinquents and the sick and mentally ill. They gave special attention to one group of Michigan's disadvantaged, the epileptics, whose numbers were increasing steadily, keeping pace with the area's skyrocketing population. Based on a careful survey conducted by several members of the Thursday Noon Group, it was revealed that people who suffered from epilepsy, popularly known as the "falling sickness," were incarcerated in jails or sent to mental hospitals. The only hospital treating epileptics was the Michigan Home and Training School in Lapeer, Michigan, but unfortunately this institution was so overcrowded that little attention was given to the proper care of those afflicted with this less common illness.[17]

After long and careful deliberations at several Thursday meetings, and with the active endorsement of the members, McGregor, Butzel, and Hulbert organized a campaign to secure legislative support for a new facility limited exclusively to the treatment of epileptics. With the backing of medical and mental health leaders, they succeeded in getting the state legislature to pass Public Act 173, "to create a farm colony for the humane treatment of epileptic persons to be known as the Michigan Farm Colony for Epileptics."[18]

The site chosen for the new facility was the W. A. Heartt farm in Wahjamega, Michigan, located on the Michigan Central Railroad, four miles from Caro and eleven miles from Vassar. Within a year, a hundred acres were cleared, and cottages, a blacksmith shop, a barn, and an icehouse were built. A hospital providing beds, schooling, and the "scientific treatment of patients" was also constructed. On May 30, 1914, twenty-four epileptic patients were transferred to the new facility from the Michigan Home and Training School at Lapeer. By 1925 the Michigan Farm Colony for Epileptics at Wahjamega had eight hundred patients and had become a pioneer in the medical treatment of persons afflicted with the illness.[19]

The members of the Thursday Noon Group took pride in their role in getting the legislature to fund the Michigan Farm Colony for Epileptics at Wahjamega, not only because it filled a real community need but also because it demonstrated their influence in bringing about social change. They hardly had time to celebrate, however, before Detroit was faced with a serious crisis—a major economic depression that struck the city and the rest of the country in the winter of 1914–15.

The "boom and bust" economic cycles that accompanied the industrialization of America were not unknown to Detroiters. The city had faced serious economic downturns in 1894 and 1907, but the depression of 1914–15 hit Detroit even harder. More than 50 percent of the work force—an estimated eighty thousand—lost their jobs, and of these, an estimated sixty thousand were European immigrants, most of whom could not speak or read English. The announcement of Henry Ford's "five-dollar-a-day" plan only served to exacerbate the Detroit crisis, bringing tens of thousands of new residents into the city.[20]

No member of the Thursday Noon Group joined the ranks of the unemployed, but the business firms with which they were associated were hit hard by the downturn. Furthermore, many members of the group were also involved with various Detroit charities that were overwhelmed by the numbers turning to them for assistance. By midwinter these charities were forced to turn away thousands of needy Detroiters because of the severity of the depression and the lack of resources.

Reacting promptly, the Thursday Noon Group devoted its full attention to the economic crisis. They invited local government officials, business leaders, and heads of Detroit charities to address the group and offer advice and counsel. The results of these sessions made it clear that Detroit was in serious trouble. Public agencies such as the Detroit Poor Commission and the welfare agencies were ill-funded and short staffed and had little information about the extent of the problems created by the business downturn. Nor were they better informed or able to develop an organized plan of action than was the Thursday Noon Group.

In January 1915, the Thursday Noon Group, acting upon the recommendation of Tracy McGregor, hired a national expert from outside Detroit to review the extent of the crisis and offer recommendations for a course of action. They chose Walter E. Kruesi to come to Detroit one week each month "to make an analysis of the unemployment situation in Detroit." The travel and living expenses and other fees were raised by individual contributions from members of the Thursday Noon Group.[21]

Kruesi was ideally suited for the task. He was a trained economist and had considerable experience in developing private and public programs to deal with unemployment. From 1905 to 1907, he had served as assistant general secretary of New York charity organizations and, from 1908 to 1912, as executive secretary of the New York Conference on Charities and Corrections. After serving for two years as commissioner of charities in Schenectady, New York, he was superintendent of the Public Employment Bureau in New York City. He also met frequently with the leaders of the Detroit Board of Commerce as well as members of the Thursday Noon Group.[22]

In his extensive study, *Report on Unemployment in the Winter of 1914–1915 in Detroit, and the Institutions and Measures of Relief,* Kruesi described his findings and recommendations. With Tracy McGregor and members of the Thursday Noon Group to provide entrée, Kruesi had met and consulted with the executive officers of most of the public and private agencies responsible for "employment and material relief."

By the time Kruesi arrived in Detroit, the economic situation had reached a critical stage. Hundreds of unemployed walked the streets daily looking for work and begging for food. Starvation was widespread, and hospitals and health clinics were crowded with the sick and infirm. Kruesi described the feeling of hopelessness throughout the city where the unemployed "have been cast overboard and constitute the flotsam and jetsam in the labor pool." He also observed that neither the mayor nor members of the city council and leaders of the public relief agencies were well informed about the crisis and did not have any realistic plans or programs to solve it.[23]

In his study, Kruesi reported on the programs that had been adopted by a few public and private agencies. The Detroit Police Department had opened a soup kitchen, which provided some assistance from February 6 to May 19, 1915. Unfortunately, it was not coordinated with the work of other relief agencies and did not provide any services to aid workers in finding employment or a "proper place to sleep."[24] Henry Ford, partly in response to the impact of his "five-dollar-a-day" plan, arranged for the Ford Hospital to "feed and bed" one hundred workers each night in his new hospital. Kruesi faulted the plan, however, because such services were to be limited to two successive nights. Ford believed that if homeless men were allowed to remain longer it could discourage them from finding employment.[25]

Walter Kruesi examined the facilities made available at the Unitarian Church on Woodward and Sibley avenues in Detroit. Cushions were placed on the pews to provide sleeping accommodations, and breakfast and supper were offered daily in the church classrooms. Commonly known as the "IWW Flop," Kruesi compared it favorably to a similar facility in New York City called the "Hotel de Gink." Kruesi was impressed that it was "run quietly and democratically" but was disappointed that the Detroit police commissioner "refused to recognize it, or even supervise it."[26]

He gave special attention to the programs provided by the McGregor Institute, and although he recommended a number of changes, his overall evaluation was favorable. He was especially impressed with the living accommodations at the institute. "Those who are able, pay fifteen cents for a clean, comfortable bed, a bath and a cleansing care of their clothes," he observed, and "excellent food is sold at cost, and a simple supper and breakfast are served free to those who cannot pay. The accommodations and care at McGregor Institute compare favorably with private lodging houses in Boston, New York, and Buffalo while the cost of the latter per man per night is from twice to several times that of the Institute." He recommended that the institute add a "smoking, reading, and game room, especially for steady patrons" and that placards describing the institute be placed in railroad and ferry stations in Detroit.[27] Kruesi criticized the institute for failing to "acquaint the public with its principles, aims and methods." "The police," he observed, "from patrolman to Commissioner," were spreading falsehoods about the institute and had urged that a "parallel institution be opened under police control."[28] He recommended that two alternative plans be considered. The first would involve turning the McGregor Institute over to the city of Detroit to be run by the present institute board of trustees, with vacancies and additional members to be appointed later by the mayor based upon recommendations by the board. The second involved adding to the institute's board the police commissioner, "the superintendent of the poor, and one representative each from the patrolmen's association, the Federation of Labor, and one from the city news writers."[29] Kruesi had praise for the Associated Charities of Detroit and especially its reorganization by Tracy McGregor in 1914. The value of a separate registration bureau, he noted, "was inestimable" for the "special work for the unemployed."[30]

It is difficult to evaluate the impact of Kruesi's report. It was widely circulated and discussed by local governmental agencies, the Board of Commerce, and the various charitable agencies involved in the aiding of the unemployed, homeless, and needy citizens of Detroit. Unfortunately, the Detroit city government, which had primary responsibility for aiding the poor and destitute, was so disorganized and poorly administered that no effective action was taken. The Detroit City Council, wracked by corruption and scandal, was powerless to provide the corrective measures recommended by Kruesi.

The Thursday Noon Group did, however, benefit from the report. Tracy McGregor and his colleagues on the board of the McGregor Institute were pleased with Kruesi's evaluation and, as a result, identified housing as one of the crises requiring immediate attention. The severe housing crisis that had already faced Detroit in the early 1900s worsened during the depression of 1914–15. McGregor and other business and community leaders had been aware for years of the severe shortage of affordable housing and lodging facilities for Detroit residents. The Detroit Board of Commerce, the Detroit Employers Association, as well as major automobile manufacturers were struggling to develop better housing for Detroit workers. Unlike eastern industrial cities, Detroit had few tenements, apartment houses, multihousing units, or inexpensive lodging facilities for single workers. Detroit was a city characterized by "single family dwellings."[31] McGregor called attention to the housing crisis at one of the early meetings of the Thursday Noon Group and, with their approval, embarked upon an investigation of Detroit's housing problems.

In 1912 McGregor spent nine weeks in Chicago reviewing that city's planning program and meeting with public and private officials who had responsibility for these activities. He visited various lodging houses, low-cost housing units, and public housing centers. He spent hours with Jens Jensen, the Chicago landscape architect, discussing Chicago's city plan and Jensen's ideas for providing "homes for residence districts of wage earners." Chicago's Municipal Lodging House was another site that attracted McGregor's interest and provided him the opportunity to spend hours with the residents. On his return to Detroit he met with city officials responsible for community housing.[32]

McGregor found that Detroit, unlike Chicago, had no comprehensive plan for the housing crisis. Except for the McGregor Institute and a few charitable organizations, there were no other facilities to provide low-cost housing for workers and their families. Furthermore, the lack of a housing code made the task of developing an overall plan for the city impossible.

The situation in the winter of 1914–15 got worse. As thousands of Detroit workers lost their jobs, without financial resources, they were evicted from their homes. In addition to the housing shortage, real estate and homeowners "raised their rents disproportionately." The population of the homeless skyrocketed, and families were split up, often with the children being placed in boarding homes.[33]

The charitable institutions of Detroit felt the brunt of this housing crisis, and McGregor, as head of the Mission for Homeless Men and the Associated Charities and as a financial supporter of many of the affiliated charitable groups, was especially affected. In 1914 he again placed the housing issue on the agenda of the Thursday Noon Group. After several meetings devoted to the issue, including a review of the reports by Walter Kruesi and McGregor, the group hired Lawrence Veillier of New York City to come to Detroit for one week each month to investigate the city's housing needs and to develop a plan of action.

Veillier was the perfect choice for the task.[34] Like Kruesi, who had worked on the Detroit scene a year before, Veillier made the rounds of the various local and state governmental agencies and boards that had responsibility for housing and neighborhood development. He also met with the leaders of the Detroit Board of Commerce, local real estate dealers, and the staffs of the charitable agencies who dealt with those in need of housing. Within a year, Veillier's efforts met with success. With the help of city agencies, he developed a revised and enlarged building code for the city, which was heartily endorsed by the Board of Commerce and by local officials of the city of Detroit. He then developed a new housing code, which was approved by the Michigan Legislature.[35]

McGregor and the Thursday Noon Group also established a private organization to assist Veillier and provide a means to implement his findings and recommendations. In 1914–15, the Detroit Housing Association was formed, and Robert E. Todd was hired to direct it. His salary was met by generous donations from Thursday Noon Group members and other local business leaders, including Roy Chapin, Walter O. Briggs, David Whitney Jr., Howard E. Coffin, Henry M. Leland, Horace Rackham, and Alec Dow.[36]

Although the Detroit Housing Association assisted in developing a more coordinated plan for new housing in all parts of the city, it did not address the needs of thousands of single factory workers, most of them recent immigrants who were not interested in a house but rather a room in an apartment, hotel, or other inexpensive facility. In 1915, responding to the urgent need, the leaders of the Thursday Noon Group formed the Men's Hotel Corporation, hired an architect, and acquired property on Beaubien between Madison and Beacon streets. The plan for the hotel, recommended by McGregor after his tour of similar facilities in several other cities, was similar to the Mills Hotel in New York City and the new YMCA hotel in Chicago. Eight to ten stories high, the facility would provide "clean, comfortable living quarters for workingmen of moderate means."[37] The cost of the property, the design and plans for the hotel, as well as the capital stock was subscribed by members of the Thursday Noon Group, Detroit business leaders, and especially Tracy and Katherine McGregor.[38]

World War I forced the delay of construction on the hotel, but plans were reactivated in 1919 with an additional $300,000 subscribed by Tracy and Katherine McGregor and $25,000 each by Richard Webber, J. B. Schlotman, E. L. Ford, and the John Gray Estate. Seventeen others, mostly members of the Thursday Noon Group, subscribed $5,000 each. The new facility, called the "Commonwealth Hotel for Men" or the "Factory District Men's Hotel" had a capacity of seven hundred rooms, with three hundred set aside at $2.75 a week and the remaining four hundred at $.50 a night. The facility also contained a restaurant, a store, a newsstand, and a billiard room. If the occupancy remained at an average of 80 percent, it was estimated that the stockholders would earn a total of $92,560 a year.[39]

Detroit's educational system also received the careful attention of the Thursday Noon Group. McGregor had been concerned about the status of education in Detroit, a result of his work with the Mission for Homeless Men, the Associated Charities, and the Detroit Board of Commerce. Not only were

Detroit schools unable to meet the needs of the burgeoning population of Detroit, especially after the automobile companies expanded operations in the greater Detroit area, but also the depression of 1914–15 brought into focus another related serious problem. Tens of thousands of new Detroiters needed educational attention because they could neither read nor write English. One of the economic downturns in the winter of 1914–15 had resulted in the layoffs of nearly eighty thousand workers, a great proportion of whom were recent immigrants who not only could not write or read English but also were ignorant of American history and the ideals of democracy. The Detroit Board of Commerce, the Detroit Employers Association, and the Thursday Noon Group were especially concerned when they recognized a pattern in that the first workers fired and the last ones rehired were usually foreign-born residents who did not possess the needed language skills. In 1916, the Detroit situation was carefully explained by one writer in the popular magazine *Outlook* when he observed that three of every four persons in Detroit were either born abroad or were of foreign-born parents.[40]

Despite the critical need for educational programs for this new generation of foreign-born citizens, the Detroit Board of Education was slow to respond. Finally, after concerted pressure from the Board of Commerce, and with the support of auto manufacturers, the Board of Education opened night schools for adult workers. Several manufacturers followed suit and began similar programs inside their factories. The Ford Motor Company, for example, developed an extensive program called "Americanization" that made attendance compulsory for those workers who could not pass tests about American history and language. This program so appealed to Henry Ford that he required his immigrant workers to take these courses to qualify for the five-dollar-a-day salary.[41]

McGregor and many of his colleagues in the Thursday Noon Group and the Associated Charities took an active role in Detroit's Americanization programs. Under a special committee chaired by McGregor, they inaugurated programs to aid immigrants in adjusting to urban life in Detroit. In addition to English language programs, they sponsored workshops to train immigrant women in their buying habits at stores and markets, their housekeeping, and the importance of sound health and nutritional practices. They mobilized attorneys, physicians, and pharmacists to volunteer their services to aid the non-English-speaking immigrants. Finally, McGregor developed a clearinghouse for all social agencies, automobile companies, and other organizations involved in Americanization programs. It publicized programs, coordinated schedules, assisted in recruiting qualified language teachers, and encouraged ethnic organizations to recruit members to enroll in the courses.[42]

McGregor's contacts with the Detroit School Board during the Americanization campaign made him aware of its inefficient and corrupt operations. This situation, however, was not new. Former mayor Hazen Pingree had earlier carried on a bitter campaign to combat "the long traditions of corruption and scandal" in the school board and had succeeded by persuading the state legislature to give him power to veto board expenditures. Pingree had forced the resignation of several board members who were later convicted and sent to prison due to the extent of their corruption.[43]

McGregor and the Thursday Noon Group got involved in school board activities when in 1913 nine Detroit teachers who had been granted sabbaticals to study abroad had their monthly allotments cancelled by the city controller after they had arrived in Europe. When the matter was brought to the attention of the Thursday Noon Group, McGregor advanced the living allowance to the teachers so that they could continue their studies abroad, and then put pressure on the city controller and the school board to resolve their differences.[44]

By 1915 it was evident that former mayor Pingree's reforms had waned and that the Board of Education was again deeply involved in an era of graft and corruption. Despite public outcries, little could be done to change board practices because of its unwieldy size. With the backing of the Thursday Noon Group, Tracy McGregor accepted the chair of the Citizen's School Board Committee, which was made up of twenty-eight prominent business and professional leaders. The committee successfully campaigned for radical changes in the board's membership, reducing it from forty-two to seven at the general Detroit election in April 1917. The Citizen's School Board Committee also persuaded a number of prominent community leaders to run for the newly created school board and campaigned for their election.[45]

By 1917 McGregor was recognized as one of Detroit's most influential citizens. His leadership in reorganizing the Associated Charities into the Detroit Community Union, as well as chairing the Patriotic Fund, was praised by Detroit's civic and charitable leaders. As a result, he was constantly invited and even pressured to assume key roles in other civic campaigns and programs. One civic leader observed, "As a community citizen of unselfish spirit, McGregor was accepted as a wise counselor and friend, whose approval of a given enterprise assured its success by attracting to its support of men of prominence with their financial subscription and personal activity."[46]

In 1919 the Thursday Noon Group gave its support to the school board for another project. The Detroit schools needed a special home for "incorrigible boys," but they could not persuade the city council to appropriate funds to purchase such a facility. The school board turned to McGregor for assistance, and he in turn persuaded the Thursday Noon Group to finance this important program until such time as the Board of Education could find the necessary resources. With contributions from Thursday Noon Group members, the home of Admiral A. G. Winterhalter, located on West Jefferson at the corner of Junction, was leased and renovated to meet the needs of the Board of Education. The board then rented the building from the Thursday Noon Group, from 1919 to 1924, until it could secure the necessary funds to purchase it.[47]

The formula that was adopted for support of the Winterhalter School and the abandoned Detroit teachers struggling abroad was typical of the approach of the Thursday Noon Group. The individual members subscribed the needed funds for a particular project and used their influence, individually and collectively, on behalf of the programs under consideration. They did not seek credit for financial contributions personally or as an organized group. These activities were kept confidential from the media and even from their business and community colleagues. Fortunately, McGregor kept detailed financial records of the Thursday Noon Group activities so that the nature and extent of their work has been preserved.[48]

In the summer of 1915, the Thursday Noon Group became embroiled in a major controversy that involved a fire that destroyed the single bridge connecting Detroit with its recreational center on Belle Isle. Since 1889, when the original bridge was built, tens of thousands of Detroiters had visited the island during all seasons—to picnic, bathe, skate, canoe on the beautiful inlets and lagoons, ride horses, and fish. But on April 27, 1915, a city-owned asphalt wagon en route to the island accidentally dropped red-hot coals on the creosote pavement, which was saturated with automobile motor oil. For four hours a fire raged, and by the time it was finally extinguished, the bridge had been completely destroyed. More than two thousand motorists and their automobiles were stranded on the island and had to hire a ferry to return them to the mainland.[49]

Detroit's mayor and members of the city council immediately responded to the public outcry for a new bridge and voted for funds for a temporary structure. This solution lasted only a few days before a major controversy erupted. Detroit's political leaders questioned whether the $100,000 appropriation was sufficient for a temporary bridge or whether the funds should be put toward a permanent structure. The proposed location of the temporary bridge was also debated, as was the issue of whether an expanded ferry service was the best solution. Within a month, a new plan emerged—a proposed 2 million dollar permanent bridge to be built without wasting funds on a temporary structure. This plan was placed on the ballot for a special election in July 1915, but it failed to get the necessary three-fifths majority of the voters. Mayor Oscar Marx then suggested constructing two 1 million dollar bridges. When this plan also failed to garner public support, he urged the construction of a footbridge for pedestrians only. Another controversy arose when local engineers and contractors objected to the hiring of several New York firms to develop plans for a "Detroit" bridge.[50]

It was at this stage in the controversy that the Thursday Noon Group became involved. Two of the group's active members were Francis C. McMath, an internationally known bridge engineer who had built the Quebec Bridge over the St. Lawrence River, and Gustavus Pope, field engineer for the Canadian Bridge Company. As one of the key members of the city's Consulting Bridge Engineer Board, McMath was familiar with all of the issues relating to the Belle Isle Bridge. He recognized also that a permanent structure would take several years to design and build at a cost of several million dollars. The only reasonable solution was a temporary bridge that could be completed and opened for automobile and pedestrian traffic within a year. Unfortunately the bids for the construction ran well over $150,000 dollars, an amount too costly for the city council to approve.

McGregor gave the matter his utmost attention and after several meetings with McMath came up with a solution to end the controversy and get the Belle Isle Bridge under construction without further delay. McMath modified the plans "without impairing the safety or usefulness of the bridge," and new bids were requested. This time the lowest bid came in at "approximately one hundred and fourteen thousand dollars."[51] McGregor and the Thursday Noon Group acted immediately. They met with the contractor with the lowest bid, "swore him to secrecy, and offered to hold him harmless" for all costs over $100,000. As a result, the contractor put up a new bid of $99,000 and it was immediately accepted. The construction began without further delay, and on August 11, 1916, the temporary bridge opened to single-file automobile traffic and pedestrian access.[52]

The approach taken by the Thursday Noon Group in resolving the Belle Isle Bridge controversy was typical of the way the group operated. They recognized the urgent need of such a bridge to satisfy the recreational interests of Detroiters, many of whom were the poorer residents of the city. They soon became aware also that the elected officials of Detroit—both the mayor, who had very limited authority under the city charter, and the city council, which was torn apart by corruption and fraudulent practices—were powerless to provide useful remedies. McGregor and his colleagues had the financial resources, the technical expertise, and the leadership to overcome the impasse and get the bridge constructed in a timely manner. They sought neither publicity nor any recognition for their assistance. It was kept a secret until "many years afterward, when an old member of the Council by accident learned of the story, introduced a resolution in Council and the money was refunded."[53]

When they organized in 1912, the leaders of the Thursday Noon Group decided that they would not get involved in the political life of Detroit. This responsibility would be left up to the Detroit Citizens League, which counted among its leadership and supporters several members of the Thursday Noon Group. But it was soon evident to McGregor and his colleagues that they needed wider support, especially with the mayor, city council, and governmental units, in order to achieve their objectives. The controversy involving the nine Detroit schoolteachers studying abroad, the Americanization programs, the bottleneck involving the construction of the temporary Belle Isle Bridge, and the ineffective city relief efforts during the depression of 1914–15 illustrated clearly the need for a more effective and responsible city government.

Under the existing governmental system in Detroit, the mayor had little effective power. The budget was controlled by the city council, and all mayoral appointments had to be approved by the council. Even in times of crisis, the mayor was unable to act decisively. The leadership role of the city council was also compromised, especially because of its cumbersome size. Each of Detroit's twenty-one wards was represented by two members, elected for two-year terms. Not only was this inefficient, but also it was thoroughly corrupt as well. Elections were controlled by saloonkeepers, who occupied one-third of council positions. On election days they used strong-arm tactics to intimidate voters, falsify ballots, and destroy tally sheets. Extensive graft was also present in the city council. Detroit government was run by council subcommittees "whose meetings were often hard to find as to time and place, even when a committee member might want to attend." The city treasury was popularly called the "Xmas Grab Bag."[54]

By 1915 McGregor, James Ingles, Henry Hulbert, and other members of the Thursday Noon Group recognized that the highest priority must be given to reforming Detroit city government, starting with the election procedures. Working with Henry Leland and Pliny Marsh of the Detroit Citizens League, they persuaded state representatives George Scott and Charles O. Flowers to introduce legislation to reform Detroit election practices. Called the "Honest Election Law," the bill provided for strict rules governing elections, the tallying of ballots, and penalties for violation of election rules.[55] The success of the election reform led to the movement to adopt a new charter for the city of Detroit. Led by Tracy McGregor, who was selected to chair the Citizens' Charter Committee, along with Henry Leland, Pliny Marsh of the Detroit Citizens League, Dr. Lent D. Upson of the newly established Detroit Bureau of Governmental Research, and Emory Clark of the Thursday Noon Group, they proposed a charter amendment that was approved by Detroit voters on November 6, 1917, to take effect by the committee and passed by voters in April 1918. It provided that the city council be reduced from forty-two to nine members, to be elected at large, on a "non-partisan basis" for two-year terms. The mayor was given increased power over city government, including full appointive power over all city officials, except the city clerk and city treasurer, who continued to be elected by the voters.[56]

The approval of "Detroit's strong mayor, small council charter plan was a radical advance for the City of that day," stated one government authority. It became the model followed by other major cities in the United States. According to one observer of the Detroit political scene, the success of the charter reform was based on "McGregor's community spirit, and Leland's industrial leadership which furnished a combination of sweetness and strength to which the factor of strategy was added by the sagacity, tact, patience and driving power of Marsh." He added, "here was a triumvirate of religious men who remembered the Bible text, 'Provoking one another to good works.'"[57]

The success of the campaign to reform Detroit's election system and adopt a new charter for the city prompted the leaders of the Thursday Noon Group to turn to another branch of city government that needed attention—the criminal court system. Established in 1883, it had provided for two courts: the Police Court, administered by three judges, handled misdemeanor cases, and the Recorders Court, consisting of two judges, was responsible for felony cases. The system had worked effectively in its early years, but by 1915 it was hopelessly outdated. Not only was there overlapping jurisdiction between the two courts, but also huge backlogs of cases resulted in long delays.[58]

Joined by Leland and Marsh of the Citizens League, the Thursday Noon Group mobilized a campaign to reform the court system. Tracy McGregor was appointed chair of the Campaign Committee and was joined by Frank Eamon, Henry Hulbert, and Edwin Denby, colleagues from the Thursday Noon Group. Although not an attorney, McGregor formerly had many encounters with the municipal courts, appearing before them on many occasions on behalf of mission men who had run afoul of the law.[59]

With support from friends in the state legislature, a Municipal Court bill was passed on April 25, 1919, for reorganization of Detroit's criminal courts. It provided for the Police Court to be replaced by a single Recorders Court. The number of judges was increased from two to seven. The task of McGregor's Campaign Committee was to convince the voters of Detroit to approve the plan. Petitions with thirty-one thousand signatures were secured and submitted to the state, and the referendum was placed on the April 1920 ballot.

Despite widespread public support for the court reform, many influential citizens opposed the legislation. Judges Jeffries and Wilkins, two of the incumbent judges, campaigned against it, as did Francis X. Martel, head of the Detroit Federation of Labor. McGregor and the Campaign Committee secured the support of many community and business leaders, and in order to secure the widespread support of Detroit's factory workers, McGregor devised the following strategy. He persuaded the leaders of the automobile companies not to take a strong public position on behalf of the reform, which would only alienate the workers. Instead, McGregor himself dealt directly with the workers. He attended neighborhood meetings and met with workers at the factories. On another occasion he persuaded the automobile companies to sponsor an "elaborate dinner" at the Board of Commerce auditorium to which only rank-and-file factory workers representing the major automobile companies were invited. Speakers explained the need for court reform and distributed literature. According to Pliny Marsh, "McGregor's cultivation of Detroit workers was a brilliant strategy on behalf of the court reform."[60] On April 5, 1920, Detroit voters overwhelmingly approved the court reform by a vote of 106,081 to 30,588.[61]

Two of the provisions of the Court Reform Act were the establishment of a psychopathic clinic and a probation department within the Recorders Court. The statutes providing for these innovative units were drafted by Frank D.

Eamon, an eminent Detroit attorney and active leader of the Thursday Noon Group. In order to ensure the successful operation of the system, Edwin Denby, a member of the Thursday Noon Group and later U.S. secretary of the navy, volunteered to accept the position of chief probation officer and director of the clinic.[62] Pliny Marsh was appointed as one of the seven new Recorders Court judges by Governor Albert Sleeper and was later confirmed by popular election.[63]

The Thursday Noon Group had reason to be proud of its accomplishments in the political arena. The Detroit city charter, the school board reforms, and the new court system were heralded nationally and gave Detroit status as one of the most progressive cities in America. The Psychopathic Clinic, the oldest clinic of its kind in the United States, won international recognition for its pioneering program. The probation department of the Recorders Court also won national acclaim for its accomplishments.[64]

Although it had not been the intent of McGregor and the founders of the Thursday Noon Group to get involved in the local and statewide political campaigns, they soon realized that such involvement was not only desirable but also absolutely necessary if they were to achieve their goals in reforming city government and make it more responsive to the needs of the community. The active participation of the group in the movement to reform the educational, political, and judicial systems as well as their behind-the-scenes role in supporting the construction of a temporary bridge to Belle Isle made them realize that better qualified candidates must be brought into the political arena if the reforms were to survive. Tracy McGregor reflected this view in his remarks that "we must find ways to encourage superior men to give themselves to public service."[65]

Several members of the Thursday Noon Group, such as Henry Hulbert, Edwin Denby, and Dexter Ferry, ran for key public offices and, with active support from their colleagues, were elected. Tracy McGregor refused all requests and pressures to run for public office, but he did take an active part in the political process. After a successful campaign to reduce membership on the Detroit Board of Education from twenty-one to seven members, McGregor headed a citizens committee to recruit and support key candidates for the new positions. In 1917, McGregor and his Thursday Noon Group, Fred M. Butzel, James Ingles, Henry S. Hulburt, Dexter M. Ferry Jr., and Gustavus Pope headed a committee to elect Ira W. Jayne for the Circuit Court of the

Third Congressional District.[66] In addition, members of the Thursday Noon Group raised funds to support Jayne's election campaign.[67]

Henry Hulburt also received major support from the Thursday Noon Group. In his 1918 campaign for election to the Detroit Probate Court, his colleagues not only actively supported his candidacy but also raised substantial funds for him.[68] Matthew Bishop also benefited from the Thursday Noon Group's support. After Bishop's appointment as prosecuting attorney for Wayne County in 1919, McGregor and other group members gave him five hundred dollars to be used in "the prosecution of the notorious Dr. Fritch . . . who was in charge of the Tuberculosis Hospital at Jackson Prison" and who had mistreated several of the inmates.[69]

The Thursday Noon Group did not fight lone battles in its concern for the serious problems facing Detroiters, their government, and private organizations. The Detroit Municipal League, the Citizens League, the Board of Commerce, and the various charitable institutions, as well as key individuals, also actively participated in programs to improve the quality of life of Detroiters and to make their government more responsible and effective. However, few Detroit organizations had the impact or the major accomplishments to its credit as the Thursday Noon Group.

The public spirit and commitment of the Thursday Noon Group's members and the leadership of Tracy McGregor deserve credit for the group's effectiveness. Both factors are often overlooked, and indeed, few Detroiters even of that period were aware of the organization. Historians of Detroit have been equally oblivious to their work and contributions, due in a large part to the decision of its leaders to work behind the scenes and avoid publicity. As one journalist observed, "The Group did its work without splurge. There was no ballyhoo because men's lips move more freely when they can speak without danger of misinterpretation." He also observed that "what went on was not made public, but what went on eventually changed the pattern of communal life for the better."[70]

In addition to the reforms championed by the Thursday Noon Group, another major contribution was the opportunity it gave its members to participate in civic affairs and develop their leadership skills. Many of the members who had joined the Thursday Noon Group in the early stages of their professional careers became leaders of the business, educational, and professional realms in Detroit throughout the coming decades. The training and experience garnered from their involvement in the group's campaign to reform city government and its philanthropic programs proved invaluable and encouraged their continued involvement in Detroit's future.

Of all of the members of the Thursday Noon Group, few had attained a wider and more respected reputation in the community than Tracy McGregor. By 1912, when the group was organized, McGregor was well known for his leadership of the Mission for Homeless Men and his support of numerous charities. As Pliny Marsh noted, McGregor was involved in all issues of a "civic nature or a sociological nature," but "he was so quiet, so unobtrusive, so self-effacing, that you couldn't always find him in the bushes. . . . He was the one," Marsh said, "who was back there and giving the benefit of his counsel and his help and assistance."[71]

McGregor's role in the Thursday Noon Group exemplified this approach. He organized the group and selected its members, but he did not dominate its meetings or its agenda. James Ingles, who chaired most of the Thursday meetings, recognized Tracy McGregor as "the main squeeze" of the group. "If there was any dominant figure it could have been Tracy McGregor," Ingles later recalled, "but that gentle soul never forced his personality on any crowd. He just naturally won them over. He was a good man."[72] William J. Norton, who headed the Detroit Community Union, observed that McGregor "towered head and shoulders above all other devoted citizens in the charitable world of Detroit."[73]

Given his unobtrusive style, his reluctance to control or dominate meetings, and his avoidance of publicity, one may wonder how he became so skilled and effective in chairing such groups and committees. Pliny Marsh later described an example of diplomacy in an extensive interview.[74] At one meeting chaired by McGregor, Marsh recalled that there was a sharp split between Charles Carson, superintendent of the Cadillac Motor Company, and James Murphy, an influential politician and director of the Murphy Chair Company. After an exchange of "vehement" opposing views between Carson and Murphy, McGregor adjourned the meeting until the following week. In opening the subsequent session, McGregor summed up the sharp differences of the two men, but purposely attributed to Carson the views earlier championed by Murphy. A heated exchange continued until McGregor tactfully explained his mistake and pointed out that they both supported the same objective. McGregor's profound understanding of Detroit's leaders and their personalities and prejudices helps explain why he was such an effective leader and why he was able to accomplish so much through the Thursday Noon Group and other organizations that he led.[75]

The Thursday Noon Group became inactive after World War I. McGregor continued to have a close association with most of its members, and several, such as Henry S. Hulbert, William J. Norton, Frank McMath, and Frank Sladen, served with McGregor on the governing boards of various community and charitable organizations.

In the early 1930s, during the Great Depression, several of the founding members of the group met to discuss the problems facing Detroit and its institutions, specifically "the police situation, the street railway fares, the upheaval over unemployed and Communistic meetings resulting from idleness."[76] They were especially troubled by the lack of public policy relating to these issues and the need for a concerted plan by "businessmen who are not merely businessmen but men of humanitarian sympathy and vision." They concluded that a new Thursday Group was urgently needed, and they wanted McGregor involved again, if not as its leader then as an advisor.

Kirby White, a close friend and colleague of McGregor and one of the Thursday Group's original founders, contacted Tracy, who was vacationing in St. Petersburg, Florida, and urged him "to overcome some of your modesty and see how peculiarly well-fitted you are to start the most useful work that has ever been undertaken in Detroit."[77] Under pressure from other colleagues, McGregor agreed and in May 1931 invited a number of associates to join him in a "meeting for old times' sake" at the Detroit Club. The group included Gustavus Pope, F. C. McMath, Kirby White, Dexter M. Ferry, Frank J. Sladen, Fred Butzel, Frank Eamon, Joseph Schlotman, Henry G. Stevens, and James Ingles.

The gathering had more the flavor of a reunion than a business meeting. They discussed in great detail the early years of the group, especially the projects and causes that they had supported. The overwhelming conclusion was that the Thursday Group was as relevant in the 1930s as it had been two decades earlier and that it should be activated as soon as possible. McGregor shared these views and agreed to participate, but he made it clear that he could not provide the leadership that he had done earlier because of his residence in Washington. He turned that responsibility over to Henry S. Hulbert, James Ingles, Fred Butzel, and Frank Eamon.

McGregor did insist, however, that the new group not be limited to the original members. New blood was needed, he stressed, especially young men who were experienced and concerned about the critical problems facing

Detroit. In this manner, he reasoned, "the spirit of service which is so evident in the old members might be passed on into the future."[78]

The monthly meetings of the new Thursday Group were held at the Statler Hotel, and the topic of the sessions related to a specific issue. The critical unemployment problems were often on the agenda as were issues relating to Detroit's charitable agencies. At the March 1935 meeting, McGregor led the discussion on "the federal transient program," and at a later session he presented his ideas on "the needs for the insane in Michigan" and a formal proposal for a statewide mental hygiene program.[79] Welfare relief, another issue of special interest to McGregor as well as to the trustees of the McGregor Fund, was the topic of a joint meeting of the Thursday Group and the Detroit Board of Commerce in April 1935.

The Thursday Group continued meeting until the close of World War II, and although it couldn't claim as long a list of accomplishments as the earlier group had done, it did provide a forum to address key social issues and train Detroit's future leaders. Fred Butzel acknowledged that "the organization is not now as strenuous as it was in the old days,"[80] but given the challenges facing Detroit during the 1930s, this is perhaps understandable. Furthermore, after 1936 it did not have Tracy McGregor as its inspired leader. George Stark, one of Detroit's leading journalists, observed that even without McGregor, the inspiration of his life and deeds still worked on quietly and effectively.[81]

10

Merrill-Palmer Institute

One of the civic responsibilities that Tracy McGregor took very seriously was his relationship to the Merrill-Palmer Motherhood and Home Training School, in which he was actively involved from its founding in 1918 until his death in 1936. During those eighteen years he served as president of the Merrill-Palmer Corporation Board of Trustees.

Senator Thomas Palmer and his wife, Lizzie Pitts Merrill Palmer, founders of the school, had roots in early nineteenth-century Detroit. Thomas Palmer was born to Thomas and Mary Witherell Palmer in 1830 in Detroit, where he grew up and attended the local public schools. After high school graduation, he attended the University of Michigan and then joined his father in 1852 in his various business ventures, which included lumbering, mining, and retail stores. A year later, young Thomas became a partner with the lumber baron, Charles Merrill, who owned vast stands of white pine in the lower peninsula of Michigan. In 1855 Thomas married Merrill's daughter Elizabeth, who insisted on being called "Lizzie."[1]

After a successful business career, which made him one of Michigan's earliest millionaires, Palmer entered the political scene of the state. In 1883 he was elected United States senator, an office he held until 1889 when he was appointed ambassador to Spain. In 1892 he became commissioner for the World's Colombian Exposition in Chicago. He died in Detroit in 1913 at the age of eighty-three.[2]

Lizzie Palmer shared her husband's interest in business and community affairs. She was especially active in the women's suffrage movement, was founder of the Michigan Humane Society, and was a patron of the Detroit Institute of Arts. Lizzie and Thomas Palmer made many generous gifts to the Detroit community, including a six-hundred-acre park located at the north end of the city at Woodward Avenue and McNichols or Six Mile Road. Of special concern to Lizzie were the serious problems facing immigrants in the early 1900s, specifically those of the women and children.[3]

After her husband died in 1913, Lizzie Palmer concentrated her attention on the disposition of the huge estate that they had developed together, including extensive real estate holdings, stocks, and bonds. She and the senator had no offspring of their own, but they had adopted two children, Lizzie and Harold. The elder Lizzie allocated 3 million dollars to establish a school to be known as the "Merrill-Palmer Motherhood and Home Training School" where "girls and young women of ten years or more shall be educated, trained, developed and disciplined with special reference to fitting them mentally, morally, physically and religiously for the discharge of the functions and service of wifehood and motherhood, direction and inspiration of the home."[4] These directives reflected her views that "the welfare of any community is divinely and hence inseparably dependent upon the quality of its motherhood, and the spiritual character of its homes."[5] In her will, she concluded, "It is my hope that before I depart this life, I shall have at least initiated my cherished project."[6]

Unfortunately, her hope was not realized. On July 28, 1916, at the age of seventy-nine, she died before the school could be launched. Under the terms of her will it was left up to the Wayne County Circuit Court to appoint a board of trustees to administer the will and establish the school. Before any action could be taken, however, the court had to resolve claims by her relatives who were dissatisfied with the amount left to them in the will. In the negotiations that followed, the executors worked out a compromise whereby the contesting parties received approximately 2 million dollars, and the remaining 3 million dollars were allocated to the Merrill-Palmer Motherhood Training School.[7]

The Palmer will was admitted to probate on June 26, 1918, followed by the court's appointment of George L. Canfield and R. McClelland Brady, the two executors of the Palmer Estate, and Tracy W. McGregor, Henry G. Stevens, and Lawrence K. Butler as the board of trustees. The specific duty of this board was to manage "properly the affairs and business of the Corporation."[8] At the January 1919 meeting, Tracy W. McGregor was elected president of the board, a position he held until his death in 1936.

It was soon evident to McGregor and his colleagues what a monumental task they faced in accepting these appointments to the board. Because there was no model to follow for the school as envisioned by Lizzie Palmer, they had to determine the scope of its educational programs, its governing policies, and the student body. Facilities were needed for classrooms, staff offices, a library, and research office, and finally a staff had to be hired, including the position of superintendent.

Under the leadership of Tracy McGregor and Henry G. Stevens, the board began its deliberations with a "survey of agencies in Detroit offering types of instruction that in any way touched the home, occupations derived from home activities, child welfare, education of girls and women, social visitors serving in any advisory capacity to home workers, or those dealing with the welfare of home and community."[9]

McGregor also turned to his friend and colleague, Lent Upson, the director of the Detroit Bureau of Governmental Research, for recommendations for the new school. He had a list of questions ready: "What and How Many Women should it be planned to reach? What territory should be covered? What type of institution or manner of teaching will be best adopted to reach the women involved?" and "With the money available will the plan adopted do the greatest good to the greatest number of women?"[10]

After a careful analysis of the potential groups of women in the community and the possible methods to reach them, Upson recommended three plans. The first was to organize a domestic science college to train "teachers and leaders to instruct in the principles of wifehood and motherhood and household arts."[11] The second plan suggested the creation of a school of household arts and domestic training for Detroit grade and high school girls. Such a program would be clearly coordinated with the existing educational programs of the Detroit school system, especially the latter's "Concentration School," which was designed for training "young girls who left school before reaching the age of sixteen and who have not completed the eighth grade." Married women would also be eligible.[12] A third proposal involved the establishment of a household art college aimed at "advanced college students." In addition to the creation of separate schools, Upson recommended a program of "Field Work and Propaganda" that involved conducting classes in "factories, stores, clubs, and other places where girls and young women work or congregate."[13]

Upson also gave attention to subsidizing existing local public schools, health departments, some public nursing organizations, visiting housekeeper associations, and neighborhood social settlements. Upson recommended that the Merrill-Palmer Board of Trustees consider a "concentration" of all of these plans.[14]

The trustees also sought the advice of Dr. Benjamin R. Schenck, a retired Detroit physician who was not only familiar with Detroit and its educational institutions but also knowledgeable about similar endowed research programs in other parts of the country. After reviewing the Lizzie Palmer will and other relevant documents and discussing this with McGregor and other trustees, he recommended: "Spend money for efficient workers and not for splendid buildings." "Keep the endowment intact, spending only the accumulated income for buildings, equipment, etc.—even if you wait a number of years." Finally, "engage as directors the most able men or women in the world." Displaying a somewhat cynical view of Detroit, Dr. Schenck added, "Whatever you do, do not turn it over to local talent to lapse into a semi-comatose condition as have so many of our Detroit institutions."[15] Dr. Schenck also suggested patience. "Draw on the whole country and whole world for ideas and for people to carry them out; go slowly and *don't build any marble memorials to Mrs. Palmer.*"[16]

Not all the reactions to the proposed agenda of the board of trustees were positive or complimentary. The Detroit Federation of Women's Clubs was highly critical of the Merrill-Palmer Corporation and its trustees "for not taking care of the provisions of the [Palmer] will" as they interpreted it. They proposed that the Palmer Estate be used either for the "education of delinquent girls at Adrian and Lapeer" or to invest the total funds from the estate in "putting up a building."[17]

Tracy McGregor was sensitive to the seriousness of the charges made by the Federation of Women's Clubs. He and his colleagues recognized that they lacked influential women on the board. McGregor diffused some of the criticism by appointing Martha Ray, the president of the Detroit Federation of Women's Clubs, to the newly established board of directors.[18]

The Palmer will, rigidly enforced by the chancery of the circuit court, limited membership on the board of directors to five. Tracy McGregor asked George Canfield, whose firm handled the legal affairs of the corporation, to find a solution acceptable to the court. The plan Canfield decided upon was to create a separate board of directors "to conduct the affairs of the school, exclusive of its capital funds, the duties of the Board to include the employment and dismissal of members of the faculty and the entire management of the activities of the School."[19] With the approval of the trustees and the court, McGregor appointed Katherine Smith Diack, Georgia Emery, Mary G. Haskins, Fanny S. Pope, Gertrude Safford, and Martha Ray to serve on this new board of directors.[20]

The appointments reflected McGregor's astute leadership abilities. Martha Ray, the president of the Detroit Federation of Women's Clubs and an outspoken critic of the Merrill-Palmer Corporation, now became an enthusiastic supporter of the work of the trustees. Also, McGregor selected the other members because of their experience in other Detroit charitable institutions.

Within a few weeks after establishing this new board of directors, the members took action. They decided that their highest priority should be finding a qualified woman to direct the school. They contacted by phone, by mail, and then in person leaders in the fields of home economics and nutrition to get their ideas and recommendations. Katherine Smith and Gertrude Safford visited educational institutions in New York City, Philadelphia, Cincinnati, and Columbus, Ohio. Dr. Haskins, Georgia Emery, and Martha Ray were assigned to Chicago and Urbana, Illinois, and Milwaukee and Madison, Wisconsin, and other western cities, and Tracy McGregor visited the educational institutions and federal agencies in Washington, D.C.[21]

The board of trustees devoted several meetings to reports of these visits. In December 1918, McGregor convened a special conference in Detroit to discuss plans for the organization of the Merrill-Palmer school. He was joined by George Stevens, Fred Butzel, Julia Grant, McAdam, representing the Detroit Board of Education, Bessie Lee of the Visiting Housekeepers Association, Gertrude Safford and Katherine Smith Diack, all from Detroit, plus three outside guests: Henrietta Calvin, specialist in education of the Bureau of Education of the U.S. Department of Interior; Josephine Marshall, instructor in home economics at Teachers College, Columbia University; and Jenny Snow, supervisor of household arts in Chicago.[22]

All of the participants strongly supported the plans for a special school for women homemakers. Calvin summed up the views of the speakers in her closing remarks: "The Trustees of the Fund have an opportunity to establish an institution of value not only to Detroit and Michigan, but which shall be an example for the whole country."[23] She concluded, "The highest priority should be to employ the very strongest women you can secure."[24]

By late summer 1919, McGregor and his colleagues on the Merrill-Palmer Board of Directors and the trustees had several strong, highly qualified candidates under consideration, based on recommendations from leading national experts. By far the most impressive and attractive was Edna Noble White, head of the home economics program at Ohio State University. She had impressive credentials. Born on June 3, 1880, and raised in Farrand, Illinois, the second of the three children of Angeline Noble and Alexander White, she was educated at the University of Illinois, which awarded her a Bachelor of Arts degree in 1906. After two years of teaching at Danville Illinois High School and Lewis Institute in Chicago, she joined the faculty at Ohio State University in 1908 as associate professor of home economics. Five years later she was appointed full professor and chair of the home economics department. White also developed a national reputation as one of the leaders in the field of home economics.[25]

One of White's most active supporters was Katherine Smith Diack, who had studied under her at Ohio State University. According to Diack, White clearly had the qualifications for the job as executive head of the Merrill-Palmer training school. She was "old enough to have demonstrated administrative ability, judgment and professional leadership, but also young enough to be dynamic, imaginative, enthusiastic and willing to 'adventure.'"[26] However, when first approached by Merrill-Palmer trustees, White assumed that she was being consulted only for advice on the program of the newly established school, and she declined the first request to come to Detroit. Only after her colleagues persuaded her that she should look carefully at the position in Detroit and the opportunities it offered her professionally did she consider the position. After several visits with the trustees and a special meeting with Tracy McGregor on October 23, 1919, she accepted their offer. On November 6, 1919, she was officially hired for a three-year appointment starting in February 1920, with a beginning salary of $7,500 a year. She insisted on the title "director" rather than "superintendent" as had been stipulated in the Palmer will.[27]

Her initial three-year appointment grew into twenty-seven years, and Edna Noble White served as executive head of the Merrill-Palmer school and directed its formation and growth into one of the premier institutions of its kind. Diack described White in the Merrill-Palmer school's report twenty years later:

> So much depended on the personality of the Director of the School, in this new enterprise, that I cannot escape being personal when trying to estimate what these years have meant under the leadership of Edna

> White—such a leadership as has been expressed in breadth of vision; in high executive ability, safely balanced by a rich human understanding; a gift for choosing the right people for work to be done. . . . She is a real leader, a grand cooperative, and an indefatigable worker, as well as a delightful friend.[28]

When Edna Noble White arrived in Detroit to formally take over her new position as director on February 5, 1920, the quarters assigned to the new school were located on the second floor of the Palmer Building on Washington Boulevard. In addition to a large classroom, which also contained desks for the staff there, the facility included a glassed office for Miss White and a small area for a library and kitchen. At the time of her arrival, the staff consisted of a secretary and two specialists, one in charge of "development of economic and social phases of home making courses" and another "in charge of nutrition." Although the facilities were extremely limited, Tracy McGregor and the trustees considered it adequate until a program could be developed to hire a more complete staff.[29]

One of the major challenges facing White and the school's trustees was that there was no educational model in the field of "home and family life" to emulate. The Merrill-Palmer school, in effect, had to begin as a pioneering venture in "method and research." After extensive consultation with McGregor and the trustees, White conducted a survey of the agencies in Wayne County that offered instruction involving "home activities, child welfare, education of girls and women" and employing "social visitors serving in any advising capacity to home workers or those dealing with the welfare of the home and community."[30]

In planning and implementing the survey, White relied heavily on McGregor for assistance and counsel. He provided White entrée with the leaders of the city's various charities and educational institutions and gave her an awareness of the special immigration problems facing the Merrill-Palmer school.

As a result of the survey, White immediately began an intensive study of the Americanization programs underway throughout the city.[31] She followed with two other projects. The first was a course for twenty-five Red Cross nurses in "Nutrition for Children," and the second involved a working arrangement with the Continuation School of the Detroit Public Schools. This program, which had been authorized by the state legislature, was aimed at a significant number of young girls, between the ages of fourteen and eighteen, who had left school to take "jobs in industry" with "little opportunity for home-training."[32] The Merrill-Palmer staff conducted "an experimental study" to determine "the type of course best fitted to give them some viewpoint regarding home and family responsibilities, and some knowledge of the economic and social background of the home."[33]

By the end of 1920, Miss White and her staff agreed that their major priority would be the establishment of a nursery school for about "12 to 20 children between the ages of three and five, with the purpose . . . of providing a laboratory for the training of girls in child care."[34] The board of trustees approved the plan at its meeting on January 21, 1921, and also authorized White to travel to England to visit nursery schools and recruit staff to operate the Detroit school. The trip, according to Miss White, exceeded expectations. She not only had the opportunity to visit the most successful English nursery schools and study their programs but also met the leaders of the schools, one of whom, Emma Henton, she hired later in 1921 to come to Detroit to head the nursery school there.[35]

After her return from England and with the approval of the board of trustees, White made plans for the first educational program of the Merrill-Palmer Institute. In January 1922, the nursery school "opened as a center for student study and practice." Also, as a part of the nursery school, an arrangement was worked out with Michigan State University, then Michigan Agricultural College, to send a group of "six qualified senior students in home economics to the Merrill-Palmer School for a quarter's work, to be credited toward their degrees." These students received training in child care and homemaking as well as supervised contacts with the social agencies in Detroit that had programs for children. This arrangement established a pattern that became an integral part of the Merrill-Palmer program.[36]

The success of the nursery school program led to the introduction of other related educational projects. In 1927 the Infant Service was inaugurated, followed by the Children's Clubs in 1929 and the Merrill-Palmer Camp in 1930, all of which offered "many and diverse opportunities to observe and work with children."[37] These programs were soon expanded to reach the parents of the children.

In addition to teaching, the Merrill-Palmer Institute also included school services, community services, and research. Within a decade the school not only was highly regarded in Detroit, especially among civic, educational, and community groups, but had attracted national attention as a pioneer in the field of home and family life.

White served as director of the Merrill-Palmer Institute for twenty-seven years until her retirement in 1947. During those years she helped develop the Merrill-Palmer Institute into a premier educational institution. Her pioneering work in "child research, nursery school education, parent education, the study of human behavior, and family life research and education" was recognized internationally. Her accomplishments would have exceeded the hopes of Lizzie Merrill Palmer.[38]

Tracy W. McGregor, who served as president of the institute from 1918 till his death in 1936, also deserves credit for its success. Despite his heavy schedule and other community commitments, he took an active role in the operation of the Merrill-Palmer Institute. McGregor was selected by the circuit court to serve on the board of trustees because of the high regard in which the Detroit business and civic community held him and because of his business acumen. The trustees discovered that although Lizzie Palmer's will was appraised at 3 million dollars, the cash resources totaled only $140,515, the stocks represented $294,870, the bonds $175,858, and mortgages and contracts $113,096. The largest segment of the Palmer Estate was in real estate holdings, which were estimated at $2,275,661.[39]

After a careful analysis of the Palmer portfolio, McGregor and the trustees decided that they should sell the real estate as "judiciously as possible and reinvest in securities exempt from taxation and suitable for trust funds."[40] They also adopted the policy that the "use of the funds of the Merrill-Palmer School for purposes and groups already provided for by public funds would be unwise—in other words that the wisest and most helpful expenditure of these funds from the standpoint of the community would be in fields where public moneys could not be applied."[41]

In its report to the circuit court in chancery in 1919, the board announced, "This is the policy of the Trustees to preserve the endowment intact and conserve the resources; to use the income for teachers rather than buildings during the formative stages at least." McGregor and his trustee colleagues were firm on one issue, echoing the sentiments of Dr. Benjamin Schenck: We will not "build any marble memorials to Mrs. Palmer."[42] The court heartily approved of the trustees' policy statement, although there was not unanimous support by other community groups.

However, the critical issue of adequate facilities eventually demanded the attention of the trustees. The several rooms allocated in the Palmer Building were suitable in the early planning stages, but after White and her staff developed specific programs, the space proved to be "inadequate." Even the use of the Palmer Homestead, or "Log House" as it was called, located west of Woodward Avenue and north of Six Mile Road did not provide the needed space. At the board of trustees' meeting on September 30, 1921, White outlined the plans for the nursery school and the homemaking courses, and additional space was essential for these new programs not only to take care of the twenty to thirty children in the nursery school, including "sleeping space, play space," but also to accommodate "the six students with a teacher or chaperon in charge."[43] With the prior approval and assistance of McGregor, White had inspected several available houses "with a view to renting or leasing" one of them. She looked at the Burton House on Brainard Street, the Moore House on Canfield, and the Freer House on Ferry Avenue. Because of the condition of the Burton and Moore properties and the extensive renovation needed to make them usable, she recommended the Freer House, which not only would require fewer changes but also would be large enough for the nursery school, the "practice-home units," and the administrative unit. Its proximity to the main public library, Central High School, one or two grade schools, and apartment houses was also in its favor.[44]

The Freer House had been the residence of Charles L. Freer, a wealthy Detroit industrialist and prominent art patron. The house contained three art galleries, including the famous Peacock Room, the contents of which had been transferred to the Freer Gallery at the Smithsonian Institution in Washington, D.C. The galleries in the Freer House would serve as the "center for all resident activities of the School."[45]

The trustees gave White's recommendations their careful consideration. They raised the issue of possibly using the Palmer homestead property but finally approved a proposal by McGregor to offer "a sum not to exceed $70,000" for the Freer House. The purchase of the Freer House was finalized in October 1921, and between 1922 and 1928, five other houses located in the same block, formerly "the homes of old Detroit families," were also purchased. In December 1934, a seventh residence at 60 East Ferry was acquired for the school.[46]

An even more demanding issue than the establishment of the school was the financial arrangements required to reinvest the estate of Lizzie Palmer.

McGregor and the trustees faced not only a limited income on the real estate investments but also a turbulent financial market in the 1920s. Practically every meeting of the board of trustees gave special attention to selling some of their real estate holdings, investing in stocks and municipal bonds, and negotiating the rental space in their buildings.[47]

However, the board faced problems in this endeavor. Disposing of the property adjacent to Palmer Park was a typical example. In 1893 Senator Palmer and his wife offered a gift of 120 acres near Woodward Avenue and McNichols Road to the city of Detroit for a park. According to the provisions of the gift, he and his wife continued to live in the "log cabin" until 1897, when all of the property was taken over by the city and renamed Palmer Park.[48] In 1921 the city of Detroit condemned additional property adjacent to the park, owned by the Merrill-Palmer Corporation, for $1,092,751. The trustees spent weeks on this transaction, engaging in lengthy meetings and conducting detailed studies to determine how the money should be invested in the best interests of the school.[49]

The trustees were also involved in many legal disputes involving the school and the Palmer Estate, which consumed a great deal of their time, especially that of Tracy McGregor. In 1929 the Merrill-Palmer Corporation was involved in a legal dispute with the Detroit Golf Club and property owners facing Palmer Park. The Merrill-Palmer Corporation had planned to approve the sale of their property for the erection of apartment buildings facing the golf course. A complicated legal issue arose as to whether the original restrictions against the construction of such buildings signed or approved by Lizzie Palmer were valid. With the assistance of the Miller, Canfield, Paddock, and Stone law firm, Tracy McGregor satisfactorily handled these difficult negotiations with the golf club and community groups. His patience and leadership skills resolved the dispute without placing the Merrill-Palmer school in an embarrassing public position.[50]

As noted earlier, Tracy McGregor served as president of the Merrill-Palmer Institute from its founding in 1918 to 1936, during the height of the Great Depression. During this brief span, the school grew from a vision described in vague terms in Lizzie Palmer's will to one of the great innovative institutions in the world devoted to marriage and family life, human growth and development, and child rearing and guidance. Edna Noble White and her colleagues on the faculty commented on McGregor's contributions and style of leadership: "His grasp of the vital needs of the School, his wonderful ability as an organizer, his fine tact, his sympathetic understanding of the problems of the School, together with his ready help and advice made him our natural leader. Despite the great demands put upon him by his broad philanthropic activities, he was ever ready to lend a hand when his aid and counsel were needed."[51]

11

The McGregor Fund

In reviewing Tracy McGregor's career in civic affairs and his reputation as a humanitarian, it is difficult to comprehend how he could accomplish so much. His supervision of the Detroit Mission for Homeless Men was a full-time job requiring a commitment of ten to twelve hours each day of the week. The Thursday Noon Club, the Provident Loan and Savings Society, as well as his active involvement in other charitable and community endeavors only added to his responsibilities and reflected his abilities as a talented administrator.

McGregor also demonstrated his business and financial acumen in a variety of other ways. After his marriage, he assumed responsibility for monitoring the multimillion dollar estate that he and his wife shared. He also served as an officer in the Whitney Realty Company. In addition, McGregor established several business firms, many designed to provide low-cost housing to the families in the Detroit metropolitan area.[1]

In 1929 McGregor founded the LaSalle Land Company on several acres of undeveloped land east of Detroit, near the Mt. Olivet Cemetery and the Detroit City Airport. After roads, sidewalks, and sewers were laid out and completed, the company built a number of houses on Blackmoor and Park Grove avenues. The cost of construction of these houses ranged from $4,500 to $5,000 and sold for $6,800 to $7,000. The profits were minimal, but the companies provided well-constructed homes and helped in a modest way to ease the housing shortage in the Detroit area. These real estate projects proved to be sound business ventures for McGregor, and with his other investments his net worth increased steadily in the 1920s.[2]

By the mid-1920s Tracy and Katherine had decided that they must find a more efficient way to manage their financial resources and to ensure that if anything happened to them their support for humanitarian and charitable programs would be continued. After careful study and consultation with friends and colleagues, McGregor decided that establishment of a benevolent foundation was the best way to ensure the continuity of their charitable programs. He was familiar with earlier such foundations, including those of John Harvard, Benjamin Franklin, and James Smithson. More recently, during his early years at the McGregor Institute, and especially after his marriage in 1901, he was attracted to the views of Andrew Carnegie, which were expressed, in his "The Gospel of Wealth" in 1889. Carnegie believed that "the rich had an obligation to share their wealth in ways which benefited the public" and that "a millionaire must be a trustee for the poor."[3] Of the several foundations Carnegie established, the one that provided for the endowment of libraries, art galleries, public parks, and concert halls was well known to McGregor. In fact, one of the Detroit Public Library's branches, financed by Carnegie and named for Henry M. Utley, was one of McGregor's favorite libraries.

McGregor was also familiar with the ideas of John D. Rockefeller, who was prompted to establish a major foundation because of the daily pressures on him for financial assistance from individuals and organizations. Also, McGregor admired the Hull House in Chicago, which he visited often, as well as the work of the Russell Sage Foundation, established "for the permanent improvement of social conditions." In addition, McGregor was familiar with the work of S. S. Kresge, who had established a foundation in 1924, followed by a similar action in 1926 by C. S. Mott.[4]

Another important consideration to McGregor, as well as to other wealthy families establishing foundations, were the changes in the tax code, prompted by the passage of the Sixteenth Amendment to the United States Constitution in 1913, which gave the federal government the power "to lay and collect taxes on income." The action by Congress in 1917 that provided for the deductions of charitable contributions encouraged many of the nation's millionaires to consider special foundations. Tracy McGregor was no exception, although his primary motive was not to evade taxes.

After carefully investigating his options in the summer and fall of 1925, and then consulting with his attorney, George L. Canfield, McGregor invited five of his close associates—Henry S. Hulbert, Frank J. Sladen, William J. Norton, Kirby B. White, and John W. Staley—to meet with him at the People's State Bank on December 29, 1925. He had, of course, discussed his plans with each of them prior to the meeting, but he needed to follow all legal requirements to establish the McGregor Fund, as enunciated in the provisions of chapter 1, part 4, of Act No. 84 of the Public Acts of Michigan for 1921. As his initial gift, he gave five thousand dollars to the fund.[5]

The specific purpose of the fund was to "relieve the misfortunes and promote the well being of mankind." The methods to reach these objectives were to be determined by the trustees. Tracy McGregor was elected president and treasurer of the fund; George Canfield, secretary; and Hulbert, Sladen, Norton, White, and Staley, members of the board of trustees. McGregor's office in the McGregor Institute at 1453 Brush Street was designated as the fund's headquarters.[6]

The McGregors' decision was part of a major movement in the United States to establish organized philanthropies. In a piecemeal way, the McGregors, working through the Detroit Community Union, had supported such community-related activities since the turn of the century. Now, in 1925, they set in motion a philanthropic endeavor that was designed to continue long into the future.

Although the fund was formally established late in 1925, and the necessary legal documents were filed with the secretary of state in the months that followed, McGregor did not intend "to begin at once the actual carrying out of the purpose he had in mind." First he wanted to work with the trustees "in discussion and in an unfolding of his own thoughts and policies" that would govern the work of the trustees.[7] During the three years following the establishment of the fund, he held frequent meetings with the trustees to develop guidelines for it. The delay also gave McGregor the opportunity to plan for the fund's financial support.

In 1929, four years after it was established, the McGregors gave their first major gift to the fund. It consisted of stock in the LaSalle Land Company, which they owned, at a par value of $88,800. An additional $100,000 in cash was given with the understanding that it would be used for loans to the LaSalle Company "to build houses and for other purposes affecting the development of its properties."[8] During 1930 the McGregors gave additional gifts totaling $316,000, and in the following two years, the totals amounted to $3,179,814.19.[9]

With this substantial endowment available, the trustees were ready to begin "the serious work of carrying out the purposes of the Trust."[10] Special attention was given to electing new trustees. Kenneth L. Moore was elected as its seventh member, and in 1929, following the deaths of John W. Staley and George L. Canfield, Edgar A. Bowen and Renville Wheat were added to the enlarged board. McGregor continued as president and treasurer, and Renville Wheat was elected secretary.

In a "Memorandum for K [Katherine]," Tracy described his views of these men, listing their strengths and what he believed they would be able to contribute to the work of the fund. Judge Hulbert, he observed, was "my own age, Chief Judge of the probate Court, closely related to the settlement of estates, all wills being probated in that court," and "Dr. Sladen and Mr. Norton about 45 and are well balanced and conservative and have unusual knowledge of social problems and of what is being done or likely to be done throughout the country." Renville Wheat, Edgar Bowen, Kirby White, and Kenneth Moore, "while having more than an average sense of duty and interest in humanity, are capable business men." He added, "I expect to find two or three younger men to be added to these."[11]

Tracy also explained to his wife his future plans for the fund. "As you know," he wrote, "my will leaves what I have to this corporation. It is my present intention in a few years if I live to turn over or deed everything to the Fund." He gave Katherine this advice: "If you were to turn over say one of the three chief parts of your estate (the three being bonds, Whitney Realty Co. stock, and Parke Davis stock) in the event of my death you would have capable persons willing to serve and assist you, and after your own death well suited to carry out your wishes."[12]

Katherine shared her husband's enthusiasm for the fund and its future, and in December 1932 gave to the fund several thousand shares of common and preferred stock. She followed in October 1934 with an additional gift to the fund of securities and bonds with a market value of $2,685,000. In return for these generous gifts, the fund agreed to pay Tracy and Katherine an annual annuity totaling $25,000 each as long as they lived.[13]

As the fund embarked on its program to carry out its mission, Tracy McGregor set forth his ideas "of the lines I am interested in."[14] The McGregor Institute, which was given priority, received generous annual grants. National organizations working for the homeless, mental hygiene programs, and various Detroit-related charitable endeavors, including the Detroit Community Union, were also recipients. In addition to philanthropic organizations, McGregor urged the trustees to support worthwhile programs "in the fields of education and science which might be open for useful work by a fund of moderate size, in relieving the misfortunes and promoting the well-being of mankind."[15]

With adequate financial resources available for the first time, the trustees began on November 10, 1932, to authorize grants for special projects. The first grant of $10,000 went to the city of Detroit for the work of the Emergency Relief Committee. The McGregor Institute received a grant of $33,000 for the year 1932. In recommending such support, which he and Katherine had been giving from their personal estate each year, McGregor acknowledged that the future of the institute was in doubt. Because of massive unemployment in Detroit and the increased number of homeless, the institute could no longer provide meals and lodging for all of the men who came there each day for assistance. Earlier in 1932 the McGregors had approached city welfare officials with an offer "to loan the Institute building to the Department of Public Welfare to be used as a municipal lodging house where the men would be dealt with more or less en masse," but this proposal was never approved by the city. McGregor also proposed that a case work bureau—to be supported by the McGregor Fund as an agency of the Community Union—be established "to deal with the men individually." The fund continued to support the institute with similar grants each year until 1935, when the "Institute discontinued its services due to the taking over of this work on a broader scale by the Government of the United States."[16]

The Detroit Community Fund also received a generous grant of $40,000 for the year 1933. Other favorite projects of Tracy McGregor's were added to the list at the November trustees' meeting. The National Committee for the Care of Transients and Homeless—which the McGregors had supported privately—received $10,000. Another grant for $3,371.52 was allocated to Carleton Wells for expenses to study in England. As noted in chapter 3, McGregor had met Wells in 1920 when he interviewed him for a job at the institute. They subsequently became golfing partners and met often on the golf courses in Detroit and Ann Arbor, and later a closer friendship developed between McGregor and Wells and his family. McGregor encouraged Wells, a young instructor in the English department at the University of Michigan, to complete his Ph.D. and helped support his research in England. Wells also assisted McGregor in building his library on English and American literature. In addition, McGregor had given financial aid to many other young students for their college education, including his nephew, Douglas McGregor, Murray's son.[17]

The McGregors strongly endorsed financial aid for mental health issues. They wanted the fund to assist "those chronically ill or in danger of serious breakdown in general health, particularly those who might be saved from permanent and continuing broken health, by a period of rest and by change of environment." They believed it was this field that "might eventually find that research would develop the most effective weapons for the prevention of disease of both mind and body."[18]

The final actions of the trustees at their November 1932 meeting were giving approval to move the fund's headquarters from Detroit to Washington, D.C., and providing a grant to the fund of $30,000 for staff and administrative expenses and the annual annuity payment to the McGregors.[19] The grants approved in 1932 totaled approximately $150,000.

McGregor decided to streamline the role of the trustees in March 1933 by establishing three main committees to oversee operations. An executive committee, "made up of a majority of the Trustees of which the President shall be ex officio a member and chairman," was to be elected annually by the trustees "and shall have all of the powers of the Trustees when the Trustees are not in session." A standing investment committee, "which shall have the power to invest and reinvest the funds of the corporation," with McGregor, Kirby White, and Edgar Bowen as members, was also approved. A standing committee on program of work consisted of McGregor appointees Henry S. Hulbert, William J. Norton, and Dr. Frank Sladen.[20] McGregor served as ex officio on all of the committees, and following his typical style of leadership, he took an active part in the work of each of the standing committees.

The investment committee was faced with the challenge of finding suitable ways to protect the substantial amounts given to the fund in 1933 and 1934, which was especially difficult given the onset of the Great Depression and the unstable condition of the stock market. It was the function of the program committee to not only review all requests for assistance but also search for other projects that merited the support of the fund. The allocations for the years 1933–36 followed in a general way the pattern set in 1932 under the broad areas of health, sickness and research, education, local and natural philanthropies, civic endeavors, and religion. Support for capital structures involving "problems of health, fresh air camps and community service" commenced in 1936.

The health, sickness, and research projects received high priority from McGregor and the trustees. The Wayne County Training School, with which

McGregor had worked closely since its founding, received grants for "two research workers in mental hygiene" and for the "salary of Dr. Thorlief G. Hegge, who was engaged in a new method of teaching the mentally subnormal to read." The Michigan State Medical Society was the recipient of a grant in 1934 to complete "an investigation and report on the subjects of cost of medical care and health insurance, with particular attention to continuing education for the doctor."[21] In 1935 and 1936 the fund supported the Detroit Orthopedic Clinics, operated by the Sigma Gamma Association, for pioneering research in the "surgical repair, convalescence, which included the training of the mind of the crippled child in independence of thought, in order to break up the well-known tendency of crippled children to feel that they are wholly dependent upon others." The Wayne County Medical Society, the Eloise Hospital and Infirmary, and the Joint Committee on Public Health Education also received grants for their educational and research programs.

Following the wishes and strong recommendation that both Tracy and Katherine McGregor presented at the November 1932 meeting, the trustees of the fund devoted special attention to "the relief of certain cases of persons not chronically or permanently ill, but rather of persons at the harder line of such condition and in imminent danger of becoming chronically or permanently ill."[22] A special health committee was formed to coordinate this program with trustees Henry Hulbert, Dr. Frank Sladen, and William J. Norton as members, along with representatives of the Visiting Nurses Association and the Detroit Community Fund. After meetings with representatives of the Board of Health, the Board of Education, the League of Catholic Women, and a number of private physicians, the committee solicited applications for assistance. During the period of January 6 to May 9, 1933, the committee received fourteen applications from individuals, and of these, seven applicants were accepted and granted from six weeks to two months of rest.[23]

Another special project endorsed by McGregor was the National Committee on the Care of Transients and Homeless. This organization was established "under the stimulus of Mr. McGregor in 1931 to provide a clearing house for study and research in this very serious national problem." The fund gave the committee grants of $1,000 in 1932 to begin its studies; $8,000 in 1933 "to broaden the scope of the work and conduct a study of methods to bring about a more humane administration of the settlement laws between the states and local communities"; and additional grants of $7,300, $5,750, and $6,000 in 1934, 1935, and 1936, respectively.[24] The studies financed by the committee were accepted by the Federal Emergency Relief Association "as a basis for the formation of a National Program."[25]

In addition to the McGregor Institute, the Detroit Community Fund, the National Committee on the Care of Transients and Homeless, the fund strongly supported the work of a number of national, state, and local charitable organizations during Tracy McGregor's presidency. Most of these grants reflected McGregor's long-standing interest in the work of these organizations while other allocations were for innovative new programs established to respond to the economic crisis of the Great Depression.

The fund sponsored the Detroit Council for Youth Service in 1935 and 1936 to develop a program for National Youth Administration's projects, and as a result of its program, several thousand "young people in Detroit and nearby metropolitan areas were put to work."[26] The fund's support made possible the establishment of the Detroit Consultation Bureau, which replaced the Case Work Department of the Associated Charities of Detroit. As a family case work agency, it provided services to families to help them meet difficulties that arose in matters of finance, health environment, and personal or family relationships.[27] It also provided consulting services to other social agencies that dealt with family issues.

The National Committee for Mental Hygiene, to which Tracy and Katherine McGregor had been substantial contributors for years, also received the fund's support. In addition, the fund issued grants to the Michigan Society for Mental Hygiene, organized in 1936. McGregor's strong endorsement of the International Migration Services also led to fund support. This organization provided services to citizens who traveled "in other countries, looked into the condition of the relatives of foreigners who are now residents of this country," and aided Americans who wanted to return to their native countries. This program appealed specially to McGregor and other trustees because of the large number of foreign-born Detroiters who needed help. The Atlanta School of Social Work of Georgia, which was the "only school for educating Negro social workers," and the National Urban League, the YMCA, and the Detroit chapter of the American Red Cross were among the recipients of fund grants.[28]

The fund bestowed several religious organizations with grants, again reflecting the McGregors' belief that religion played a special role in alleviating the burdens of the needy and disadvantaged. The Federal Council of Churches of Christ in America received support for its program "to bring about a spiritual awakening in America," the National YMCA for its role in "religious field work," and the First Congregational Church in Detroit was an additional recipient.[29]

The support of education and science was always high on Tracy McGregor's agenda, and it remained a major interest of the McGregor Fund. For years Tracy and Katherine had supported young students entering college and those working on advanced graduate degrees. Under the auspices of the fund, a more extensive scholarship program "for college and post graduate study and for professional and vocational training" won approval.[30] Grants were given mainly to students selected by the trustees and "to various small colleges which selected the recipients for this assistance."[31] Special emphasis was also given to "Young men and women who are willing to make sacrifices for an education and training."[32]

Although the majority of grants given by the fund between 1932 and 1936 were initially recommended and strongly endorsed by McGregor, the fund did give financial aid for favored projects of trustees. One of these related to Henry S. Hulbert's personal interests in astronomy, a hobby that caught his interest when he was a young man. Hulbert and Francis McMath, who was elected to the board of trustees in 1933 following the death of Kirby White, built and equipped an observatory on the shores of Lake Angeles near Pontiac, Michigan, which had been founded "for research in the field of motion picture photography of celestial bodies."[33] In 1931, Hulbert and McMath gave the observatory to the University of Michigan, and when the Depression curtailed the university's support for this field of science, they persuaded the McGregor Fund "to give major grants to the University to assist it." One of the major grants underwrote the purchase of "a 97 1/2 inch blank disc of a special Pyrex glass with a low co-efficient of expansion for the primary mirror, and a .28 inch disc of the same glass for the secondary mirror of a Cassegraine reflecting telescope, which, when completed, became the third largest reflecting telescope in the world."[34] A few years later the fund financed the construction "of the new design of Solar Tower . . . developed at the Observatory at Lake Angeles."[35]

Another project was the establishment of the Institute of Public and Social Administration in Detroit by the University of Michigan in 1935. This graduate program was the brainchild of William J. Norton, one of the founding members of the fund's board of trustees. McGregor heartily supported Norton's proposal because of McGregor's long interest "in the training of students in the practical field of social work."[36] The Merrill-Palmer Institute, for which McGregor served as trustee and president until 1936, also received major grants from the fund in support of its educational programs.

Capital structures and equipment relating to health, fresh air camps, and community service received support during McGregor's presidency of the fund. These projects included settlement houses, camps, and schools that needed additional property, improvement of existing facilities, and additional equipment. The Detroit Girl Scouts, for example, received a generous grant for its camp at Metamora, Michigan, as did the Bay Cliff Health Camp at Big Bay, Michigan, "for undernourished and underprivileged children." The Detroit Urban League was given a grant "towards the acquisition of property and the completion of its settlement houses," and the Salvation Army was assisted in operating expenses for its fresh air camp on Lakeville Lake, Michigan. The Bay Court Camp near Mt. Clemens, one of Katherine McGregor's major charities, was given a grant to enlarge its facilities. The Society of Perpetual Health, which was "organized for the care and treatment of cancer patients in an advanced stage," was given two grants in 1936 and 1937 "toward the purchase and rehabilitation of a suitable building for hospital use in the care of such patients."[37]

Tracy McGregor did not live long after the fund established an active grant program in 1932, but he firmly launched its mission "to relieve the misfortunes and promote the well being of mankind." Under his leadership, the projects he sponsored and others he endorsed set a pattern that firmly guided the trustees of the fund.

PART 4

Books, Libraries, and Education

12

Books and Libraries

By the 1920s Tracy McGregor was well known in Detroit and Michigan for his leadership in the charitable movements of the state, his efforts to aid the homeless and to reform Detroit's political and judicial system, his statewide campaigns for better health services for the disabled, needy, and mentally incompetent and the improvement of statewide prison and juvenile facilities. Few Detroiters–even his close associates and friends—knew of another interest that dominated much of his time and personal resources—book collecting.

McGregor's interest in books began while he was a student at Oberlin College. His studiės of English literature, American history, Greek, Latin, and the classics first stimulated his interest, which continued even after he had to drop out of college in 1891 to manage the Mission for Homeless Men in Detroit. Shortly after he arrived in Detroit he joined a local literary group and often gave talks on books that interested him. He often stressed the importance of books and reading, which he believed "strengthens the mind and procures intellectual health."[1] In planning the new headquarters for the McGregor mission in 1900, he insisted that it contain a special facility for a library and adequate space for the men to come and read in quiet.

He presented his ideas on the value of books in a speech he gave at one of the meetings of the Mission Brotherhood, an organization of former mission men that held weekly meetings at the McGregor Institute. Titled "Books and Reading," his speech stressed that reading books "imparted useful knowledge" and developed a "noble character." He urged his associates to "read only the best books, selecting them carefully after visits to libraries and bookstores," a practice he always followed. “Select only a few books,” he advised, reading them “thoroughly and repeatedly.” Read a little each day, “even a page or two and use special times such as Sunday afternoons, holidays, and vacation periods” and perhaps “one evening per week. . . . Give small attention to newspapers and current magazines . . . as the daily paper induces harmful mental habits and yields no lasting good.” McGregor also urged the men to “practice reflective after thought.”[2]

McGregor also recommended a list of nine categories of books that should be considered on any “list of standard books.” The Bible, he stressed, should be read every day. Religious books, including such titles as *The Imitation of Christ* by Thomas á Kempis, *The Christian's Secret of a Happy Life* by Hannah W. Smith, and *Christian Doctrine* by R. W. Dale were on his list. History books, including Edward Channing's *The United States,* John Richard Green's *History of England,* George P. Fisher's *History of the Christian Church,* and books on Greece, Rome, and the Reformation were also on his list. He recommended biographies such as Henry Cabot Lodge's *Washington,* Benjamin Franklin's *Autobiography,* Booker T. Washington's *Up from Slavery*, and Norman Hapgood's *Lincoln.* He suggested works of poetry, including those by Shakespeare, Wordsworth, Coleridge, Burns, Longfellow, and Whittier.

“Books of wisdom, moral inspiration and advice” were more difficult, he observed, and “should be read but little at a time.” For Ralph Waldo Emerson's *Essays and Poems*, “a page or two . . . per day would be splendid,” and he specifically recommended the works of John Ruskin, Thomas Carlisle, and Francis Bacon. He gave nature books special attention in his speech, no doubt as a reflection of his keen interest in hiking, bird-watching, and studying plants and flowers, and highly recommended John Burrough's *Nature Poems* and *Wake Robin* and Henry David Thoreau's *A Week on the Concord and Merrimac.*

“Books upon the principles of government and questions of the day” was the category in which he included Edward Everett Hale's *Foundations of the Republic,* James Bryce's *American Commonwealth*, and W. E. B. DuBois's *The Souls of Black Folk.* He devoted the ninth category to fiction, and despite his warning that “many unworthy story books have been written” and “all novels are sometimes held in ill-repute,” McGregor considered novels as “some of the greatest books.” Many were written “to teach history and the best historical novels set forth the customs, manners and spirit of foreign lands and times as no other writings.” He listed Sir Walter Scott's *Ivanhoe,* George Eliot's *Romola,*

Charles Dickens's *A Tale of Two Cities,* James Fenimore Cooper's *The Last of the Mohicans,* Victor Hugo's *Les Misérables,* Nathaniel Hawthorne's *Scarlet Letter,* and Alexandre Dumas's *Three Musketeers* were among the twenty-five fiction titles listed. McGregor ended his speech with this entreaty: "Here then is spread a banquet for the soul of what princes and sages have partaken. Determine what shall be best for yourself and eat."[3]

McGregor's speech to the Mission Brotherhood was significant because it reflected not only his great interest in the men of the mission and their intellectual growth but also his own interest in books. The entries in his diaries and his journals also reflect this interest. On his frequent trips to New York, Philadelphia, Baltimore, and Washington, D.C., for example, he visited local libraries and bookshops and examined and purchased hundreds of books. Not only did McGregor spend several hours a day reading, but also, on many evenings during their lengthy vacation sojourns, Katherine read aloud sections of books to him.

Chicago was one of McGregor's favorite cities, largely because of the University Club, which had a library that contained twenty thousand volumes available to borrow. During a four-week visit from December 23, 1921, to January 19, 1922, he spent hours at the club reading books on American and English literature and world history.[4] On his frequent visits to Washington, the Library of Congress and the Folger Library were always on his itinerary, and at those institutions he had the opportunity not only to examine their holdings but also to spend hours reading his favorite volumes and talking to staff members.

McGregor frequently made the rounds of local Detroit bookstores and spent hours in the Detroit Public Library and its branches. The Henry M. Utley branch was his favorite, not only for its beautiful architecture but also for its facilities, which encouraged quiet study. The McGregors also made themselves familiar with the public libraries in the Detroit suburbs.

The McGregors had a special interest in the public library system in Highland Park, an incorporated city that lies within Detroit's city limits. By 1916, Katherine and Tracy McGregor recognized that the Highland Park Home for Orphans and Children that Katherine had earlier established was no longer adequately serving its purpose and that there were other well-run charitable facilities in Detroit that were better staffed and able to take care of orphans. Furthermore, all of the thirty children who had lived at the orphanage had "reached the age of independence" and had left to begin new lives in the

Detroit area.[5] The possibility of using the site of the orphanage building for the proposed Highland Park YMCA was explored, but local officials wanted that new facility to be "nearer the business section of Highland Park," and moreover, they anticipated that the selection of the Stevens homestead site "might be opposed by local residents."[6]

When these alternatives were rejected, McGregor turned to his friend Pliny Marsh for advice. Marsh was not only an influential resident of Highland Park but also a prominent judge in the Detroit Recorders Court and a former executive director of the Detroit Citizens League. He and McGregor had worked together on a number of community projects and shared many of the same interests in political reform and Prohibition. Marsh responded immediately to McGregor's inquiry. "We have no library in Highland Park, and I feel quite confident the people in that community would not object to a library being located there. Furthermore," he added, "that would be a very good use for the property." McGregor liked the suggestion. He recognized the value of a library to a city like Highland Park, which was just emerging as one of the most attractive residential communities in the greater Detroit area.[7]

Two days after Marsh's response, McGregor replied. "I've talked to Mrs. McGregor, and she is thoroughly in accord with the idea. We would be glad to offer the property to the city of Highland Park for a library if they would be willing to accept it." Their only condition was that the city build a "suitable building within a period of five years." The "old stone house," once used as the orphans' home, became a temporary library until the city was ready to build the new facility.[8] Marsh raised the issue of whether the McGregors wanted their name attached to the library, and Tracy responded after giving the matter some thought. "Well," he replied, "if they want to call it that, I wouldn't object to it, but that certainly would not be a condition."[9]

Marsh, acting on behalf of the McGregors, proceeded to contact Mayor Royal Milton Ford and key members of the Highland Park City Council. The terms of the proposed gift were most attractive to the council, and city officials were delighted at the prospect of a new library. Up to that time the city's library was located in the high school and was limited to two thousand volumes that were rarely used except by high school students. It was hopelessly inadequate for a community that was rapidly expanding as a result of the introduction of the Ford Motor Company factory in 1910. Not only was the population of the city skyrocketing, but also hundreds of beautiful homes, including mansions for Ford executives, were being built.

The only issues raised by the council were the amount of land to be given to the city and the exact location of the new library. Originally, the McGregors had planned to provide a plot of land on the corner of Woodward and Massachusetts avenues, but the council countered with a request for the whole site, which stretched from Massachusetts to Rhode Island avenues. With Katherine's approval, McGregor responded, "Yes, I think it would be good. It would be a marvelous site. They could put it right in the center and have wonderful grounds."[10]

Once the matter of the site was resolved, the McGregors and their attorneys drafted a formal agreement outlining the terms of their gift. It provided that the land given to the city be maintained as a library in perpetuity and that, by June 1919, Highland Park demonstrate its commitment by allocating five thousand dollars to renovate the old Stevens homestead, ten thousand dollars for the purchase of books and reading materials, and five thousand dollars each year for five years for the general needs of the library. The agreement also provided that a "competent librarian and assistants" be hired and given adequate salaries and that the city improve and adorn the surrounding grounds "in a manner in harmony with the principles of landscaping gardening and suitable to the surroundings of a public place." Finally, the agreement prepared by the McGregors provided that if the "lands conveyed" were no longer suitable for a library, they could be sold and the proceeds placed in a trust fund "to be used in perpetuity for public library purposes." Katherine McGregor signed the deed on June 29, 1918, and on July 18 the city council of Highland Park accepted the gift.[11]

The final stages of World War I delayed measures for the proposed library, but by the spring of 1919 the city of Highland Park was able to proceed. The McGregor Public Library Commission was created in March 1919, with Mrs. W. C. Dora M. Miller appointed as chair. The first meeting of the commission convened on May 17, 1919, in the upstairs rooms of the Stevens homestead, already being renovated for the temporary library. Unfortunately, the building was locked on the day of the meeting, so an enterprising assistant climbed to a second-story window for access. When it was further discovered that there were no chairs available, nail kegs were overturned and used for seating. For subsequent meetings, the commission used the facilities at the Detroit Athletic Club.[12]

Following the advice of Adam Strohm, the director of the Detroit Public Library who met often with the Highland Park Library Commission, the appointment of a librarian was given highest priority, and on his recommendation Katharyne G. Sleneau, then librarian at the Port Huron Public Library, was hired effective August 1, 1919. By October 11 the temporary library opened with its two-thousand-volume catalog, all of which were signed out to local patrons by the end of the first week. Within twenty months the library had increased its holdings to 12,762 volumes and had opened branches in fire engine houses, the police station, and a local Knights of Columbus hall.[13]

The library commission and Sleneau gave considerable thought to the proposed new library structure. The McGregors had recommended that the Henry M. Utley branch of the Detroit Public Library, which had cost $255,000, be used as a "standard," but the commission decided that "they should not be limited" to that amount and that "something entirely worthy of the modern city of Highland Park and its progressive citizens should be constructed."[14] In order to locate a suitable model, the commissioners visited "every eastern and central city of the country containing library buildings of the type sought."[15]

After months of investigation the commission unanimously chose the public library of Wilmington, Delaware, as their model and immediately hired its architects, Edward L. Tilton and Alfred Githens, and several local architects to plan a building for Highland Park. Once this was accomplished, a bond issue of $500,000 was submitted to the city's voters. On March 5, 1924, it was approved by "the largest majority ever given to a bond issue in this City."[16]

With this strong local support, the architects immediately drafted plans, which were approved on February 4, 1925. Groundbreaking ceremonies took place on February 7, 1925, the cornerstone was laid on March 28, and the library was "ready for equipment, decoration and furnishing by October 13, 1925."[17]

Based on the Wilmington structure, the McGregor Public Library was classic Roman in style, "the interior showing more markedly its Greek derivation." The basement provided shelving for two hundred thousand volumes, and the huge open main floor was devoted to open stacks "with twenty-five thousand book capacity" along with "a well equipped reference room, a children's room and toilet facilities for patrons." The second floor was designed for staff offices, cataloguing, meeting rooms, and an "assembly room comfortably seating 400 with stage, footlights and a fine proscenium curtain." Public voting booths were also constructed in the library. The commission described the building proudly: "In general no effort has been spared to furnish the citizens of Highland Park an attractive and homelike building; one which will be inviting alike to old and young, which will create a desire to linger and produce an atmosphere of quiet dignity and refinement."[18]

The formal dedication of the McGregor Public Library took place on March 5, 1926, featuring speeches by members of the library commission, the city council, the mayor, the architects, and Sleneau. Dr. Warner W. Bishop, head of the library at the University of Michigan, presented the main address: "The Place of the Public Library in the Community."[19]

The McGregors were invited to be on the program, but they were in Washington, D.C., and were unable to attend. In their place, Tracy's secretary, Hugh Montgomerie, attended to express their regrets and read a letter from the McGregors. They wrote of their pleasure in being partners in the completion of "this beautiful structure" and added, "It is fitting that books, containing as it were, the very soul of man and capable and guiding in ways of wisdom, should be safely and notably housed. Even the building itself, as you have planned and built this one, may well be a monument to the great, whose lives and thoughts are herein preserved."[20]

At some point during the early 1920s, Tracy McGregor changed from relying on public libraries for his favorite authors to purchasing copies for his own library. English literature was his earliest interest. He acquired first and early editions of eighteenth- and nineteenth-century poets, playwrights, novelists, essayists, and philosophers. He purchased for his growing home library in Detroit editions of works by Charles Lamb, Sir Thomas More, James Boswell, John Milton, Henry Tomlinson, Samuel Pepys, Thomas Carlyle, William Wordsworth, John Galsworthy, Sir Walter Scott, Alfred Lord Tennyson, Percy Shelley, Lord Bryon, John Keats, William Butler Yeats, and Robert Burns. Later he turned his attention to American writers and developed a collection of the first editions of Ralph Waldo Emerson, Henry David Thoreau, James Fenimore Cooper, Walt Whitman, Henry Wadsworth Longfellow, and Washington Irving.

American history had always been a favorite subject of McGregor's, but it was not until about 1925 that he started to collect and intensely study it. In September of that year he met Claude Van Tyne, professor and chair of the Department of History at the University of Michigan and a distinguished scholar of the American Revolution. His book *Loyalists and the American Revolution,* published in 1902, was widely acclaimed as one of the major studies on this era. Van Tyne was impressed with McGregor and spent hours encouraging him to read extensively in early American history before embarking upon collecting. He recommended that McGregor read and concentrate on Vernon Parrington's *Main Currents in American History.* He also gave him a list of thirty books on American history to acquire as a core for a collection of Americana. Three days after this meeting, Van Tyne invited McGregor to join him at the William L. Clements Library at the university to meet its director, Randolph Adams.[21] McGregor accepted the invitation with great anticipation, for he had heard about this new library, which had opened just two years earlier. He had not yet met its founder, William L. Clements, the wealthy Bay City industrialist and University of Michigan regent, nor did he have any idea of the library's rich holdings on American history. Not only was he given a tour of the library, but also he spent several hours discussing the library and its founder with Adams and Van Tyne. He thanked Van Tyne for the special invitation and expressed his admiration, which, he wrote, "grows as I recall the valuable books and the fine spirit of you two who prize them so."[22]

McGregor's contact with Van Tyne was propitious, but even more important was his meeting with Randolph Adams. Like Van Tyne, Adams specialized in the American Revolution, having received his Ph.D. from the University of Pennsylvania in 1920. His first book, *Political Ideas of the American Revolution,* published in 1922, was followed by *History of American Foreign Policy,* which appeared in 1924. Adams had been recruited from Duke University, which was then called Trinity College, to fill the positions of director of the Clements Library and professor of history in the university history department. Adams was a man of great personal dynamism, and his enthusiasm for American history was infectious. During his tenure at the Clements Library, which lasted from 1923 to 1951, he won international recognition for his development of the library and as an expert on Americana.

Curiously, Randolph Adams's recollection of that visit was slightly different from McGregor's in minor respects. He recalled the visit but placed it in the "early autumn of 1928," not 1925. McGregor "came as a casual visitor," Adams wrote, "who wanted to know what the library was, and why Mr. Clements had placed it at the University." Adams at first thought that McGregor was interested only in English literature and nineteenth-century poets, but "rather suddenly, Mr. McGregor turned to the subject of Americana, and began asking questions." "He listened courteously," Adams remembered, "and then, almost abruptly, rose to leave, remarking that he would call again soon."[23]

McGregor kept his word and "reappeared a few weeks later." On this occasion, Adams recalled, "he stated quite definitely that he intended to build up a collection of rare books on American history." He then asked Adams to repeat remarks he had made at their earlier meeting—an idea that had "stirred his fancy." Adams again expressed his strong view that a "few people collect rare books simply because they are rare; people collect important books." Adams then emphasized that "important books of the past usually exist today in a quantity in inverse ratio to their original importance." "If a book was important when first printed," he stated, "it is apt to be rare today." Because the "supply of incunabuia" that was sought after by nineteenth-century collectors was practically depleted, he advised McGregor that it would be wise to concentrate his efforts on books published "about the New World" after 1500.[24]

This meeting with Adams, as well as the frequent ones that followed, solidified a close relationship between the two men. Adams became McGregor's mentor in his quest of Americana. He met often with McGregor at the Clements Library and in Detroit. Adams recommended book dealers in New York, Boston, and Philadelphia, as well as in England, and put McGregor in contact with the heads of the Library of Congress, the Folger Library, the American Antiquarian Society, the Massachusetts Historical Society, the John Carter Brown Library at Brown University, the Huntington Library in San Marino, California, and the New York Public Library. Not only did Adams supply the names of these key experts, but he also contacted them personally and asked them to extend every courtesy to McGregor.

McGregor's frequent visits to the Clements Library also involved meetings with the staff. They made available to him their extensive files on book catalogs, book auctions, and the names of private collectors. They gave McGregor privileged access to the priceless books in their library for his personal examination, and they enhanced his training in the examination of rare books. They showed him how to collate each book by comparing his new acquisitions leaf by leaf with a different copy or a bibliographic description.

McGregor turned to Adams constantly for advice on the cost of books offered to him by dealers. At first he was somewhat confused by the varying prices for a particular rare volume, until Adams, with his vast knowledge of books as well as the background and practices of certain dealers, was able to advise him on how to determine a fair price for a particular volume. Adams also gave McGregor valuable advice on how other collectors had refined their interests and methods to amass major collections of Americana. McGregor was fully aware that he could not duplicate the collecting opportunities of pioneer Americanists such as John Carter Brown or James Lenox or match the expenditures of Pierpont Morgan or Henry Huntington. But using the same collecting instincts and even the same dealers, he could emulate William L. Clements or Henry C. Folger. Adams was delighted to assist McGregor in achieving his objective.

Adams and his dedicated assistants at the Clements Library also gave McGregor invaluable advice on the care and preservation of his books. Many of the volumes McGregor acquired had minor defects such as torn pages, foxing (discoloration), or loose bindings. The Clements staff explained and demonstrated to McGregor the best way to restore these volumes and advised him on when to seek the assistance of professional book conservators. McGregor was also concerned about the storage conditions for his books, which he housed first at his apartment in Detroit and, after 1931, in his office in Washington, D.C. He noticed that some of his books suffered from "undue dryness." Following Adams's recommendation, McGregor contacted William Hammond at the Library of Congress for advice but discovered that even that distinguished library faced the same problem. "The Library of Congress," Hammond reported, "had no mechanical devices in the present building for regulating the amount of moisture in the stacks" and, as a result, "there is excessive dryness in the winter and at other times excessive moisture." McGregor sought to monitor and control the temperature and humidity in his storage facilities.[25]

It was obvious to McGregor by 1930 that, although he spent hours each day with his books, the care of his Americana collection required the assistance of a trained staff. After his move to Washington in 1931, he hired Georgiana Crowther, Virginia Rittenhouse, and Kathryn Slagle to work with him on the book collection.[26]

McGregor studied the work of other great collectors, including Junius Beal, Lucius L. Hubbard, and William L. Clements, all regents of the University of Michigan. During one of his visits to the library in June 1930 McGregor finally met Clements in person. Clements gave McGregor a personal tour of the library and selected several choice items from his collection for McGregor's review, including John Smith's *History of Virginia*, published in 1624, still in its original vellum binding.[27]

The friendship between the two collectors matured after McGregor expanded his collecting activities and was able to demonstrate the seriousness of his commitment. With considerable pride, McGregor informed Clements of his new acquisitions, including "the first issue of the unique Molyneaux map and a nice copy of the complete Peter Martyr Decades, 1530."[28] Later he happily advised Clements of his purchase of a rare Increase Mather pamphlet, *The Life and Death of the Reverend Man of God, Mr. Richard Mather,* published in 1670. Clements warmly congratulated McGregor on these rare acquisitions and encouraged him to continue his quest for rare Americana.[29]

After Clements was defeated for reelection to the university board of regents in 1932, McGregor responded with a tribute to Clements's impressive accomplishments. "The impermanence of political office, so much in evidence since last November," he wrote, "suggests by contrast the enduring quality of the great library which you have established in Ann Arbor. You have built a house not to be cast down by a shift of an election—a house 'not for Time's throwing.'" McGregor added, "It stabilizes my own soul to think of something so sure and strong."[30]

Lawrence Wroth, the director of the John Carter Brown Library at Brown University, also shared his expertise with McGregor, despite the fact that they often competed for acquisition of the same books. Wroth was impressed with McGregor, not only for his enthusiasm for books but also for his candor and the gentlemanly way he dealt with colleagues. He shared with McGregor his extensive files on rare books, conducted research for him, and advised him on book prices. On one occasion in 1932, after McGregor reported to Wroth that he had just purchased a John Smith, *True Relation,* the latter replied, "It is always a pleasure to learn of someone buying a John Smith book, especially so when this happens to be a true copy of the *True Relation.*" McGregor was pleased with these comments.[31]

At the Library of Congress McGregor worked closely with William B. Hammond; Herman H. B. Meyer, the director of the Reference Legislative Service; and Colonel Lawrence Martin, chief of the Map Division. These men generously assisted McGregor in a variety of ways, sharing information on forthcoming book auctions, book prices, and their expertise involving rare Americana and maps. Hammond and McGregor cemented their friendship on the golf course in Chevy Chase, Maryland, and Martin and Meyer, both private collectors, were even more eager to assist McGregor. It was Meyer who nominated McGregor for membership in the prestigious Cosmos Club in Washington in 1931.[32] Louis Karpinski, professor of mathematics at the University of Michigan, was another collector whose assistance McGregor valued. As a major advisor to Clements and a friend and colleague of Adams, Karpinski enjoyed his contacts with McGregor and met with him often to discuss their mutual interests in rare books and maps. Karpinski encouraged McGregor to include rare maps in his collection of Americana, and he gave him invaluable information on forthcoming map sales. In return, McGregor kept Karpinski informed of his major purchases, especially those involving rare maps. When McGregor purchased the rare Wright-Molyneaux map at the Lothian auction in February 1932, he notified Karpinski, along with Wroth, immediately. Later in that letter McGregor responded to the news that Karpinski was planning to sell his own collection to Yale. He wrote, "Though you may lose the books, the personal cultivation, friends and other values will remain with you, while scholars will profit by what you have done long after you are gone to rest."[33] Tracy's advice was consistent with his own plans to place his collection in a major library where it would be accessible to scholars.

Once McGregor made his decision to develop collections of rare books on English and American literature and Americana, he directed his undivided attention to this task. He acquired and studied numerous reference books relating to rare books and collecting, conservation of books, bookbinding and binders, and bibliographic studies on English literature and American history and discussed them with Adams, Karpinski, and members of the staff at the Clements Library.

After reviewing the techniques and methods used by Clements, Folger, Lennox, Huntington, and other notable collectors, McGregor commenced a serious and organized collecting program. The first step was to visit major book dealers. The Sign of the Mermaid in Detroit was one of the first on his itinerary, followed by bookstores in Chicago, Cincinnati, New York, Philadelphia, and Washington, D.C.

Of all of the cities he visited, New York proved the most rewarding in his search for rare Americana and English literature. From the Cadmus Post Box Bookshop, Brentano's, and the Brick Row Bookshop he acquired many rare first editions and rare volumes. His visits to New York publishers such as the Oxford University Press, Scribner's, Putnam's, Duttons, Houghton-Mifflin, and MacMillan also resulted in the acquisition of important books. At Laudermilk's and Meegan's Rare Book Shop in Washington, D.C., and the Haunted Bookstore in Cincinnati, Ohio, he located other prized volumes.[34]

Following the advice of Adams, McGregor contacted several recognized dealers in rare books, announced and explained his collecting objectives, and asked for their newsletters and catalogs. He also solicited information on upcoming auctions that featured Americana, as well as auction sale catalogues that indicated the prices paid for particular items. McGregor placed advertisements in local newspapers in Washington, D.C., and other cities, announcing his interest in locating rare books on literature and Americana, but this approach failed to meet his expectations, and he soon abandoned it.

With the assistance of Adams and Clements, McGregor made contact with the distinguished, internationally recognized firm of Stevens and Stiles of London, England. This firm was established in 1845 in London by Henry Stevens, a young Vermonter, who had earlier graduated from Yale University and Harvard Law School. Stevens's original plan was to tour England and the continent searching for both American and European books to sell to American universities and libraries. His quest was so successful that he opened a bookstore in London and soon represented a number of American institutions. Stevens became the major source of Americana for the John Carter Brown Library at Brown University, the James Lenox Collection at the New York Public Library, and the libraries at Harvard and Yale universities. Later, Stevens's firm assisted J. Pierpont Morgan, Henry Huntington, and William Folger in developing their major libraries. At the same time with his contacts in the United States, he became the supplier of American books for the British Museum and major university libraries in Great Britain. As a result of Stevens's efforts, "the rarest books such as the Bay Psalm Book, the Gutenberg Bible and Shakespeare folios and quartos" found their way into major American research libraries.[35]

Following Stevens's death in 1886, the firm was taken over by his son, Henry Newton Stevens, who remained in charge until his death in 1930. In 1895, Robert Stiles joined as partner, and the firm's name changed to Stevens and Stiles. The additions of Henry Stevens, grandson of the founder, in 1907, and later his brother-in-law, Roland Tree, rounded out the company's leaders with whom McGregor worked.

Clements was intimately familiar with the Stevens and Stiles firm, as they were the main source of many of his rare American items, including the magnificent manuscript collection relating to the American Revolution. These included the papers of Lord Shelburne, Sir Henry Clinton, and Lord George Germain. Indeed, it was at Clements's recommendation that Henry Newton Stevens received an honorary master's degree from the University of Michigan in 1923. Adams also developed not only a fine working relationship with Stevens but also a true friendship.

Once Adams, who had developed not only a fine working relationship with Henry Newton Stevens but also a true friendship, was aware of McGregor's interest in developing a rare Americana library and recognized the seriousness of his quest, he contacted Stevens and asked him to send to McGregor a large shipment of rare Americana books for his review, with the understanding that he could return any items he did not want. In August 1929, to McGregor's great pleasure, the books arrived, and he reviewed and purchased a number of them.[36] More importantly, this signaled the beginning of a close business relationship between McGregor and Stevens and Stiles that resulted in the acquisition of hundreds of rare books on both English literature and Americana. From August 15, 1929, until McGregor's death in May 1936, hardly a week went by without an exchange of letters, cables, and telegrams. During these years, Stevens and Stiles represented McGregor at various book auctions in England and the continent and, moreover, provided detailed information on various books that McGregor desired.[37]

One of the rarest publications Tracy acquired from Stevens and Stiles was a set of *Grand Voyages*, published by Theodore DeBry between 1590 and 1644. Designed and conceived by DeBry, a Frankfort, Germany, engraver, the twenty-seven volume, thirteen-part set, published in Latin, German, French, and English, included accounts of the historic exploratory voyages to the New World. Among the editions within the set was Thomas Harriot's *Brief and True Report of the New Found Land of Virginia* (1590), the "earliest English book to describe the first English colony in America," a book many regard with the same kind of reverence accorded Shakespeare's first folio; Girolamo Benzoni's *History of Early Discoveries and Travels by Columbus and others in the New World;* Americus Vespuccius's *Second and Third Voyages;* and the *Voyages of Drake, Hawkins, Cavendish and Raleigh.*[38] The DeBry set was particularly important because of the faithful copies of original drawings made on the spot by artists who actually accompanied the various expeditions. At first McGregor was hesitant to purchase this set because of its cost, but after examining the set at the Clements Library and consulting Adams, he accepted Stevens's offer. Moreover, Stevens was the recognized expert on DeBry publications, and his endorsement meant a great deal to McGregor. Stevens had advised him that "this notable work is undoubtedly the showpiece of any Library of American history, illustrating as it does, the whole course of early discovery and travel in that Continent."[39]

With Stevens acting as his representative, McGregor was able to acquire a number of valuable items at various book auctions held in England. In 1932 at the Lothian auction in London, he secured a copy of the 1589 edition of Richard Hakluyt's *The Principall Navigations, Voyages and Discoveries of the English Nation,* which contained the second issue of the rare Wright-Molyneaux map of the world, the first one based on Mercator's projection.

A year later, on March 31, 1933, at the Hodgson auction, Stevens purchased for McGregor the first issue of the Molyneaux map. This was a major coup for McGregor, and he immediately won the admiration and envy of other collectors. The distinguished New York rare book dealer, Lathrop Colgate Harper, wrote, "Yours is the only library in the World where both issues of this map may be seen side by side."[40] Adams was even more congratulatory. "You are certainly to be congratulated upon your acquisition of the John Smith and the Hakluyt," he wrote. "Do you know that even the John Carter Brown [Library] did not have the Molyneaux until about three years ago?"[41] Wroth, president of the Bibliographic Society of America in addition to librarian at the John Carter Brown Library, which owned the second state of the Molyneaux map, added his compliments to McGregor. "It is, indeed, most unusual for a single individual or institution to possess the map in both states. I do not know of anyone who has achieved this distinction."[42]

After the news of McGregor's acquisition circulated, he received numerous requests for copies. Without hesitation he made several photographic copies of the map and presented them to the Library of Congress, which featured it in a special exhibit; the Clements Library; the John Carter Brown Library; the James Lennox Collection of the New York Public Library; and the International Hydrographic Bureau in Monaco.[43]

In addition to rare publications on the explorations, discovery, and settlement of the New World, the Stevens and Stiles firm also assisted McGregor with purchases from the Colonial period and especially the American Revolution. The earliest publications describing the first settlements in Florida, the Carolinas, Virginia, Maryland, New York, and the New England colonies were obtained by Stevens and Stiles from sources in England, especially during the 1930s when the worldwide depression had forced many prominent English families to break up their personal libraries. Also available from the same source were hundreds of books, tracts, and publications relating to the American Revolution. From these, McGregor purchased a limited number of rare manuscripts to supplement and enrich his published items.

While Stevens and Stiles provided McGregor with his invaluable partnership in England, Lathrop Colgate Harper of New York City became

McGregor's trusted associate and mentor in the United States. Like the London firm, Harper, one of the nation's leading rare book dealers, was recommended to McGregor by Clements and Adams. Harper had helped Clements build his collection and provided many leads to Adams for rare books for the Clements Library.

It did not take long for McGregor and Harper to become fast friends and business colleagues. Harper recognized immediately that McGregor had a careful plan for his collection, that he was open to suggestions for book purchases, and that he had the resources for a long-term commitment. Similarly, McGregor trusted Harper and recognized his deep understanding of rare and important books.

Starting in 1930 when they first met, they were in constant contact with each other. They phoned, wrote, and cabled every few days, and hardly a week went by when a shipment of books did not arrive from Harper. McGregor often went to New York to meet with him, and after 1931 Harper made special visits to see McGregor in Washington, D.C. Once Harper had a clear understanding of the scope of McGregor's book collection, he made many helpful suggestions and made available titles from his own extensive collections. He also contacted other book dealers in search of books McGregor needed and often attended book auctions on McGregor's behalf.[44]

Harper not only sent McGregor lists of books he thought he should consider but also sent detailed information on books, including the differences, however slight, between the various editions. He also advised McGregor what not to buy, either because certain volumes did not fit into his collection or because the books were overpriced. For example, in November 1931, he suggested that McGregor not collect Revolutionary War military orderly books because there were too many of them on the market, and most of the "good ones" were in the Library of Congress, the New York Historical Society, and the Huntington Library.[45] On another occasion, Harper told McGregor not to purchase the "English Marco Polo" because that edition "had no direct American interest." "If you want a good Marco Polo for your collection," Harper explained, "get one of the 15th Century editions, preferably one printed at Gauda in 1483."[46] By giving this advice, Harper lost sales on two valuable books. In response to McGregor's question about whether he should purchase the forty-volume set by Edward Curtis, *The North American Indian,* which Harper had for sale at three thousand dollars, Harper expressed his personal reservations about the book. He explained that he did not approve of the practice of dressing the Indians in clothes not worn in their native villages. McGregor agreed with Harper's reasoning and decided not to purchase the set.[47]

When McGregor asked Harper for advice on setting prices on books offered to him by a prospective dealer, Harper advised, "Don't be a buyer and a seller too, don't set prices, have them set prices and then if they are too high, you can negotiate." In the same vein, Harper refused to set prices when representing McGregor at a sale.[48]

In August 1932 he purchased from Harper an early edition of Americus Vespucius's letter describing his third voyage, which took the merchant-astronomer to the American coast and south to Antarctica.[49] He later acquired from Harper Ptolemy's *Cosmographia,* printed in 1475 and representing "prediscovery science and geography."[50] Peter Martyr's *First Three Decades,* containing an account of Cabot's voyage and Balboa's sighting of the Pacific, and *The Cobler of Aggawam,* published in 1647, were other volumes McGregor purchased from Harper in 1932.[51]

Representing McGregor at the Lothian sale on January 28, 1932, Harper acquired Captain John Smith's rare *The True Relation of Such Occurances and Accidents of Noate as Hath Hapned in Virginia Since the First Planting of That Colony.*[52] Harper was also responsible for many of McGregor's rare holdings on the American Revolution.

There were other dealers in addition to Stevens and Harper that McGregor relied upon in developing his collection. Abraham S. W. Rosenbach of Philadelphia; Gabriel Wells and Ernest Dressel North of New York City; Hugh Tregaskis, Bernard Quaritch, William Robinson, all of London; and Martenus Nijhoff of the Hague allocated and sold him unique items for his library. But by far the overwhelming number of rare books was acquired through the efforts of Stevens and Harper.[53]

Once in a while McGregor operated on his own and made contact with collectors without the assistance of Stevens, Harper, or other book dealers. In fact, one of his most valuable acquisitions resulted from his dealings with William German Mather of Cleveland. Mather was a descendant of Increase Mather and Cotton Mather, two of the most prominent seventeenth-century clergymen. William Mather had possession of the family papers. Because of financial reverses during the Great Depression he was forced to sell his family collection and was persuaded that McGregor would not only pay a fair price for it but also properly preserve the materials in his library of Americana. Furthermore, unlike many other private collectors of Americana or major research libraries whose budgets were seriously cut during the Depression, McGregor had the funds to make such a major purchase.[54]

The Mather Collection consisted of more than fifteen hundred books, pamphlets, maps, manuscripts, and portraits relating not only to the prominent Mather family but also generally about life in the early New England colonies. Among the seventeenth-century imprints was the rare first edition of *A Platform of Church Discipline*, published in 1649, which served as the basis of New England Congregationalism, and Increase Mather's *Brief History of the War with the Indians in New England,* with the rare "White Hills" issue of the "Map of New England," considered the first map engraved and printed in America. A large percentage of the Mathers' sermons were included in the collection, many of which were once owned by the family. The collection included a print of Richard Mather (ca. 1670), struck from a woodcut by John Foster—the first portrait printed in British North America.[55]

Fortunately for McGregor, he was able to expand his competent and dedicated staff that assisted him with his rapidly growing book collection. In addition to Georgiana Crowther, Virginia Rittenhouse, and Kathryn Slagle, he hired Mildred White to assist in the acquiring, inventorying, and collecting of his collection. After 1931, when he moved his residence and his collection to Washington, D.C., he rented a large apartment at 1901 Connecticut Avenue, which also became the headquarters of the McGregor Fund and his private family business operations. Because he traveled often to Detroit, New York, Philadelphia, and other East Coast centers on McGregor Fund business and in search of rare books for his collection, he remained in almost daily contact with his staff by phone, letter, and cable. The communications describe the new books received, sometimes numbering in the hundreds; contacts with dealers in the United States and Europe; and announcements of forthcoming book auctions. It is obvious from the letters exchanged that he not only depended greatly upon his Washington staff but also had developed close friendships with them. He ended a letter written on November 8, 1934, with the postscript, "I am thinking of the office at 1901 and of the lovely and spirited people hooked up with me there."[56]

The staff also expressed in almost every letter their love, admiration, and respect for McGregor. On June 3, 1935, Mildred White wrote to him in Detroit, "We are getting along well here at the office—all of us—but not so well as if our leader were here."[57] The following day Miss Slagle wrote, "We miss our teacher and helper very much."[58]

McGregor's success as a collector can be credited in large part to his shrewd business acumen. The economic situation in the United States and Europe in the early 1930s forced market prices down and encouraged many collectors to break up or sell their collections, often at reduced prices. When McGregor began his quest for Americana and English literature in the late 1920s, he paid top prices "for a number of expensive items," but by 1932, according to Slagle, "few could have struck better bargains than he did. . . . Mr. McGregor almost never wanted a book so much that he would pay a price higher than what he thought it should be when he reached the point of knowing. He always had the patience to wait until he could find a copy at a reasonable price."[59]

McGregor's association with Adams and the Clements Library became even closer in 1933 when he was appointed to the Committee of Management of the library. This governing group, established by the board of regents under the terms of Clements's gift agreement and, similar to the one at the John Carter Brown Library, consisted of five members: the president of the university, the university librarian, a senior member of the Department of History, and "two men of recognized standing and ability from diverse parts of the country."[60] Serving on the committee with McGregor, who had replaced George Parker Winship of Harvard University, was William Warner Bishop, university librarian; Vernor W. Crane, professor of history; William Smith Mason, owner of the principal private collection of Benjamin Franklin material in the United States; Alexander Ruthven, president of the university; and Adams, the library director.[61]

The selection of McGregor to serve on the governing board of the Clements Library was based on more than his friendship with Adams and Clements. By 1933, McGregor had amassed an outstanding collection of Americana, was knowledgeable about the rare book market, and had developed close contacts with Harper and Stevens. McGregor's business experience and his wealth might also have been factors, especially because of the critical financial problems the university was facing at that time. The stock market crash in 1929 and the onset of the Great Depression had seriously eroded the financial stability of the university. State appropriations for the university and other educational institutions had plummeted, student enrollments had declined, and gifts from once wealthy alumni had dwindled.

In 1930 the Clements Library had lost two of its major supporters with the deaths of Claude Van Tyne, the ranking member of the Committee of

Management since it was officially established in 1923, and Henry N. Stevens, the head of the prestigious London rare book firm. An even more severe crisis arose in September 1931 with the closing of the Bay City Bank. Clements, who was president of the bank and its major stockholder, suffered heavy financial losses, which, with earlier stock market losses of a "disturbing magnitude," had a direct impact on his association with the library.[62] Clements suffered another disappointment in the fall election in 1933 when he was defeated in his reelection bid for regent of the university. This was followed by a serious heart attack in the winter of 1933–34, and on November 6, 1934, he died at his home in Bay City. Adams paid tribute to him when he described him as "a born connoisseur, whose good taste was apparent in whatever he touched. Like other successful American businessmen of the period, he was essentially a builder with somewhat of the soul of an artist."[63]

In addition to the death of its benefactor, the Clements Library faced another grave crisis relating to the status of the magnificent historical manuscripts that Clements had acquired in the 1920s and that had never been transferred to the library. They included the official and personal papers of several leading English government officials and military officers who served during the American Revolution: Sir Henry Clinton, Governor George Clinton, Lord George Germain, and Generals Nathaniel Greene and Thomas Gage. Although Mr. Clements had planned to place these manuscripts in the library, the great financial losses he suffered during the stock market debacle and the closing of his Bay City Bank forced him to reconsider. In the spring of 1933 he informed Adams that he now planned to sell these manuscript collections to the university at a reduced price.[64] Adams, who understood the difficult financial situation that Clements faced, responded favorably to his proposal, and in September 1934 the Clements Library paid Clements fifteen thousand dollars for the papers of John Wilson Croker, secretary of the British Admiralty from 1809 to 1830, a collection which Clements had purchased in England in 1924.[65]

At the meeting of the Committee of Management on November 13, 1934, the first one that McGregor attended, Mr. Clements's last will and testament, dated April 16, 1931, and the codicil dated March 17, 1932, were reviewed and discussed in detail. The documents confirmed what Clements had earlier told Adams: that if the university wanted his manuscript collections, it must purchase them or they would be sold at auction.[66]

After a lengthy discussion, the committee instructed the secretary to notify the board of regents that the university must acquire the material under the terms of Clements's will; that the collections "should be saved and preserved as a whole for the benefit of scholarship; that the failure of the University to acquire them and their possible resulting dispersal would be nothing short of disaster for American historical scholarship as well as for the University of Michigan." Furthermore, it "would seriously diminish if not destroy the relative values of these collections and those held in Ann Arbor." The committee also recommended that the board of regents "make every effort to secure a waiver of the interest provision in Mr. Clements's will and a reduction of the payments specified within."[67]

McGregor left the meeting of the Committee of Management deeply concerned about the controversy. He was aware of the great historical as well as monetary value of the manuscript collections. Adams, Harper, and Stevens had on several occasions told McGregor about these collections, their value and their great significance to the holdings of the Clements Library. McGregor was also fully aware and understanding of not only the financial plight of Clements but also the economic crisis facing the university. As president of the Detroit Community Union and responsible for its fund-raising efforts with Detroit's leading business and community leaders and as trustee and major financial benefactor of the McGregor Institute, he understood the impact of the stock market crash and the Depression upon the state and its taxpayers.

McGregor's first response was to persuade the trustees of the McGregor Fund to lend its support to the Clements Library. On November 11, 1934, the fund approved a grant of five thousand dollars to the Clements Library for 1935, with the understanding that it was not to be used "to lessen any part of the University's regular appropriation to the Library." In March 1935 the fund authorized similar appropriations to the library for the years 1936 and 1937.[68] The McGregor Fund also gave substantial financial support to the university for the establishment of its Institute of Health and Social Sciences in Detroit and its McMath-Hulbert Observatory at Lake Angeles.[69]

Following the Committee of Management meeting in November 1934, President Ruthven turned to McGregor for assistance in resolving the impasse involving Clements's will. Despite the strong position taken by the committee to abide by the terms of Clements's will, the university, on the advice of its legal counsel, challenged the provisions relating to the Clements Library. "The University considers it had a contract with Mr. Clements," President Ruthven informed McGregor, and that it had lived up to its obligations with the "very large sum of money" that since 1923 it had appropriated for the maintenance of the library.[70] Ruthven also reported that Clements "repeated over and over again that the material is ours." He continued, "Mr. Clements was a curious man and I am firmly convinced that practically up to the last, he expected the papers to go to us. Why he left matters in a way to arouse controversy I do not know except that it is just the kind of thing he delighted in doing."[71]

The Clements family, however, did not accept the university's position. They hired Charles Goodspeed, the highly respected Boston antiquarian book dealer to appraise the manuscript collection before setting the asking price at $350,000. If the university could not find the necessary funds, it could easily raise them from its wealthy alumni or benefactors, they argued. President Ruthven, acting on advice from the university's legal counsel, responded promptly. The university could not, he said, contact prospective donors and say, "Please give us some money to pay for something which Mr. Clements told the world he had given to us."[72] President Ruthven's response infuriated the Clements family. They charged that the university's position was "disparaging to the original gift and its value and significance" and "the value of the manuscripts themselves was belittled."[73]

McGregor recognized immediately the seriousness of the impasse. After a series of meetings with President Ruthven, board of regent members, Adams, colleagues on the Committee of Management, and Renville Wheat, attorney for the Clements family, he proposed to President Ruthven that the university offer the Clements family $250,000 and ask them to make a contribution so that the total amount would be reduced.[74] Neither side was enthusiastic about McGregor's compromise proposal, but it was finally accepted because both sides agreed that the manuscript collections should be a part of the Clements Library.

The next obstacle, raising the funds, proved formidable. Few alumni or benefactors of the library had money to spare at that time. Again McGregor found a solution. He arranged for the McGregor Fund to give $100,000 toward the settlement, and the Clements family "agreed to accept the balance in installments of $15,000, the amount of the yearly University appropriations to the Library for Acquisitions."[75] The McGregor Fund paid the university in installments of $25,000. The regents of the university approved the compromise contract on March 26, 1937, and immediately thereafter the manuscripts were transferred to the Clements Library.[76] Mrs. Clements also gave the library gifts of her husband's furniture and his "collection of prints," including four that had hung on the walls of his residence: those of Charles James Fox, Lord Cornwallis, Sir Henry Clinton, and General Nathaniel Greene.

McGregor died before the compromise agreement had been approved, but President Ruthven, Adams, and the Clements family never forgot his guiding spirit in solving the controversy. His generosity ensured that future generations of scholars would be able to use the magnificent collection that Clements had accumulated.

13

The McGregor Plan

In the spring of 1932 Tracy McGregor had made a special visit to the Clements Library to see Randolph Adams about "a plan he wanted to discuss." In the words of Adams, written soon after this visit, McGregor "talked of the pleasure and profit he was deriving from his avocation, and seemed to be grasping for some connecting link between that and his life work with humanitarian charities in Detroit." He told Adams that his recent intensive studies revealed the close association between the "story of early American history which was related to his work with hopeless and homeless humanity. . . . Perhaps," he noted, "it was the fact that in the days when the world was smaller, the unfortunate, the wastrel, the desperate could win a place in life as discoverer, conquistador or pioneer." He also expressed his admiration for the late William L. Clements and the library that bore his name in helping the University of Michigan "make up those four centuries of printing which it naturally lacked by reason of it being born nearly four hundred years too late." He shared his concerns for "the less fortunate American institutions, which because of the exigencies of the war, or because of late development, found themselves outclassed by older institutions."[1]

McGregor then unfolded his plan for helping colleges develop collections of rare Americana. He proposed to favor the colleges in the region "outside of New England, and in the main, outside of the metropolitan cities." He planned to give five hundred dollars a year to certain "selected college librarians on the condition that they would contribute a like sum, the resulting thousand dollars to be spent annually on rare Americana."[2]

He sought Adams's advice on how such colleges should be selected, what books should be chosen, and the overall management of the program. It was McGregor's view, strongly endorsed by Adams, that the program should be administered by one of the "great learned societies or associations." They discussed the American Library Association but decided that it would not be a good choice "because of the predominant concern of that organization with public libraries and their problems." They also decided against it because of the "relatively small amount of attention devoted by the American Library Association to the field of collecting, the preservation and the proper use of rare books."[3] Adams expressed his views on the subject in a splendid but controversial article, "Librarians as the Enemies of Books," which was published in the *Library Quarterly* in July 1937.[4] Since McGregor's plan involved the collecting of rare books on American history, the American Historical Association (AHA) was selected as the first choice, and in January 1933, McGregor wrote formally to Charles A. Beard, its president. He outlined his proposal, and Beard, after consulting with his colleagues on the board of trustees, appointed the Committee on Americana for College Libraries under the chairmanship of Dr. J. Franklin Jameson, for many years the editor of the *American Historical Review,* a leading advocate for the establishment of a national archives in the United States and also chief of the Manuscript Division of the Library of Congress. Joining him on the committee were Dr. Conyers Read, executive secretary of the AHA; Dr. Lawrence Wroth, librarian of the John Carter Brown Library; Samuel Flagg Bemis of George Washington University; and Adams. A year later, William Warner Bishop, librarian of the University of Michigan, and Leonard Machall, a distinguished book dealer and president of the Bibliographical Society of America, were added. McGregor was appointed to the committee in January 1934 and at the same time was elected to the board of trustees of the AHA.[5]

A unique feature of the "McGregor Plan for the Encouragement of Book Collecting by American College Libraries" was that he would buy all of the books selected as eligible and make them available at cost to the various participating college libraries. He decided upon this provision for several reasons. First, he recognized that the average institutional librarian representing the selected colleges was "little practiced in the highly technical business of buying rare books." Librarians, he observed, "could buy books, but there were comparatively few who have had experience in buying *rare* books." Second, McGregor had excellent relationships with the leading dealers in rare books both in the United States and abroad and he had become an "extremely able buyer." His recent experience in building his own collection of Americana during the depths of the Depression had made him especially knowledgeable about the intricate nature of the rare book market. Finally, his own personal experience in supporting charitable endeavors convinced him that he must do more than merely finance the plan; he must be an active participant as well. He would be involved in the selection of colleges, the purchase of the books, the evolution of the plan, as well as the provision of funds.[6]

To finance the plan, McGregor turned to the McGregor Fund. On his recommendation they appropriated sufficient funds to the AHA to provide for the overhead costs incurred to administer the program and five hundred dollars a year per college for the purchase of books, which would be matched by each participating institution.[7] With the aid of Lathrop Harper, Wroth, Leonard Machall, and Adams, McGregor began to purchase a supply of rare books that were considered suitable for a rare Americana book collection. In establishing the criteria for the selection process he decided to concentrate on rare books relating to the discovery, exploration, and colonial settlement of North America; the American Revolution; and early western exploration and settlement.[8] McGregor was aware from his own recent collecting activities that books dealing with those epochs were "still obtainable and at prices not beyond the reach of $1,000 per year."[9] To represent the period of the American Revolution, for example, McGregor chose "three small books covering the Clinton-Cornwallis Controversy relating to the surrender of Yorktown, published in 1783." They could be purchased in 1934 for anywhere from ten dollars to twenty-five dollars per volume. General Burgoyne's *State of the Expedition from Canada* (London, 1780) and Tarleton's *History of the Campaign of 1780–1781 in the Southern Provinces* (London, 1794), both written by British officers, was also included on the approved list. In addition, McGregor acquired a supply of the "controversial pamphlets of Samuel and John Adams, Jonathon Boucher, John Dickinson, Daniel Dulony, Joseph Galloway, Alexander Hamilton, James Otis, Thomas Paine, Samuel Seabury, and many others on the American side, as well as those of Francis Bernard, Edmund Burke, Soame Jenyns, William Knox, William Pitt and others on the British side." These volumes were, with "one or two exceptions, available at prices from $10 to $50."[10]

For the period of western travel and exploration, he was able to acquire a wide selection of rare books "still available below $100." Among these were

Portlock's *Voyage around the World* (London 1784), Captain Anburey's *Travels* (London, 1789), Long's *Voyage on Travels of an Indian Interpreter* (London, 1791), and the account of the Lewis and Clark *Expedition to the Pacific Coast* (published in Philadelphia in 1814 and London in 1815). Most of the rare volumes that had been published in the fifteenth and sixteenth centuries were too expensive to be included in the plan, although McGregor was able to locate copies of Smith's *Generall Historie of Virginia* "with one or two maps in facsimile" for $100 to $125.[11]

On special occasions, the committee approved the inclusion in the plan of books other than "source material." In 1937 they purchased six sets of Joseph Sabin's *Dictionary of Books Relating to America,* published in installments from 1867 to 1937, and distributed them to participating college libraries "in accordance with a careful survey of the present geographical location of known sets."[12]

As soon as McGregor, with the active assistance of Harper and Adams, had acquired a large supply of books, a catalog was prepared listing the titles and costs per book for distribution to the eligible libraries. The librarians then promptly selected the titles they wanted, and their accounts with the Committee on Americana for College Libraries were adjusted accordingly.

McGregor listed in the catalog additional requirements for the participating libraries. All books acquired under the plan must be "regarded and treated as rare books." They must not be placed in a library's general open stacks, but "into its Treasure Room, Rare Book Room, or equivalent section even if that is only a locked case in the librarian's private office." McGregor also insisted that the library be in "a modern fire-resistant building, with provisions for locking the books in a separate room or case, and the enforcement of a rule giving access to the books only in the presence of a responsible teacher or library assistant."[13] The AHA committee endorsed McGregor's recommendation that the college libraries "should be enjoined against the defacing of the books by stamps, embossing, or perforation, and that the books should never be let out of the library, but used therein, and under observation of suitable authorities."[14]

The selection of eligible college libraries proved to be more of a challenge to the committee. It was evident from its first meeting in 1934 that special attention must be given to certain criteria. The committee readily agreed that the colleges should not be located near another major research institution or near one of the eastern metropolitan areas where collections of Americana were readily available. Furthermore, to be eligible, a college must be of "substantial character with a well-managed library" that had a nucleus of books on American history. The committee also recommended that colleges raise the matching five hundred dollars per annum from alumni and other outside sources and not take it from their regular library budgets.

The Committee on Americana for College Libraries prepared a list of about thirty colleges that it considered eligible and assigned to individual committee members the task of making the initial contact and explaining the plan. By September 1934 about fifteen colleges had applied or expressed interest, and of these, six were approved: Allegheny College, Dartmouth College, Emory University, Mount Holyoke College, Lafayette College, and Wesleyan College for Women, in Macon, Georgia. Later that year, Wake Forest University was also approved. By the end of 1936, nine additional libraries had been selected: Albion College, Baylor University, Mills College, Pomona College, Western Kentucky State Teachers College, College of William and Mary, College of Wooster, Florida State College for Women, and Carleton College.[15]

As information about the McGregor Plan spread, scores of additional applications were received. Some were rejected because of their location near established Americana collections, including the University of California, Stanford University, Rutgers, Temple University, Smith College, the University of Texas, and the University of Maryland. Others met all of the necessary criteria except that they could not raise the necessary five-hundred-dollar annual match.

In March 1936, Adams, who had taken an active role in the administration of the plan, met with McGregor to review the progress made. McGregor was especially pleased. He had been successful in purchasing at very reasonable costs an extensive collection of rare Americana. In some instances, though, he had paid more than one hundred dollars per volume, but by balancing the costs of the books under his policy of price equalization, he was able to make them available to colleges within the annual budget. In order to assist some of the colleges who lacked the support staff to administer these rare book collections, McGregor established a special scholarship fund to allow those colleges to hire "bibliographically inclined, but needy students."[16]

McGregor urged Adams to visit the approved colleges to witness firsthand the operation of the plan. In the spring of 1936 Adams visited Allegheny College, the College of William and Mary, Wake Forest University, Emory University, Wesleyan College for Women, Florida State College for Women,

Lafayette College, Mount Holyoke College, and Dartmouth College. The report of his tour, submitted to the Committee of Americana, was extremely positive. All of the colleges had met the requirements of the plan, and several had received generous grants from alumni for their rare book collections. Adams also reported that the Americana collections had been enthusiastically used by members of the college faculties and their students. At several colleges special rooms were established for the proper care and security of the rare books. Unfortunately, Adams was not able to share his positive findings with McGregor. When he returned to Ann Arbor early in May, "he was greeted with the tragic news of Mr. McGregor's death."[17]

The sudden death of McGregor on May 6, 1936, came as a complete shock to both the members of the Committee on Americana for College Libraries and the trustees of the McGregor Fund. The fund was aware of the McGregor Plan, at least in a general way, and they had approved several grants for its operation since it was established in 1934. But they were not familiar with the detailed work of the AHA committee. In June 1936 they asked Adams to prepare a detailed report on the origins and operation of the plan and a proposed budget "for carrying on the work."[18]

On behalf of the AHA committee, Adams made a detailed account of the plan, including the fifteen participating colleges and a proposed budget request of $14,600 for the year 1937. Responding to a request of the McGregor Fund trustees, and with the approval of Alexander Ruthven, president of the University of Michigan, the headquarters of the McGregor Plan were moved to the Clements Library. Adams was appointed director, and Kathryn Slagle, who had worked as McGregor's assistant at the Washington office, was appointed assistant director. At the December 1936 meeting, the committee was reorganized. Adams, William Warner Bishop, J. Franklin Jameson, Leonard Machall, Conyers Read, Wroth, and Slagle were appointed for four-year terms, and the trustees approved the proposal of sending a framed photograph of McGregor to each of the fifteen colleges participating in the plan.[19]

Under Adams's leadership, the McGregor Plan continued to flourish. As the news of its successes spread, an increasing number of colleges applied for membership. By 1937 an additional sixty-five colleges had asked for support. In order to facilitate the selection of rare books, Adams and Slagle prepared a new book catalog, which contained about 250 titles. The University of Michigan Press announced its endorsement in June 1937 by offering each participating college complimentary copies of any of its publications still in print.[20]

World War II, however, interrupted the operation of the plan. Some of the colleges faced financial difficulties, and the McGregor Fund decided that other funding priorities should be given attention. In November 1942 the fund trustees decided to "suspend the work of the Americana Committee effective August 31, 1943, until the duration of the War and the necessary readjustment period thereafter."[21] The issue of renewal was raised again in 1947, but there was little support for it among the McGregor Fund trustees.[22]

McGregor did not have an opportunity to review the long-range impact of the plan even on those initial fifteen colleges that had participated during his lifetime. Based on his long years at the McGregor Institute and his work with the homeless of Detroit and the rest of the nation, he believed that providing a man with a "thought or an idea" through books was just "as important as giving him a square meal, or a new suit of clothes." McGregor also believed that his plan would "remove some of the artificial prejudices which had been created, largely by the professional scholar, against the true book collector."[23]

Randolph Adams perhaps best summed up the success of the McGregor Plan when he described a meeting with McGregor and his staff a few weeks before McGregor's death. "After lunch," McGregor informed Adams, "we usually have a chapter—at present it is Pickwick." Adams was reminded of "Sam Weller's famous remark when he dashed out to Fleet shouting, 'I can see some good in this.'" Adams concluded, "All the Committee on Americana for College Libraries can do is echo Sam's statement and say, 'we can see some good in this.'"[24]

14

The McGregor Library of American History

UPON TRACY MCGREGOR'S DEATH, the trustees of the McGregor Fund assumed the responsibility for the disposition of McGregor's library of Americana. Although the development of this collection of rare books, articles, maps, and manuscripts had occupied much of Tracy's time since 1925, none of the trustees had any idea of the library's scope, size, or research and monetary value. The trustees had only heard about this collection in a general way before June 1932, when he shared with the trustees his wishes for the ultimate disposition of his collection after his death. He advised them that he wanted his "collection of books, particularly Americana[,] to be given to a college in the southern part of the country, the northern states being much more fully supplied with rare books in the field of American history." He recommended to the trustees that they contact Randolph Adams of the Clements Library and William Boyd, head of the history department of Duke University "for good advice in this connection."[1]

Shortly after McGregor's death, Henry Hulbert confided in Adams that the trustees of the fund "knew and know nothing of books, book collecting or bibliography." Hulbert added, "Quite frankly the Trustees were puzzled by the manner in which Mr. McGregor spent the last eight years of his life."[2] It is possible, of course, that when he brought up the matter of his personal library on Americana, they assumed he was referring to the volumes he had acquired for distribution to the college libraries participating in the AHA's Committee on Americana for College Libraries. Since 1934 the fund had made annual appropriations for this project.

Within a few weeks after his death, the trustees finally learned of the scope, size, and value of his personal collection of Americana. The prestigious Goodspeed's book firm in Boston appraised the collection, which consisted of several thousands of books, pamphlets, maps, and historical manuscripts worth more than $300,000, a very substantial sum in 1936. With this information, the trustees acted promptly to determine if McGregor had made any definite commitments as to a specific college or university. They contacted a number of McGregor's friends and colleagues with whom he had been in recent contact, including Conyers Reed, executive secretary of the AHA; J. Franklin Jameson, head of the Manuscripts Division of the Library of Congress; Adams, director of the Clements Library; Dumas Malone, director of the Harvard University Press and formerly professor of history at the University of Virginia; Anson Phelps, former secretary of Yale University; Lawrence Wroth, librarian of the John Carter Brown Library; and Lathrop Harper, the prominent New York book and manuscript dealer. Frank Perley, the fund's Washington, D.C., financial advisor, and the staff at McGregor's Washington office were also consulted. The subject of McGregor's plans for his library had been the topic of discussion with many of his close associates, although not with the trustees of the fund.[3]

Henry Clemons, librarian of the University of Virginia, added more missing pieces to the puzzle. He advised the fund trustees that McGregor had first shown an interest in the University of Virginia on July 25, 1933, when he wrote to Clemons for information about his library and especially its Americana holdings.[4] McGregor contacted Clemons again in March 1936 and told him of his impending visit to Charlottesville. He requested information on the library, a place to stay near a golf course, and the name of someone connected to the university medical school who had "an interest in psychiatry." He also told Clemons that this would be his first visit to Charlottesville.[5] During his twelve-day visit, McGregor met several times with Clemons and the library staff as well as President John L. Newcomb and members of the faculty.

Kathryn Slagle emphasized that McGregor had expressed a "sentimental feeling" about the University of Virginia and had mentioned "his respect for Jefferson's plan for it. It stood for something very fine and worthy in McGregor's mind." He also planned to invite the students to his library on weekends to examine the books in order "to inspire young minds with the ideals for which our country has stood, to stimulate interest in the finest things in life, good literature, beautiful printing and a keen feeling for old and rare books," and at regular intervals, "perhaps on Saturday or Sunday afternoons," he planned special sessions "when he could talk and teach them some of the things so close to his own heart." "He felt confident," Slagle added, "of the good that could be accomplished in this way, knowing that original source material can do so much more for one working with other prepared studies." Also, from his library and under the guidance of his librarian he could "carry on . . . the work of the Committee on Americana for College Libraries."[6] Although McGregor had not yet made a definite commitment to give his library to the university, according to Slagle, he seemed satisfied in his own mind "to give it a try, but would have moved slowly, tested well, and seen to it that the whole scheme was properly organized before he would have let it go out of his hands into those of others."[7]

Despite the wealth of information obtained in their contact with associates of McGregor, the trustees were not convinced that McGregor had made a definite decision for a depository for his library. It was obvious that he was "leaning" toward the University of Virginia and a move to Charlottesville in the fall of 1936, but by the end of 1936 the trustees were still undecided as to the disposition of the library. The trustees' investigation did, however, reveal McGregor's keen interest in Americana and book collecting, of which none of the trustees were heretofore aware, and his method of facing and resolving problems.

The impasse faced by the fund trustees did not deter officials at the University of Virginia from pursuing their interest in becoming the home of the McGregor Collection. At the urging of Dumas Malone, former history professor and a distinguished Jefferson scholar, President John Newcomb contacted the McGregor Fund Board of Trustees and provided information about the university, its financial situation, and its faculty and students. Newcomb also informed the fund that the university was building a new library facility, which would have ample space for the McGregor Collection. To reinforce the university's interest, Harry Clemons, the university librarian, came to Detroit in September 1936 to meet with the McGregor Fund trustees.[8]

The University of Virginia was not the only educational institution that expressed an interest in the McGregor Collection. As news spread of McGregor's death and the sudden availability of his personal Americana collection, several other universities contacted the fund. It soon became obvious to the trustees that the challenge would not be in finding a southern university to accept the collection, but in selecting the most appropriate one.

Before a final decision could be made, however, the trustees were faced with another dilemma involving the disposition of the Mather Collection.

This rare collection of rare books, pamphlets, and manuscripts relating to Cotton and Increase Mather, two early New England Puritan religious leaders, had been purchased by McGregor in 1933 from William G. Mather of Cleveland, Ohio. Several fund trustees raised the issue of whether this rare collection so vital to the early history and religious and intellectual development of colonial New England should be placed in a southern institution. Trustee Cleveland Thurber wrote, "It is highly illogical to place the Mather Collection in the University of Virginia, nor would I, incidentally, place it in Phoenix, Arizona or Butte, Montana. The place where the Mather Collection really belongs is in Boston," he concluded.[9] Renville Wheat, the secretary of the fund's board of trustees also endorsed the view that the Mather Collection belonged in the Boston area, but he proposed that the fund consider selling the Mather Collection and establish an endowment to be used to "round out the holdings" of the McGregor Collection.[10]

Other trustees expressed similar reservations, especially after they learned from Adams and others that McGregor had had doubts about giving it to a southern institution. McGregor had known that Harvard was interested in the Mather Collection, as was the American Antiquarian Society in Worcester, Massachusetts, which already had an extensive collection of Mather materials and which had tried unsuccessfully to raise the funds to purchase the collection from the Mather family when it came up for sale in 1931.[11]

To resolve the dilemma of the disposition of the Mather Collection and the location to which it most appropriately belonged, the trustees once again sought advice from Conyers Read and J. Franklin Jameson, who were familiar with the Mather Collection. They both recommended that the Mather Collection be separated from the McGregor library and placed in a research library in New England. Read preferred Harvard as a depository because it was "more accessible to scholars and much better equipped to serve them."[12] Jameson concurred that Harvard was the best choice.[13] Read added the caveat that if the fund planned on "developing a really significant Library around the nucleus which Mr. McGregor's collection will provide . . . in that case I should hang on to all the treasures."[14]

Hulbert also sought the advice of President Newcomb regarding his interest in the Mather Collection should the McGregor library go to the University of Virginia. After having his faculty review the collection, he replied that they were "convinced that the Mather is definitely related if not an integral part of the whole McGregor Collection and for this reason we should like to have the

Collection as it exists." If the fund decided to sell it, however, Newcomb recommended that the funds be used "to build up the McGregor Collection."[15]

A decision on the Mather Collection was further delayed when the fund received a communication from William G. Mather that he would like to repurchase the collection and give it to the American Antiquarian Society so that it could be combined with their extensive Mather holdings.[16] The trustees were pleased with this proposal, as it solved their dilemma and ensured that the collection would find a home in a responsible institution. Unfortunately, in February 1938, William Mather informed the trustees that "the fall in the value of his investments" had negated his plan of "recovering possession of the Mather Collection."[17]

Before the Mather issue had been resolved, the fund trustees moved ahead with a decision on the McGregor library. Since the fall of 1936 the trustees had been gathering information on the University of Virginia from a variety of sources. President Newcomb had provided financial reports, faculty resumes, and student body profiles. Fund trustee Kenneth Moore, executor of the McGregor Estate, had visited three potential southern universities and had "discussions of this matter with various persons in eastern cities."[18] On January 25, 1938, the trustees appointed a committee on library disposition, which consisted of Henry S. Hulbert and Kenneth Moore, the assignment of negotiating with officials of the University of Virginia "with respect to the probable gift of Mr. McGregor's Library."[19] On March 18, 1938, Moore reported that the university was willing "to expend $7,500 per year for the salary of a special curator and assistants, repairs, re-bindings, etc., and accessions to the Library."[20] The trustees responded that the fund was prepared "to grant $7,500 per year for three years for accessions to the Library, and at the end of such time the accomplishments and needs of the Library would be reviewed again . . . and a like grant for an additional four years considered."[21]

The University of Virginia Board of Visitors accepted the gift of the McGregor library on June 11, 1938, including the Mather Collection, which the fund had decided to retain "as part of Mr. McGregor's library."[22] In addition to the provisions that were in the "Deed of Gift," the trustees approved an appropriation of $25,000 for the "remodeling, founding and furnishing the present rare book room of the University of Virginia Library" to provide suitable quarters in which to house the McGregor Collection.[23]

After the renovations were completed on the McGregor Room and new furnishings were installed, the fund trustees and President Newcomb made plans for the dedication of the library. April 14, 1939, McGregor's birthday, was chosen. With the approval of the university, the fund trustees hired Frank O. Salisbury to paint a portrait of McGregor "to be hung in the space over the fireplace in the McGregor Room." It measured approximately three feet six inches wide by four feet ten inches high.[24]

With the concurrence of the University of Virginia, the trustees withheld four valuable items from the McGregor Collection. The Clements Library was given the *Cambridge 1649* volume, and the astronomical libraries of the University of Michigan received three items relating to Nicolai Copernicus and Galileo Galilei. In return, the Clements Library gave the University of Virginia a number of "rare and interesting broadsides, maps, and manuscripts" for addition to the Tracy McGregor Library of American History.[25]

The dedication at the University of Virginia was a well-attended affair and demonstrated the high regard in which the university treated the McGregor Library. President Newcomb "hailed this day as the dawn of a new era in graduate works and scholarly research in the field of American history at the University of Virginia."[26] Henry S. Hulbert delivered the presentation address in which he highlighted McGregor's remarkable career. In attendance at the ceremony were fund trustees, members of McGregor's family, several officials from the University of Michigan, business associates, prominent book and manuscript dealers, and colleagues from the historical profession.[27]

The dedication of the library did not end the McGregor Fund's keen interest in the McGregor Library. After the dedication, two of the McGregor Fund's members served on the library's advisory committee, and the fund has continued to provide financial support to the University of Virginia for the care and expansion of the McGregor Library of American History. When formally presented to the university in 1939, the collection consisted of 12,500 items, including 3,500 rare books, the unique Mather Collection (2,000 books and pamphlets), and 7,000 books of general literature. The appraisal value was $339,000. Fifty years later the McGregor Collection had grown to 17,000 volumes and 12,000 manuscripts—a tribute to the accomplishments of McGregor and especially to his astuteness as a premier collector of rare books.[28] To the credit of the McGregor Fund trustees, they made certain that not only would this remarkable collection be kept intact at a prestigious southern university but also would fulfill McGregor's objective of creating a truly notable rare book library and research collection.

William J. Norton, first director of the Detroit Community Union and Children's Fund of Michigan and member of the Board of Trustees of the McGregor Fund from 1925 to 1975. Courtesy Walter P. Reuther Library, Wayne State University.

Joseph L. Hudson, Detroit business leader, served as president of the McGregor Institute for twenty years. He was also one of McGregor's closest friends. Courtesy McGregor Collection, Walter P. Reuther Library, Wayne State University.

Henry Schoolcraft Hulbert, close associate of McGregor in the Thursday Noon Group and founding member of the board of trustees of the McGregor Fund. Courtesy McGregor Fund.

Mildred R. White, executive secretary to the McGregor Fund and the Student Aid Society of Michigan, in a 1958 photo. *Detroit News.* Courtesy Walter P. Reuther Library, Wayne State University.

Thursday Noon Group, 1915. Top row, from left: Frank J. Sladen, Frank D. Eaman, J. B. Schlotman, Hugo A. Freund, Fred M. Butzel; middle row, from left: Gustavus D. Pope, J. Walter Drake, D. M. Ferry Jr., Francis C. McMath, William R. Kales; front row, from left: M. Hubert O'Brien, Willard Pope, Tracy W. McGregor, James Inglis, Henry Schoolcraft Hulbert. Courtesy: McGregor Collection, Walter P. Reuther Library, Wayne State University.

Following the fire on the Belle Isle Bridge in 1915, McGregor and the Thursday Noon Group provided funds for the new temporary bridge. Courtesy Walter P. Reuther Library, Wayne State University.

Katherine McGregor (holding child in photo) established the McGregor Home for Children (1903–16), purchasing the Stevens homestead in Highland Park for the orphanage. The McGregor Library later occupied the building. Courtesy McGregor Collection, Walter P. Reuther Library, Wayne State University.

The McGregor Public Library, Highland Park, Michigan. Courtesy McGregor Collection, Walter P. Reuther Library, Wayne State University.

Randolph Adams, longtime director of the William L. Clements Library, was McGregor's mentor in collecting Americana. Courtesy William L. Clements Library, University of Michigan.

The McGregor mission building, occupied by Goodwill Industries, burned on March 10, 1938. Courtesy Detroit News Collection, Walter P. Reuther Library, Wayne State University.

The Tracy W. McGregor Room at the Alderman Library, University of Virginia. Courtesy University of Virginia Library.

The McGregor Memorial Conference Center on the campus of Wayne State University was dedicated in 1958. Courtesy Walter P. Reuther Library, Wayne State University.

EPILOGUE

The McGregor Legacy

THE DEATH OF TRACY MCGREGOR shocked scores of his personal friends and business associates in Detroit, Washington, D.C., and other parts of the country. But no one was more devastated by his passing than his wife, Katherine. Even though she was aware of his health problems, especially during the winter and spring of 1936, she was unprepared for his death. For several years she had urged him to resign from the various boards and commissions on which he served and to cut back on his work for the Detroit Community Fund. She was willing for him to continue his active role as president and treasurer of the McGregor Fund but encouraged him to implement his plan to hire an administrative assistant to take over much of the work of the fund, as well as a librarian to help him arrange his growing collection of Americana. Katherine was hopeful also that his stay in the Garfield Hospital in April 1936 under constant medical supervision would lead to the recovery of his health.[1]

Katherine's reaction to Tracy's death was reflected in a letter she wrote to Murray McGregor in September 1936: "Do consider your own interests," she urged, "particularly your health—remembering the tired one who bore too many burdens and went to rest with plans for others' good, his unfinished task."[2] She also confided in Murray that she and Tracy had "talked very often of what separation would mean to both of us, and of the spiritual relations which truly unite us, how whatever comes to us here, we were inseparable forever." She then continued, "We do not know the strength of our faith, until we are tested. I am thankful for the teaching in childhood which laid the foundation for what we all must have when sorrow comes."[3]

Katherine's adjustment to Tracy's death might have been easier if she had been in good health herself, but she too had serious health problems. For more than a decade she had suffered from severe headaches, abdominal pains, and depression, and despite frequent visits to medical specialists and the Kellogg Battle Creek Sanitarium in Michigan and clinics in New York and Baltimore, no cures were found for her ailments. By the late 1920s her condition had worsened.[4]

Her strong dislike of Detroit and her life there with Tracy was undoubtedly a factor in her unhappy state. She blamed Tracy's Detroit friends and associates for his hectic schedule and for ruining his health. Katherine had also become increasingly reclusive and lost contact with the few remaining friends she had in the Detroit area, in addition to becoming estranged from members of her own family. Katherine's situation had become so serious that Tracy feared that "a mental problem would eventually develop." In 1931 he decided to move his residence to Washington, D.C., "for Katherine's privacy and seclusion."[5]

The departure from Detroit and the new residence in Washington improved Katherine's physical condition, but Tracy continued to worry about her state of mind. She made no attempt to develop new friendships, she refused to entertain Tracy's friends and associates, and she would not accept invitations to social engagements. She did, however, continue to take an active interest in the charitable and humanitarian activities of the McGregor Fund.[6]

By the fall of 1937, Katherine's health had suffered a noticeable decline. She suffered from malnutrition, she refused to leave her apartment, and she was reluctant to seek medical assistance. Fortunately, Tracy's friends and associates learned of her situation and offered their help and counsel. The McGregors' Washington friends and colleagues Frank Perley, Virginia Rittenhouse, Mildred White, and Kathryn Slagle kept in close contact with her and ran errands for her when needed. Murray McGregor visited her often and had phone conversations with her several times a week. Henry Hulbert made frequent trips to Washington to discuss McGregor Fund business and provide other assistance. Frank Sladen, Ford trustee and director of Ford Hospital, arranged for nurses to go to Washington to live with and care for Katherine.[7] Some of Katherine's associates urged her to return to Detroit where she could be nearer to members of the Whitney family and other friends, but she refused. She identified that city with the main cause of Tracy's illness; furthermore, she was completely alienated from her family. She decided to remain in Washington.

Fortunately, Tracy had made careful plans in the event of his death. He had kept all of his business activities and records in good order, and as early as 1932 he had carefully outlined to the trustees of the McGregor Fund his recommendations for future priorities of the fund if anything should happen to him and his wife.[8]

McGregor had also provided a will to take care of his family and other interests. Under its terms, which he signed December 19, 1930, McGregor appointed Kirby B. White and Edgar W. Bowen as executors. Both were business associates of McGregor and members of the board of trustees of the McGregor Fund. In the event that neither was available, the responsibility was to be assigned to Kenneth L. Moore, also a trusted friend and McGregor Fund trustee. Following McGregor's death, Moore filed the will in Wayne County Probate Court on May 29, 1936.[9]

The document reflected McGregor's concern for his family, as well as his confidence in the fund trustees to carry out his wishes. It first created a trust fund of $250,000, the income of which was to be set aside for his family. Murray McGregor, "in some recognition of his long and faithful services to the McGregor Institute," was to receive $6,000 a year "so long as he shall live, and upon his death . . . then $4,000 per year to his widow so long as she shall live." Murray's sons, Douglas and Donald McGregor, were to receive $1,000 a year until they reached the age of twenty-five. Ruth and George Brown's children, Thomas and Tracy, were also to receive $1,000 a year until they reached the age of twenty-five.[10] Ruth's husband was also included in the will and received a sum "to give him for his own uses an income of at least $2,000 per year from all sources, including his own earnings."[11] To Hugh D. Montgomerie, "in recognition of his long and faithful service" at the McGregor mission and as assistant to McGregor relating to other community activities, the will allocated a sum of $1,800 a year.[12] In addition to the specific annual payments, Tracy advised the McGregor Fund that these sums were to be considered "minimum amounts" and that the trustees could increase these payments "for their special needs and opportunities, and in order to recognize their special worthiness, and to encourage their wholesome ambitions." In more specific terms, McGregor added that he "would approve of advances for the higher education of my nephews, and of advances to my nephews to start them in a business, trade or profession."[13] He authorized the McGregor Fund "to devote the income of such portions to the principal" of the McGregor family fund, "as it shall from time to time deem proper to relieve the misfortunes and promote the betterment and well being of mankind."[14]

McGregor directed that his wife be given "such of my personal and household goods and effects as she may desire, including furniture, furnishings, pictures, automobiles, wearing apparel and the books that we have bought and enjoyed together."[15] Tracy had earlier established a special annuity for Katherine, administered by the McGregor Fund, whereby she would receive $25,000 a year during her lifetime."[16]

McGregor gave careful attention to the disposition of his Americana library, which is discussed in detail in chapter 14. He assigned to the McGregor Fund the responsibility of finding a suitable college or university, preferably "a small institution of higher learning having fine ideals of education and reasonable means and likelihood of achieving those ideals." He also authorized and encouraged the fund to "provide a modest but suitable endowment for the care of such books and for reasonable additions to my library."[17]

In carrying out his role as executor of McGregor's will, Moore first devoted his attention to determining the extent and monetary value of the estate. This proved to be a formidable and time-consuming task because of McGregor's extensive holdings and because his business files and personal papers were divided physically between Washington, D.C., and Detroit. With the assistance of Slagle and White of the McGregor Fund's Washington office, Moore reviewed and settled all of the outstanding claims against the estate, especially the bills from numerous book dealers and book publishers in Europe and the United States. He sent notices to all those indebted to McGregor, even though he was aware that McGregor never planned to collect them.[18] Inheritance and property taxes were promptly taken care of by Moore, as were the family annuities under the McGregor family trust.[19]

In May 1937, Moore, accompanied by Henry Hulbert and Renville Wheat, visited Washington, D.C., to complete important estate business. At the American Security and Trust Company they opened McGregor's safe deposit box and transferred the securities to the National Bank of Detroit. After reviewing and inventorying all of the items at the McGregor Fund's Washington office, they arranged delivery to Mrs. McGregor of the furniture, furnishings, books, and photographs that she had selected. The strong box located at the Washington office was also carefully examined. It contained several scarf pins, cuff links, dress shirt studs, and collar buttons. Also included were a number of items of sentimental value to McGregor—his first watch, his 1886 graduation pin from Toledo High School, "an old locked pocket book containing two old coins," and specimens of confederate money.[20] Slagle also reviewed with Moore the items found in the clothing he wore to the Garfield Hospital late in April 1936, which included a coin purse and billfold containing seven dollars in bills and six dollars in change.[21] Moore delivered these items to Katherine along with a package of old letters and an envelope containing photographs of her. Unfortunately none of the latter survived, perhaps because she destroyed all such photographs of herself.[22]

Tracy's death was deeply felt by the trustees of the McGregor Fund. They were his close friends who had worked with him on fund projects and who, as Henry S. Hulbert observed, "shared his own hopes and dreams of relieving misfortune and promoting the well-being of mankind."[23] As most of the trustees were unaware that he had a serious heart problem, his death came as a shock to them. He had been in daily contact with members of the board for weeks before his death, but only Judge Hulbert and Frank Sladen were aware of his critical health situation.

Following the funeral, the board of trustees met immediately to discuss the future of the McGregor Fund. As president and treasurer of the fund, Tracy had personally supervised several of its major grants, including the Special Gifts Fund, the Student Aid and Scholarship Fund, and the AHA Committee for Americana in College Libraries. In addition, the McGregors had financed several charitable projects with their personal accounts. These issues were carefully reviewed at the board's meetings in May 1936, in addition to deciding who had the responsibility of directing the fund. On the twenty-seventh of that month Henry S. Hulbert was elected president; William J. Norton, vice president; and Kenneth L. Moore, treasurer. They were joined on the board by Renville Wheat, Francis C. McMath, and Cleveland Thurber, who were elected in June 1936. Mildred R. White was appointed manager of the fund's Detroit office, and Kathryn Slagle was chosen as manager of the Washington office. Frank Perley, trust officer of the American Security and Trust Company in Washington, D.C., continued as financial advisor to the fund.[24]

The trustees invited Katherine McGregor to replace Tracy as its president, but she declined, "feeling unable to accept the responsibility of the office and to undertake its duties and activities."[25] Katherine did advise the trustees, however, that she wanted to be kept informed of the work of the fund, especially its financial activities. She requested copies of all board minutes and the "various statements prepared by Price, Waterhouse," and for the major fund grants, she asked for the "historical background of each activity together with current information, and also the names of the people in charge of their present administration."[26] Katherine was particularly interested in the work of the Detroit Community Fund, which received major grants from the McGregor family as well as from the McGregor Fund. She requested copies of not only the Detroit Community Fund annual reports but also detailed information on the donors "to the Chest's drives and what activity was taken by certain of the wealthy people there in Detroit."[27]

Tracy McGregor's will also assigned the trustees the tasks of finding a suitable depository for his personal collection of Americana, the administration of a special family trust benefiting Murray and Jessie McGregor and their families, the management of the LaSalle and Warren Farms Land Development Companies, and the supervision of the Provident Loan and Savings Society. In addition, they were responsible for the investment of bonds having a market value of $2,685,000, a gift from Katherine.[28]

Fortunately, under the guidance of Tracy McGregor, the trustees had established its major annual funding categories. In response to the Great Depression, relief activities received major attention from the McGregor Fund. The McGregor Institute, founded and supported since its inception in 1891 by the McGregor family, received strong support from the fund until 1935 when "it discontinued its service, due to the taking over of the work on a broader scale by the government of the United States."[29] The fund continued to assist Detroit's homeless men with grants to the Detroit Emergency Relief Committee, the Goodwill Industries, and various local mission and settlement houses. The generous grants given to the Detroit Community Fund also assisted Detroit's needy and at the same time served as a tribute to Tracy, who helped found the Detroit Community Fund and served as its president for many years. On a national level, the fund continued to support the National Committee on the Care of Transient and Homeless, which had earlier been established "under the stimulus of Mr. McGregor to provide a clearinghouse for study and research on this very serious national problem."[30]

Science and education, two fields actively supported by McGregor, were also endorsed by the fund. Prior to his death, McGregor had mediated the dispute between University of Michigan president Alexander Ruthven and members of the William Clements family regarding the acquisition of the priceless manuscript collections of British Revolutionary War political and military leaders. In addition to the original grant of fifteen thousand dollars in 1935, the fund approved an additional one hundred thousand dollars in 1937 to consummate the acquisition and thus ensure the Clements Library's position as the preeminent research center on the American Revolution. The fund also gave generous grants to the University of Michigan in support of several other programs initiated by McGregor, including the Department of Astronomy, the McMath-Hulbert Observatory at Lake Angelus, and the Institute of Public and Social Administration.[31] The fund supported the Merrill-Palmer Institute of Detroit, on which McGregor had served as its president and trustee from its establishment in 1920 until his death in 1936, and the Detroit Bureau of Governmental Research, with which McGregor had a long association, received fund grants for its research in the social sciences.[32]

Tracy and Katherine McGregor had always taken an interest in health- and medical-related projects, and the McGregor Fund continued to heartily endorse these causes after 1936. In fact, one of the first programs presented to the fund in 1932, after it received its first major gift, involved financial "assistance of those chronically ill or in danger of serious breakdowns in health, particularly such as might be saved from permanent or continuing loss of their ability to work by a period of convalescent care and rest."[33] Because of the McGregors' strong support for this project, the trustees gave it high priority, and, in 1936 and 1937, 384 individuals were given assistance. In 1939 the McGregor Health Foundation was established, and a separate board of trustees was appointed to administer the program. A year later the foundation established "a model convalescent home on East Jefferson Avenue in Detroit."[34]

Other local health organizations received McGregor Fund support. The Michigan State Medical Society, the Farrand School of Nursing at Harper Hospital, the Detroit Council on Community Nursing, the Detroit League for the Handicapped, and the Detroit Orthopaedic Clinic, sponsored by the Sigma Gamma Association, were the recipients of fund grants designed to aid the "near indigent sick . . . crippled, blind and deaf." The trustees also eagerly continued their support of another of the McGregors' special projects—the Society of Perpetual Help, "organized for the care and treatment of cancer patients in an advanced stage."[35]

The trustees also focused their attention on public welfare projects as a tribute to their founder's long-standing commitment to the "army of homeless men," the unemployed, the destitute, and the youth of Detroit. Among the early recipients of grants in honor of McGregor's memory was the Detroit Council for Youth Services, the State Association of Young Men's Christian

Associations, the Michigan Council of Social Work, the International Migration Service, and the Consultative Bureau of the Detroit Community Fund. Responding to Katherine McGregor's sustained interest in African Americans, the fund gave grants to the Atlanta School of Social Work, "a center of social work, at which institutes and round table discussions are conducted and research investigations are carried on concerning many social problems relating to the Negro population of the Country."[36]

The McGregors' religious interests were also recognized, at least in a minor way, by the fund. The Federal Council of the Churches of Christ in America and its National Preaching Mission were given support "to bring about a spiritual awakening in America." The religious fieldwork activities of the National Council of Young Men's Christian Associations received fund contributions. The First Congregational Church in Detroit, where Tracy had been a long-standing member, received a grant in 1937, and in the following years the Woodward Avenue Presbyterian Church, "in which the founder and benefactress of the Fund for years had been interested," received a grant for the repair of the organ that years earlier had been given to the church by Katherine. In addition, the Convent of the Sacred Heart of Grosse Pointe Farms was granted money to purchase a Hammond organ.[37]

Another category of funding during the years following McGregor's death included "Contributions to Capital Structures and Equipment in Problems of Health, Fresh Air Camps and Community Services." The fund approved, often acting on Katherine's recommendation, grants of more than forty thousand dollars "to help in the building programs of several worthwhile camps, settlement houses and schools . . . the erection of new buildings and the improvement of old ones." The recipients included the Detroit Girl Scouts for its camp at Metamora, Michigan; the Detroit Area Boy Scouts of America for its camp at Brighton, Michigan; the Salvation Army for its fresh air camp on Lakeville Lake, Michigan; Port Huron Welfare Camp on Lake Huron; and the Bay Cliff Camp at Big Bay, Michigan. Bay Court, the recreational center near Mt. Clemens, Michigan, which was founded by Katherine in 1911 "for dependent mothers and children," was given a grant to expand its facilities, and two organizations, the Detroit Urban League and the Franklin Street Settlement, in which Tracy McGregor had taken a special interest, also received capital structures grants.[38]

In addition to the major grant areas that were supervised by the trustees, Tracy had established several major accounts that he administered on his own.

The Student Aid and Scholarship Fund was set up in 1932 to assist young men and women who needed financial aid to enroll and attend classes in college. McGregor remembered well the difficulties he and his family had faced when he attended Park College and Oberlin, and during his years at the McGregor Institute he encountered many young men who were not able to attend college because of lack of funds. With the aid of Mildred White, they reviewed scores of applications from needy students, met with the finalists and their families, and assisted in the college admission process. McGregor also followed the academic careers of the sponsored students. The trustees continued the student aid program, supporting sixty-three students in 1938.[39]

The Special Gift Fund, under the personal administration of the president, was used to assist individuals and families who faced family crisis, health problems, and unemployment. Many former "mission men" were beneficiaries. Although such loans were accompanied by a formal agreement, including a schedule for repayment, McGregor never expected or sought repayment. As Slagle, his assistant explained, McGregor "intended to let the loan recipients struggle for awhile thinking it might be good for them, but I know his general idea was opposed to burdening people with debts." Slagle concluded, "Mr. McGregor always preferred to make gifts rather than loans."[40]

A special project to support the establishment of rare Americana collections in college libraries was administered by McGregor, with the assistance of Randolph Adams of the Clements Library. It was only after McGregor's death that the trustees learned of the scope of these special funds and the amount of time and effort that McGregor had devoted to them and especially to the recipients of the grants. Fortunately, White had worked closely with McGregor in administering these grants and was able to take over the programs after his death.

The McGregors also supported with their private accounts a number of national charitable and humanitarian organizations independent of the McGregor Fund. For the most part, McGregor had long associations with those groups and had served as a trustee and officer on their governing boards. Among the recipients of annual gifts was the National Committee for Mental Hygiene, the National Council of Social Work, the National Municipal League, the National Consumers League, the National Committee of Prison Chaplains, and the Washington Urban League. Katherine's special interest was reflected in their joint support of the National Council for Mothers and Babies, the University of Michigan Presbyterian Committee, the Detroit Episcopal Mission, and the Universal Church Council.[41]

Two Detroit area public institutions received attention from McGregor and the fund: the Wayne County Training School at Northville—devoted to the education of "feeble minded children of higher mental grades, who under proper supervision may be returned to a useful life in the Community"—and the Eloise Hospital and Infirmary. At the latter, McGregor had financially supported the work of Dr. Franz Blumenthal and his research on dermatology and allergy.[42]

After McGregor's death the trustees assumed the formidable task of reviewing and evaluating all of the grants supported by the fund and the McGregor family. For several years they attempted to continue to support all of the projects originally endorsed and approved by the McGregors, due both to the major gift to the fund from McGregor in his will and to their deep affection for him. By 1940, however, the board decided that it had to review its overall granting program and concentrate on "fewer fields." This decision was prompted by two factors. One was the recent controversy with the Internal Revenue Service, which began in 1934 when the U.S. Internal Revenue Service challenged the fund's tax exempt status and demanded that it pay its "tax liability for the years of 1925 to 1933 inclusive, including income taxes, excess profits taxes, capital stock taxes and all other taxes and assessments of every kind and nature." The fund successfully disputed the challenge and on February 8, 1939, the U.S. Treasury Department ruled that the McGregor Fund "was exempt from taxation under the Federal Revenue Acts and reversed prior rulings to the contrary."[43]

A second factor was the onset of World War II and the host of problems it created for Detroit, its needy, and the agencies related to the war effort. The amount of fund grants increased from $1,174,804 during 1931–39 to $2,851,410 in the 1940–49 period. In the 1930s, more than 39 percent of the grants went to local philanthropic and charitable agencies; in the 1940s, only 22 percent was allocated to local organizations. The amount appropriated to the health field increased from 12 percent to 25.5 percent, and "a new item, War service, was added and this accounted for more than 12 percent of the grants." A slight increase for educational projects and research also occurred in the 1940s.[44]

Despite the changes in the grant allocations during the 1940s, they did not represent a major departure from the original mission of the McGregor Fund. McGregor and his colleagues on the board of trustees devoted the early years of the fund to "a careful study of the opportunities and possible achievements in the fields of philanthropy, education, religion, and science, which might be open to a fund of such moderate size."[45] The demands during the decade of the Great Depression differed from those of the previous decade, and as a result, the trustees adjusted their grant priorities to meet these needs.

The World War II years raised new critical issues and new community crises that the trustees responded to in a dramatic and timely manner. Within weeks of the attack on Pearl Harbor, the trustees authorized the first of several major grants to the American Red Cross, to the War Chest of Metropolitan Detroit, and to several foreign war relief agencies. Just as in World War I, when McGregor chaired the Patriotic Fund and coordinated war relief programs, the resources of the McGregor family provided the impetus for many innovative programs. The decision of the trustees "to consolidate commitments in relatively few fields of endeavors," especially in those areas "which Mr. and Mrs. McGregor had directed much time and money," was based on sound and responsible policy and was followed consistently in the trustees' decisions during the following half-century.

The question of a suitable memorial for the McGregors was raised shortly after Tracy's death. The trustees of the McGregor Fund received numerous inquiries from community leaders, officers of both national and local charitable groups, and public institutions regarding a memorial. The issue had been raised often during Tracy's lifetime, but he and Katherine did not want any public recognition—they preferred to remain anonymous. The name of the Helping Hand Mission for Homeless Men was changed to the McGregor Institute in 1911, but this was done, in fact, to recognize Thomas McGregor's role in founding the mission in 1891.

The issue of recognizing the McGregors rose again in 1924 when the Highland Park Library Commission notified Tracy and Katherine of their plan to name the library after them. The McGregors reluctantly agreed to this action but made it clear that it wasn't necessary. In addition, the University of Michigan on several occasions wanted to recognize the McGregors' support for the McMath-Hulbert Observatory, the Institute of Public and Social Administration, and the William Clements Library, but again McGregor made it clear that he preferred anonymity. The fund's trustees respected McGregor's preference and adopted the policy that the recipients of fund grants not use the McGregor name.

In 1937, when the AHA requested that its Committee on Americana in College Libraries be changed to the McGregor Plan, the trustees objected to this proposed alteration.[46] They relaxed this policy, however, regarding the gift of McGregor's Americana library to the University of Virginia. They authorized the title "Tracy W. McGregor Library of American History" and the designation "McGregor Room" in the new Alderman Library building. They also commissioned the portrait of Tracy McGregor to be hung over the fireplace in the room and in 1953 a bas-relief by the distinguished Detroit sculptor, Marshall Fredericks.[47]

By 1950 the trustees recognized that they needed to devote more attention to the founders of the fund. The directors and staff of the local community, educational, and charitable organizations that had been recipients of grants from the fund asked for information about the McGregors, and several newly appointed fund trustees who had never met or worked with the McGregors wanted to learn more about them and the origins of the fund. In addition, Detroit community leaders expressed an interest in a public memorial honoring Tracy and Katherine McGregor. In 1949 the Detroit School Board, which had benefited often from fund support, decided to name its new school, located at 16276 Edmore, after Tracy McGregor. The trustees approved this action and participated in the school's dedication on May 10, 1955. William J. Norton, the president of the fund, gave the main address honoring Tracy McGregor.[48] The fund hired the distinguished Detroit sculptor Marshall Fredericks to create a bas-relief of McGregor to be placed in the school.[49]

After Katherine McGregor died on June 9, 1954, the trustees again considered creating an appropriate memorial for the McGregors. They had on earlier occasions approached Katherine for permission to have portraits made of her and Tracy, but she always refused to be photographed even with her husband. In fact, she advised the trustees that there existed only one photographic likeness taken in 1901.[50]

Mildred White, the assistant secretary of the McGregor Fund who had worked closely with Tracy in the Washington office during the last two years of his life, was the inspiration of a project to collect and preserve records relating to the lives and careers of the McGregors. As manager of the fund's Detroit office, she had to constantly answer questions about its founders and their views and plans for the fund. Moreover, she was inspired by this "wonderful man who did so much to improve conditions for people who were not as fortunate as some of us."[51]

White's search for Tracy's personal and official papers began within hours of his death. She systematically brought together his business and personal family papers and arranged to have them transferred to the fund's Detroit office where she could care for them. She also contacted Murray McGregor and arranged for the preservation of records relating to the McGregor Institute. In 1954 White proposed to the trustees that a "book on Mr. and Mrs. McGregor" be written "even if it were available only for our Board."[52]

White was concerned not only about the paucity of information relating to the career and accomplishments of McGregor but also about what she considered misunderstandings about his early life. For example, she had questioned the opinion of several of McGregor's associates who believed that he "had been in his younger days, almost a religious fanatic."[53] In order to clear up this issue, White contacted McGregor's friends who had known him during his early years in Toledo. From Eliot Talmadge, a high school classmate of McGregor's and, in 1955, a retired Episcopal minister, she learned "that he and Tracy were rather austere in their young days but it never prevented their having a lot of fun."[54] Another classmate, Harriet N. Gleason, told of "the singing and skating parties" and described Tracy McGregor as "a fine moral young man but certainly without any sign of fanaticism."[55]

White also contacted the "children who were taken in by Mr. and Mrs. McGregor and given a home" at their orphanage in Highland Park. She asked them to describe their experiences there, including the games McGregor had played with them and his strong views that the children were never allowed to use slang.[56] Through Murray McGregor she was able to locate McGregor's diaries, journals, and financial records as well as the early papers of the McGregor family. She informed Murray McGregor about her success in locating so much relevant material about Tracy, even though she added, "it may be some time before the trustees decide who will write the book."[57]

The trustees were impressed and pleased with the records and information on the McGregors that White had collected and preserved. Norton, the president of the McGregor Fund, immediately recognized the value and importance of her work and appointed a committee to investigate the feasibility of a biographical study of the McGregors. Norton, a student of history by avocation and a longtime friend of Tracy McGregor, decided to take the biography a step further and establish an "oral history" project to interview on tape several close associates of McGregor. He was familiar with the oral history project at the newly established Ford Motor Company archives and contacted its director, Owen Bombard, to see if he could coordinate the McGregor project. When Bombard declined, Norton appointed the fund's program director, Mark Beech, to supervise the interviews. In the months that followed,

Norton and Beech conducted a number of oral history interviews, including those with Murray McGregor, Pliny Marsh, and James Redhouse.[58]

With the extensive files gathered by White and the oral history interviews, the trustees proceeded to search for an author to write the biography of Tracy McGregor. They approached Cyril Arthur Player, who had written biographical studies of Hazen Pingree, J. L. Hudson, and James Scripps, but when these negotiations failed, the trustees asked Henry Hulbert to undertake the biography. Hulbert, who had been one of McGregor's closest friends, carefully considered the proposal but declined because of health reasons. The biography project was tabled until another writer could be located.[59]

A suitable memorial in the city of Detroit was also considered by the trustees. In August 1953, the McGregor Fund made a formal proposal to the city of Detroit for a "Tracy W. McGregor Memorial Fountain" in the planned reflective pool at the Civic Center at the foot of Woodward Avenue. This proposal was endorsed by Charles Blessing, director of the City Planning Commission, and Weld S. Maybee, executive director of the Memorial Hall Commission, but unfortunately a decision on the proposal was delayed for eighteen months "because of the uncertainty of the City's plans for the area."[60]

The trustees withdrew their offer on March 14, 1954, and turned their attention to another alternative—a memorial to Tracy and Katherine McGregor in the Cultural Center near the Detroit Institute of Arts, the Detroit Public Library, the Detroit Historical Museum, and Wayne State University. On March 8, 1955, the trustees met with Dr. Clarence Hilberry, president, Provost Arthur Neef, and other Wayne State University officials to review the proposed campus development. The trustees were so impressed with the university's plans for a community conference center to be located adjacent to the music building and the Community Arts Auditorium that on April 11, 1955, that they appointed a committee consisting of Norton, Cleveland Thurber, and Renville Wheat to confer with President Hilberry and develop a formal proposal for a memorial to the McGregors.[61]

In the weeks that followed, the trustees and the university officials agreed upon a definite proposal. They wanted the memorial to include a community conference center and a sculpture pool to be designed to "represent Mr. McGregor's reflective nature and appreciation of the value of beauty and repose."[62] At the request of the McGregor Fund, the architectural firm of Leinweber, Yamasaki, and Hillmost was hired with Minaro Yamasaki "in personal charge" of the conference center project.[63]

The McGregor Fund trustees and university officials negotiated the final terms of the gift. The building and court, which were to be financed exclusively by the McGregor Fund, would be dedicated as the "McGregor Memorial: A Community Conference Center and Sculpture Court given in Memory of Tracy W. and Katherine McGregor." It was also agreed that the building was to be used "primarily of groups having civic, cultural, educational or professional interests and not used in the academic programs of the University in any way which shall interfere with or prejudice this primary use." It was agreed also that "the other buildings in the Center be constructed in substantial accordance with such a model and that any changes of substance in the memorial structure or in the other buildings in the Center require McGregor Fund approval."[64]

The cost of the conference center building and court was originally estimated at $975,155, but the bids from the contractor resulted in an adjustment to $1,270,000. The fund also provided and additional $50,000 for the furniture and furnishings in the building.[65]

The formal dedication of the McGregor Memorial Conference Center and Sculpture Court took place on May 18, 1958. Fund president William J. Norton formally presented the facility to university president Hilberry and was followed by speakers James M. Hare, the secretary of state who represented Governor G. Mennen Williams; Detroit mayor Louis Miriani; Dr. Robert Hill McRae, executive director of the Welfare Council of Metropolitan Chicago; and Arthur Neef, university provost. During the months that followed, thousands of visitors including community leaders, students, and friends of the McGregors visited and inspected the facility.

Although many of the charitable and humanitarian programs supported by the McGregors, such as the Mission for Homeless Men, are no longer in existence, their legacy remains. The McGregor Library—now the core of the magnificent research collection at the University of Virginia—is a visible testimony to his remarkable work as a collector of Americana. The McGregor Memorial Conference Center and Sculpture Court on the campus of Wayne State University is another tribute to the lives and work of the McGregors. Perhaps the most lasting legacy to Tracy and Katherine McGregor is the McGregor Fund, which they established in 1925 "to relieve the misfortunes and improve the well being of people." More than eighty years later, the fund supports its original mission of providing financial assistance to nonprofit emergency human service agencies and health care programs, especially for low-income individuals and innovative educational and cultural initiatives.

NOTES

ABBREVIATIONS

ALUA	Archives of Labor and Urban Affairs, Wayne State University, Detroit
BHC	Burton Historical Collections, Detroit Public Library
HHM	Helping Hand Mission
MC-RL	McGregor Collection, Reuther Library, Wayne State University, Detroit
MFA	McGregor Fund Archives, Detroit
MPC-RL	Merrill-Palmer Collection, Reuther Library, Wayne State University, Detroit

CHAPTER 1

1. James D. Taitt, "Historical Reminiscences of the Presbyterian Church at Oxbow, New York," *Early History of Oxbow and the Scotch Settlement* (Oxbow: Presbyterian Church of Oxbow, 1921), 10, 15; Murray McGregor, Oral history interview, 1954, 1–3, by William J. Norton and Mark Beach, MC-RL. See also Minnie Preston, "Thomas McGregor," HHM, Home Report, 1893, MC-RL.

2. Taitt, "Historical Reminiscences."

3. Murray McGregor, Oral history interview, 3–4, 29–30.

4. W. J. Perman, "Thomas McGregor As I Knew Him," MC-RL; Thomas McGregor, "Autobiographical Sketch," MC-RL.

5. Perman, "Thomas McGregor As I Knew Him."

6. *Detroit Free Press,* March 30, 1896; Murray McGregor to Frank Eamon, May 10, 1954, MC-RL.

7. Murray McGregor to Frank Eamon, May 10, 1954, MC-RL.

8. Murray McGregor, Oral history interview, 6.

9. Perman, "Thomas McGregor As I Knew Him."

10. Ibid.

11. Murray McGregor, Oral history interview; Minnie Preston, "Thomas McGregor," HHM, Report, 1893, MC-RL.

12. Murray McGregor, "Founding of the Toledo and Detroit Missions," MC-RL.

13. Preston, "Thomas McGregor"; Murray McGregor, Oral history interview, 8–10.

14. "Report of Work Done at Toledo Helping Hand Mission from February 19 to March 31, 1890," MC-RL.

15. Ibid.; Thomas McGregor, "Autobiographical Sketch."

16. Ibid.

17. Ibid.; Thomas McGregor, "Autobiographical Sketch."

18. "Helping Hand Mission," Toledo *Commercial,* March 1891, MC-RL.

19. Ibid.

20. Ibid.

21. Ibid.

22. "Everybody's Column": Facts about the Helping Hand Mission," Toledo *Commercial* [date not shown in clipping], MC-RL.

23. Toledo *Commercial,* March 1891. Dr. William, pastor of the First Congregational Church, and Dr. Bacon, pastor of the Central Congregational Church, praised McGregor for his work and urged members of their congregations "to aid him in his work."

24. McGregor, "Founding of the Toledo and Detroit Missions."

25. Thomas McGregor, "The Detroit Mission," MC-RL; Thomas McGregor, "Autobiographical Sketch."

26. Preston, "Thomas McGregor."

27. McGregor, "Founding of the Toledo and Detroit Missions."

28. Ibid; Preston, "Thomas McGregor"; Thomas McGregor, "Autobiographical Sketch."

29. Ibid.; "A Tramps Paradise, Mr. McGregor of Toledo prepares a Free Hotel for Floaters," Detroit *Journal,* December 20, 1890; "A Free Lodging House," *Detroit News,* December 19, 1890.

30. Preston, "Thomas McGregor."

31. Ibid.

32. Ibid.

33. Ibid.

34. Ibid.

35. Ibid.; Thomas McGregor to Tracy McGregor, April 14, 1891, MC-RL.

36. Preston, "Thomas McGregor."

37. Thomas McGregor "The Gospel for the Masses," 1891.

38. Murray McGregor to Frank Eamon, May 10, 1954, MC-RL.

39. Ibid.

40. The Toledo Helping Hand Mission closed in November 1892; Toledo *Daily Blade,* November 10, 1892, 2.

41. Kate McGregor to Tracy McGregor, January 18, 1907, MC-RL; Thomas received an offer in March 1891 to manage a mission in New York City. He responded that he "could not leave Detroit at present until God sends me." Thomas McGregor to Tracy McGregor, April 14, 1891, MC-RL.

42. Preston, "Thomas McGregor."

43. Ibid.; *Detroit Free Press,* April 28, 1923. J. L. Hudson paid for Thomas's funeral expenses. Elizabeth McGregor to Tracy McGregor, July 11, 1891, MC-RL.

44. Murray McGregor, Oral history interview, 14–15.

45. Murray McGregor to Frank Eamon, May 10, 1954, MC-RL.

46. In a letter written to Tracy on December 17, 1890, Thomas McGregor described the difficulties he faced in renovating the mission building on Larned Street; letter in MC-RL.

47. Murray McGregor, Oral history interview, 14–15.

48. Murray McGregor to Frank Eamon, May 10, 1954, MC-RL. Shortly before his death, Thomas wrote to Tracy, "I enjoyed your presence and fellowship, Tracy, very much this time with me in Detroit, and I have been wondering if God could not let us work together in some way after a while."

49. Ibid.; Toledo High School, Class of 1886, "Graduation Booklet," MC-RL.

50. Elliott Talmadge to Mildred White, October 23, 1954, MFA.

51. Ibid.

52. Harriett Gleason to Mildred White, October 21, 1954, MC-RL.

53. On March 15, 1887, at the twenty-sixth anniversary of the Washington Street Congregational Church, Tracy McGregor gave the salutary address. *Programme,* 1887, MC-RL.

54. E. Talmadge to Mildred White, October 23, 1954, MC-RL.

55. Ibid.; Murray McGregor to Frank Eamon, May 10, 1954, MC-RL.

56. Murray McGregor, Oral history interview, 14.

57. S. Frederick Starr to W. Calvin Patterson, June 19, 1992, MFA. Included was Tracy McGregor's academic record at Oberlin.

58. Tracy McGregor to Elizabeth McGregor, June 9, 1891, MC-RL.

59. *McGregor Helping Hand Mission after One Year,* Detroit, 1892, 10, MC-RL.

60. Tracy McGregor to Elizabeth McGregor, May 1891, MC-RL.

CHAPTER 2

1. The mission went through several name changes over the years. From 1890 to 1891 it was called—at least informally—the Detroit Helping Hand Mission. In 1891 it became the Mission for Homeless Men and, in 1892, the McGregor Mission for Homeless Men. In 1911 the name was officially changed to the McGregor Institute.

2. R. E. Knowles, *Detroit Journal,* June 1908; and Warren Stanley, "A Scot's Arithmatic [*sic*]," *Detroit Free Press,* April 2, 1961, MC-RL.

3. "Detroit's Lady Bountiful," *Detroit News-Tribune,* November 9, 1902; Mildred White to Murray McGregor, March 30, 1955, MC-RL.

4. *Detroit Evening News,* November 29, 1900; "Detroit's Big Land-Owners," *Detroit News-Tribune,* June 30, 1895.

5. For an account of the Whitney House, see "An American Palace," *Detroit Free Press,* February 4, 1895.

6. Carolyn Patch, *Grace Whitney Hoff: The Story of an Abundant Life* (Cambridge, MA: Riverside Press, 1933), 3, 16.

7. Ibid., 19. The book details Grace Whitney's numerous accomplishments and charitable activities.

8. "Detroit's Lady Bountiful."

9. Ibid.

10. Ibid.

11. McGregor Mission, Board of Trustees, Minutes, January 12, 1901 [hereafter cited as McGregor Mission, Minutes, date]; and Murray McGregor to Mark Beach, September 21, 1954, MC-RL. According to Harriet Gleason, a lifelong friend of Tracy McGregor, David Whitney gave money to Tracy so that he could be "on his own feet." Mildred White to Murray McGregor, n.d., MC-RL.

12. Murray McGregor, Oral history interview, 73.

13. *Detroit News-Tribune,* November 20, 1901.

14. Ibid.

15. Tracy McGregor, Diary, May 20, 1907, MC-RL [hereafter cited as Tracy McGregor diary].

16. Tracy McGregor diary, April 3, 1907.

17. Ibid., November 11, 1908.

18. Ibid., April 19, 1907.

19. Ibid., April 2, 1907.

20. W. R. Richards, "Tracy W. McGregor," *Detroiter,* February 20, 1928.

21. Tracy McGregor diary, November 11, 1908.

22. The resignation was announced at the meeting of the McGregor Mission board of trustees, on October 25, 1915. Minutes, October 25, 1915. Murray McGregor was appointed superintendent at the same board meeting.

CHAPTER 3

1. Tracy McGregor diary, April 18, 1921.

2. Ibid., April 14, 1922.

3. Ibid., November 19, 1923.

4. Ibid., March 31, 1924.

5. Ibid., April 14, 1925.

6. Dr. L. F. Barker to McGregor, April 13, 1926, MC-RL.

7. Ibid.

8. Tracy McGregor diary, November 6, 1927; December 25, 1927.

9. Ibid., May 11, 1928.

10. Ibid., August 15, 1929.

11. Ibid., January 18, 1921.

12. Ibid.

13. Katherine McGregor to Tracy McGregor, n.d., MC-RL.

14. McGregor and Wells remained close friends during the remainder of McGregor's life. They played golf often, met frequently to discuss literature, and in 1932–33, McGregor financed Wells's research trip to England and Europe. See correspondence files, MC-RL. See also Carleton Wells Collection, Bentley Library. In one diary entry in 1933, Wells commented after meeting with McGregor: "He looks fairly well, though he is aging . . . but he finds considerable happiness along the way." Wells, Diary, December 5, 1933, Bentley Library, University of Michigan, Ann Arbor.

15. Tracy McGregor diary, December 31, 1920.

16. Ibid., October 19, 1920.

17. Sandy Fugate, *For the Benefit of All*: A History of Philanthropy in Michigan (Battle Creek, MI: W. K. Kellogg Foundation, 1997), 46.

18. See "Financial Loan" file, MC-RL.

19. Slagle to Kenneth Moore, July 28, 1936, MC-RL.

20. McGregor to Fred Butzel, December 30, 1932, MC-RL.

21. Butzel to McGregor, January 3, 1933, MC-RL.

22. W. J. Norton to McGregor, January 1, 1934, MC-RL.

23. Tracy McGregor diary, September 16, 1929.

24. Katherine McGregor to Tracy McGregor, n.d., MC-RL.

25. Tracy McGregor diary, April 14, 1930.

26. McGregor to Murray McGregor, April 9, 1934, MC-RL.

27. Tracy McGregor diary, August 15, 1929.

28. Katherine McGregor to Tracy McGregor [1930], MC-RL.

29. McGregor to K. Slagle, November 11, 1934, MC-RL.

30. For an account of Douglas McGregor's academic career, see Andrea Gaber, *The Capitalist Philosophers* (New York: Times Books, 2000), 153–85. There is extensive correspondence between Douglas and Tracy McGregor in the McGregor Collection.

31. Tracy McGregor, *Towards a Philosophy of the Inner Life* (Detroit: n.p., 1934).

32. McGregor to K. Slagle, November 27, 1935, MC-RL.

33. McGregor Fund, Board of Trustees, Minutes, 1932, MFA [hereafter cited as McGregor Fund, Minutes, date].

34. Katherine McGregor to Murray and Jessie McGregor, April 7, 1936, MC-RL.

35. Ibid.

36. *Detroit Free Press,* May 7, 1936; *Detroit News,* May 6, 1936.

37. Ibid.

38. Henry Hulbert, McGregor "Obituary," MC-RL.

39. *Detroit Free Press,* June 8, 1954.

40. McGregor Fund, Minutes, June 14, 1954.

CHAPTER 4

1. Murray McGregor, Oral history interview, 64.

2. Murray McGregor, Oral history interview, 13, 70.

3. Tracy McGregor to Elizabeth McGregor, June 9, 1891, MC-RL.

4. Tracy McGregor to Elizabeth McGregor, June 15, 1891, MC-RL.

5. Henry S. Hulbert, *Tracy W. McGregor* (Detroit: McGregor Fund, 1939), 9–10. Although Tracy McGregor never identified the business leader, Hulbert and Murray McGregor believed that it was Joseph L. Hudson, who became one of the strongest supporters of the mission.

6. J. L. Hudson, who joined the board of trustees in 1891 and served as its president until his death in 1912; Murray McGregor, Oral history interview, 44.

7. *Detroit Free Press,* October 8, 1900.

8. McGregor Institute, "McGregor Institute: A Review of Forty Years," *Annual Report for 1930,* 4–6, MC-RL; *The McGregor Helping Hand Mission after Two Years* (Detroit, 1892), 12–13, MC-RL; Edward W. Pendleton was closely associated with the McGregor Institute for thirty years. A. C. Angell, "Eulogy of E. W. Pendleton," MC-RL.

9. *Detroit News,* April 16, 1893.

10. McGregor retained copies of many of the sermons he delivered at the mission's evening and Sunday chapel services. See MC-RL.

11. James Redhouse, Oral history interview, 11, William J. Norton Collection, Bentley Library, University of Michigan, Ann Arbor; McGregor to Frank D. Eamon, May 10, 1954, MC-RL.

12. *McGregor Helping Hand Mission after One Year.*

13. Ibid.

14. Ibid.

15. *Detroit Free Press,* March 30, 1896.

16. *McGregor Helping Hand Mission after One Year,* 17. Murray McGregor, Oral history interview, 24–25, 27; *Detroit Free Press,* December 16, 1893; June 23, 1895.

17. Ibid.

18. *Detroit Free Press,* December 16, 1893; June 23, 1895; *Detroit News,* April 16, 1893.

19. Murray McGregor, Oral history interview, 28–29; *McGregor Helping Hand Mission after One Year.* The mission printed a number of brochures publicizing the employment bureau and its service. See MC-RL.

20. James Redhouse, Oral history interview, 5–6; Murray McGregor, Oral history interview, 35–36.

21. *McGregor Helping Hand Mission after One Year.*

22. Tracy McGregor sent hundreds of letters and brochures to residents and business leaders, describing the KindlingWood program. See MC-RL. Murray McGregor, Oral history interview, 37–40; James Redhouse, Oral history interview, 4–5, 14.

23. Murray McGregor, Oral history interview, 37.

24. Ibid., 45–46.

25. *McGregor Helping Hand Mission after Two Years,* 8–9; *Detroit Free Press,* December 16, 1893.

26. Ibid.; *Detroit Free Press,* "McGregor Michigan Survey, 1893–1894," MC-RL; Murray McGregor, Oral history interview, 51.

27. "Survey of Mission Men," March 1892–March 1894, MC-RL.

28. Ibid.

29. Ibid.

30. James Redhouse, Oral history interview, 4–6; "A Life Crisis," McGregor HHM, Report, 1902, 5–7, MC-RL.

31. Ibid.

32. Ibid.

33. George Whipple to Tracy McGregor, November 16, 1892, MC-RL.

34. The case files of the Detroit Association of Charities, ALUA.

35. *Detroit Journal,* October 20, 1894; Thomas McGregor, "Gospel for the Masses," unpublished Mss, MC-RL.

36. Ibid.

37. "Tracy McGregor to Friends," January 25, 1899, MC-RL.

38. Murray McGregor, Oral history interview, 17–19.

39. Ibid., 17; Vittorio Re, *Michigan's Italian Community: A Historical Perspective* (Detroit: Wayne State University Press, 1981), 42–43; McGregor HHM, Annual Report, 1892, 18, MC-RL.

40. *Detroit Free Press,* October 8, 1905; Murray McGregor, Oral history interview, 16–18.

41. Pendleton served at the mission for thirty-five years.

42. Murray McGregor, Oral history interview, 78–81; McGregor Institute, Annual Report, 1927, 7, MC-RL.

43. Murray McGregor, Oral history interview, 78–81.

44. Murray McGregor, Oral history interview, 43–44; Jean Petrone, *Hudson's Hub of America's Heartland* (West Bloomfield, MI: Altverger and Mandel, 1991); "Eulogy" of Joseph L. Hudson, Tracy McGregor diary, 1907.

45. Murray McGregor, Oral history interview, 43–49; John Howarth, "J. L. Hudson, An Appreciation," *Detroit Saturday Night,* July 20, 1912.

46. *Detroit Free Press,* August 18, 1907; *Detroit News,* April 1, 1903; May 15, 1913; *Detroit Times,* January 2, 1904.

47. Clarence Burton, *The City of Detroit, Michigan, 1701–1922,* vol. 3. (Detroit: S. J. Clarke, 1922), 628; *Detroit Free Press,* August 8, 1897; *Detroit Journal,* March 4, 1912; *Detroit News-Tribune,* February 13, 1898.

48. Lem W. Bowen, "Obituary," September 9, 1925, BHC; *Detroit Free Press,* August 8, 1907.

49. Burton, *City of Detroit,* 4:784–88.

50. McGregor HHM, Report, 1898, MC-RL; Tracy McGregor to "Dear Friends," January 22, 1900, MC-RL.

51. Murray McGregor, Oral history interview, 42; McGregor Institute, Annual Report, 1915, MC-RL; "Brush Street Building," October 19, 1901, MC-RL.

52. Ibid.; McGregor HHM, Report, 1899, MC-RL. McGregor kept a detailed journal listing the contributions for the new mission building. See also "Address of Mr. Hudson," June 9, 1901, for an account of the fund-raising campaign; and Sidney T. Miller, "The McGregor Mission in Detroit," MC-RL.

53. For detailed accounts of the purchasing, planning, and construction of the Brush Street building, see McGregor Mission, Minutes, June 15, September 12, October 19, 26, November 7, December 4, 1899; January 3, February 7, March 15, April 25, May 3, 8, June 21, July 23, October 1, 1900; January 12, 1901; McGregor HHM, Report, 1902, 4, MC-RL.

54. Ibid.

55. Murray McGregor, Oral history interview, 77.

56. *Detroit Free Press,* June 10, 1891; "Mr. Hudson's address," June 9, 1901, MC-RL.

57. Ibid.; McGregor Mission, Minutes, May 24, 1901.

58. McGregor Mission, *The Year 1900 at The McGregor Mission,* MC-RL.

59. *Detroit Free Press,* October 8, 1905.

60. Ibid.

61. McGregor Mission, "Statement for the Year 1904"; Murray McGregor, Oral history interview, 74; McGregor Mission, Minutes, February 14, 1901, all in MC-RL.

62. McGregor Institute, "Statement for the Year 1911," MC-RL.

63. Ibid.

64. Ibid.

65. McGregor Institute, Annual Report, 1915, 8, MC-RL.

66. Walter E. Kruesi, *Report on Unemployment in the Winter of 1914–1915: In Detroit and Measure of Relief* (1915), 8, MC-RL.

67. McGregor Institute, "25th Anniversary," February 1916, MC-RL.

68. Ibid.

69. Ibid.

70. Ibid.

CHAPTER 5

1. The McGregor Institute "Monthly Newsletter" noted that although Murray McGregor was appointed superintendent, Tracy McGregor "will not in any way drop out as managing Trustee" and that "he will plan and advise as heretofore." November 1915, MC-RL.

2. Tracy McGregor's financial records document the loans and gifts to former mission men. See MC-RL.

3. Murray McGregor, Oral history interview, 47.

4. Ibid.; McGregor Institute, Annual Report, 1919, 4, MC-RL.

5. James Norton, "Persons and Problems of Many Years Ago," February 1968, 39–41, Prismatic Club Archives, ALUA.

6. McGregor Institute, Annual Report, 1916, MC-RL.

7. Ibid.

8. "An Introduction to 20,000 Institute Men," McGregor Institute, Annual Report, 1914, 2–15, MC-RL.

9. McGregor gave a detailed account of the life of Ofstendal in *The Story of A Man Without A Home* (Detroit: McGregor Institute, 1910).

10. Ibid., 27–28.

11. Ibid., 31.

12. Tracy McGregor, *Twenty Thousand Men (*Detroit: McGregor Institute, 1916), facsimile edition was published in 1962. A similar analysis of the men of the McGregor mission appeared in its annual report for 1914.

13. Ibid., 3.

14. Ibid.

15. Ibid., 7–8.

16. Ibid., 11–12.

17. Ibid., 13–15.

18. Ibid., 15–16.

19. Ibid., 15–29.

20. McGregor Institute, "Monthly Newsletter," MC-RL.

21. McGregor Institute, "Monthly Newsletter," May 1916, MC-RL.

22. Tracy McGregor diary, May 27, 1907.

23. "The Fellowship Club Season, 1908–9," MC-RL.

24. Tracy McGregor diary, October 27, 1912; and Tracy McGregor, "J. L. Hudson," MC-RL.

25. McGregor Institute, "Monthly Newsletter," October 1917, MC-RL.

26. McGregor Institute, "Monthly Newsletter," October 1917 and November 1, 1917.

27. The minute book of the Brotherhood from May 11, 1912, to April 24, 1913, describes the programs during those years. See also Tracy McGregor diary, May 27, 1907; and Tracy McGregor, "History of Mission Manuscript" [1930], all in MC-RL.

28. McGregor Mission Brotherhood, "Programme," May 2, 1910, MC-RL.

29. McGregor Institute Brotherhood, Programme, Season 1911–12. J. L. Hudson was the featured speaker at the December 4, 1911, meeting of the Brotherhood.

30. McGregor Mission, Annual Report, 1902, 2.

31. McGregor Mission Brotherhood, Minute Book, May 12, 1912, MC-RL.

32. Ibid., November 4, 1912.

33. Ibid., September 12, 1912.

CHAPTER 6

1. For biographies of Murray McGregor, Edward Carrabin, and David Scott, see McGregor Institute, Annual Report, 1915, 8; 1927, 7; 1933, 5.

2. At the annual meeting of the McGregor Institute on February 5, 1920, it was reported that "Managing Trustee Tracy McGregor was conspicuous by his absence, this being the first annual meeting in the history of the corporation that he has not been present." McGregor Institute, Annual Report, 1920.

3. *Detroit Free Press,* May 5, 1921.

4. Murray McGregor, Oral history interview, 47–48; Richards, "Tracy W. McGregor," 14.

5. McGregor Correspondence File, 1917–18, MC-RL; McGregor Institute, "Monthly Newsletter," 1917–18.

6. McGregor Institute, Annual Report, 1917, 3.
7. Ibid.
8. Ibid.
9. Murray McGregor to Tracy McGregor, June 27, 1919, MC-RL.
10. Ibid.; McGregor Institute, Annual Report, 1920.
11. Tracy McGregor, Financial journals, 1900–18, MC-RL.
12. McGregor Institute, "Monthly Newsletter," November 1916.
13. Ibid., May 1918.
14. Ibid.
15. Ibid.
16. Ibid.; *Detroit Free Press,* February 26, 1925.
17. Murray McGregor, Oral history interview, 49–50.
18. McGregor Institute, Annual Report, 1918, 4.
19. Ibid.
20. Ibid.
21. Philip P. Mason, *Rum Running and the Roaring Twenties* (Detroit: Wayne State University Press, 1995).
22. Ibid.; Frank and Arthur Woodford, *All Our Yesterdays* (Detroit: Wayne State University Press, 1969), 301–8.
23. James Couzens Papers, Box 136, Manuscripts Division, Library of Congress, Washington, DC.
24. Tracy W. McGregor, "The Effects of Prohibition on Homeless Men," speech given over Radio CKOK, October 11, 1932, MC-RL.
25. Ibid.
26. Ibid.
27. Ibid.
28. Ibid.
29. Ibid.
30. Ibid.
31. McGregor Institute, "Monthly Newsletter," March 20, 1920.
32. McGregor Institute, Annual Report, 1921.
33. Ibid.
34. Ibid.
35. Ibid.
36. Ibid.
37. McGregor Institute, Annual Report, 1928.
38. "Review of Forty Years," 4–6.
39. *Detroit Daily,* November 3, 4, 1930; *Detroit Saturday Night,* November 8, 1930.
40. *Detroit Evening News,* November 6, 1930.
41. Ibid.; *Detroit News,* November 6, 1930; Detroit Common Council, *Journal,* November 5, 1930, 2856–57.
42. Henry F. Vaughan to R. W. Reading, November 5, 1930. Printed in *Detroit Legal News,* November 6, 1930.

43. *Detroit Free Press*, November 6, 1930.
44. *Detroit News*, November 6, 1930.
45. *Detroit Evening Times*. November 6, 1930.
46. McGregor Institute, Annual Report, 1930, 9; 1933, 7.
47. "The Year 1932 at the Institute," MC-RL.
48. Ibid.
49. Ibid.
50. Ibid.
51. Detroit Rescue Mission, First Annual Report, 1910, MC-RL.
52. Sidney Fine, *Frank Murphy: Detroit Years* (Ann Arbor: University of Michigan Press, 1975), 273–76.
53. Ibid., 276–77.
54. Ibid., 280–81; Daniel M. Robbins "Eloise, the Finest Poorhouse in the World," *Michigan Christian Advocate* (February 15, 1934), 9.
55. Tracy McGregor to Murray McGregor, June 24, 1935, MC-RL.
56. *Detroit Times*, September 28, 1935.
57. McGregor Institute, Annual Report, 1932.
58. McGregor Institute, Annual Report, 1927.
59. Ibid.
60. Ibid.
61. Tracy McGregor to Murray McGregor, June 24, 1935, MC-RL.
62. Ibid.
63. Ibid.
64. Ibid.
65. *Detroit News*, July 27, 1935.
66. *Detroit Times*, July 7, 1935.
67. *Detroit News*, July 24, 1935.
68. *Detroit News*, March 11, 1938.
69. Murray McGregor to McGregor Institute Trustees, 1938, MC-RL.
70. Murray McGregor to McGregor Institute Trustees, March 11, 1938, MC-RL.
71. Murray McGregor to McGregor Institute Trustees, 1938, MC-RL.

CHAPTER 7

1. James H. Norton, "Persons and Problems of Many Years Ago," February 1968, 10–12, Prismatic Club Archives, ALUA. The records of the Associated Charities of Detroit, including the extensive case files, are in the Archives of Labor and Urban Affairs at Wayne State University, Detroit. "General Hints and Suggestions to Visitors of the ACD," *Proceedings of the Second Annual Meeting* (Detroit: n.p., 1882), 33–35, ALUA; Oliver Zunz, *The Changing Face of Inequality: Urbanization, Industrial Development, and Immigrants in Detroit, 1880–1920* (Chicago: University of Chicago Press, 1982), 263–68; see also the annual reports of the board of trustees of the Associated Charities of Detroit, ALUA.
2. McGregor financial records, MC-RL.

3. "A New Home for Children: Mrs. McGregor's Infant Charity," *Detroit Journal*, April 14, 1905; "A Detroit Woman's Philanthropy," *Detroit Free Press*, February 28, 1909.

4. "A Detroit Woman's Philanthropy."

5. Ibid.

6. John Gruesel, "Tracy McGregor, Practical Philanthropist," *Detroit Free Press*, October 8, 1905.

7. "A Detroit Woman's Philanthropy."

8. Associated Charities of Detroit, Report, 1913–16, ALUA.

9. "Detroit's Lady Bountiful," *Detroit News-Tribune*, November 9, 1902.

10. Ibid.

11. Ibid.

12. "A Detroit Woman's Philanthropy."

13. Zunz, *Changing Face of Inequality*, 286–89.

14. Walter Kruesi, *Report on Unemployment in the Winter of 1914–1915 in Detroit, and the Institutions and Measures of Relief* (Detroit: n.p., 1915), 20–26.

15. Alfred Crosby, *America's Forgotten Pandemic: The Influenza of 1918* (Cambridge: Cambridge University Press, 1989); Gina Kolata, *Flu: The Story of the Great Influenza Pandemic of 1918 and the Search for the Virus That Caused It* (New York: Farrar, Straus and Giroux, 1999).

16. Associated Charities of Detroit, Report, 1913–16, 3, ALUA.

17. Ibid.

18. Ibid.

19. Associated Charities of Detroit, Board of Trustees Minutes, January 1, 1914, 2, ALUA.

20. Ibid.

21. Ibid., 5.

22. Associated Charities of Detroit, Report, 1914–15, ALUA.

23. Ibid.

24. Detroit Community Fund, *Social Service Directory of Detroit*, 1917, 120–21.

25. Associated Charities of Detroit, Report, 1914–15, ALUA.

26. Associated Charities of Detroit, "Federated Clinics."

27. Associated Charities of Detroit, "Registration Bureau."

28. *Social Services Directory of Detroit*, 1917, 37; John Dancy, *Sand against the Wind: The Memories of John Dancy* (Detroit: Wayne State University Press, 1966); Zunz, *Changing Face of Inequality*, 319–23; Associated Charities of Detroit, Report, 1915, 1916, 1917, ALUA.

29. "Prominent Business Men Promise to Work for Approaching Red Cross Campaign; City Will Cooperate," *Detroiter*, April 1917, 4; James Norton, "A History of the Detroit Community Fund and the Council of Social Agencies of Metropolitan Detroit" (master's thesis, University of Michigan), 1940, 32–33.

30. Biographical data on William Norton can be found in the William J. Norton Collection at the Bentley Library, Box 1, University of Michigan, Ann Arbor; Norton, "History of the Detroit Community Fund," 32–33.

31. John Ehrlich, "William J. Norton," Prismatic Club Archives, ALUA.

32. *Detroiter,* March 1937, 2–3.

33. Associated Charities of Detroit, Executive Committee Minutes, May 7, 1917, ALUA.

34. Associated Charities of Detroit, Executive Committee Minutes, October 17, 1917.

35. Detroit Community Fund, The First Sixty Years (Detroit, 1917), 2.

36. Ibid.; Associated Charities of Detroit, Minutes of Trustees, December 13, 1917, 1–4, ALUA.

37. Associated Charities of Detroit, Minutes of Trustees, December 13, 1917, 4.

38. Ibid.

39. Detroit Patriotic Fund, Board of Directors, Minutes, February 6, 1918, 11, MC-RL; Detroiter, May 28, 1918, 1.

40. Ibid.

41. The Detroit Community Union and the Patriotic Fund, which became the Detroit Community Fund in 1921, merged in 1932 into the Council of Social Agencies. In 1949, the United Foundation was established as an independent agency to raise funds for community service organizations. The Council of Social Agencies and the Community Chest merged in 1951 to become the United Community Services of Metropolitan Detroit, which in turn merged with the United Foundation to become the United Way in 1995.

42. James Norton, History of the Detroit Community Fund, and the Council of Social Agencies of Metropolitan Detroit, 1917–1938" (Master's thesis, University of Michigan, 1940), 32–38.

43. Ibid., 71.

44. Ibid., 57; Detroit Community Fund, Board of Directors, Minutes, October 17, 1921.

45. Norton, "History of the Detroit Community Fund," 57.

46. *Detroit News,* January 8, 1939.

47. Hulbert, *Tracy W. McGregor,* 22–23.

48. Ibid.

49. *Detroit News,* October 18, 1925; William Norton, "Tracy McGregor Dedication Address," May 10, 1955, MC-RL; Tracy McGregor diary, October 1, 1925; *Detroit Free Press,* June 19, 1925; Wayne County Training School, Second Annual Report, July 1, 1928, MC-RL.

50. Hulbert, *Tracy W. McGregor,* 23.

51. McGregor Fund, Minutes, December 6, 1931.

52. Richards, "Tracy W. McGregor," 12; Detroit Bureau of Governmental Research, *The Detroit House of Correction* (Detroit: Council, 1934); *Detroit News,* May 6, 1936, November 18, 2001.

53. Fred Butzel to Hugh Montgomerie, April 23, 1921, MC-RL.

54. Hulbert, *Tracy W. McGregor,* 25; Norton, "Tracy McGregor Dedication Address."

55. Hulbert, *Tracy W. McGregor,* 26.

56. Tracy McGregor diary, August 5, 1930.

57. Ibid., September 12, 1925. Kevin Boyle, *Arc of Justice: A Saga of Race, Civil Rights, and Murder in the Jazz Age* (New York: Henry Holt & Co., 2004), 140–43.

58. George Stark, "Tracy McGregor," *Detroit News,* May 6, 1936. In 1908 Katherine Whitney endowed a home for orphaned boys at the Good Will Charitable facility in Hinkley, Maine. It was named as a memorial to her father, David Whitney. Tracy and Katherine continued to give money for the upkeep of the facility. *Good Will Record,* April 1909.

59. See McGregor, Financial journals.

CHAPTER 8

1. Matthew Josephen, "Dynamic Detroit," *Harper's,* December 30, 1930, reproduced in Melvin G. Holli, *Detroit* (New York: Franklin Watts, 1976), 117–22; Raymond Fragnoli, "Progressive Coalitions and Municipal Reforms," *Detroit in Perspective* 4 (Spring 1980): 33; Zunz, *Changing Face of Inequality*, 287.

2. For an account of the political life of Detroit in the 1890s, see Melvin Holli, *Reform in Detroit: Hazen S. Pingree and Urban Politics* (New York: Oxford University Press, 1969); Fragnoli, "Progressive Coalitions."

3. Holli, *Reform in Detroit*; William P. Lovett, *Detroit Rules Itself* (Boston: Garland, 1930), 61–62.

4. Lovett, *Detroit Rules Itself.*

5. Holli, *Reform in Detroit,* 3–10.

6. Ibid., 110–111.

7. Ibid., 81–82.

8. Hazen Pingree, "Mayor Pingree Reforms in Detroit," *Outlook* 55 (February 6, 1897), 437–42, cited in Melvin G. Holli, *Detroit* (New York: Franklin Watts, 1976), 110–16.

9. John Davis to Clarence Burton, February 27, 1902, Clarence Burton Papers, BHC; Lovett, *Detroit Rules Itself,* 53; Henry Leland, *Master of Precision* (Detroit: Wayne State University Press, 1966), 156; "A Biographical Sketch of Joseph Lothian Hudson," *Detroit Free Press,* October 17, 1946; Fragnoli, "Progressive Reforms," 18–20.

10. Lovett, *Detroit Rules Itself,* 71–72.

11. Ibid.

12. Henry Leland, *Master of Precision,* 155–156; Lovett, *Detroit Rules Itself,* 72–73; Fragnoli, "Progressive Reforms," 20.

13. Lovett, *Detroit Rules Itself,* 72–73, 78–79; The archives of the Citizens League (formerly the Civic Uplift League) are in the Burton Historical Collections of the Detroit Public Library.

14. Leland, *Master of Precision,* 160–61.

15. Lovett, *Detroit Rules Itself,* 23, 61, 85; *Civic Search Light* 3 (November 1916).

16. Fragnoli, "Progressive Reforms," 96; Lovett, *Detroit Rules Itself,* 93.

17. Woodford and Woodford, *All Our Yesterdays,* 279–80; *Civic Searchlight* 1 (October 1913).

18. *Civic Search Light* 6 (January 1919); 9 (May 1922); Fragnoli, "Progressive Reforms," 192–95; Lovett, *Detroit Rules Itself,* 154–55, 211; Pliny Marsh, Oral history interview, 24–25, W. J. Norton Collection, Bentley Library.

19. Richards, "Tracy W. McGregor," 14; Murray McGregor, Oral history interview, 47–48.

20. The signed governor's appointment, December 18, 1900, is in MC-RL.

21. Hulbert, *Tracy W. McGregor,* 11; Provident Loan Society File, MC-RL; *Detroit City Directory,* 1913, BHC, State Library of Michigan and other research libraries.

22. Norton, "Tracy McGregor Dedication Address."

23. George Stark, "Tracy McGregor," *Detroit News,* May 4, 1936; Lovett, *Detroit Rules Itself,* 108.

24. "McGregor gave substantial financial support to the Citizens League from 1912 to 1916." McGregor, Financial journals.

25. Tracy McGregor "Speech before Michigan Senate," March 1911, MC-RL; Richards, "Tracy W. McGregor," 12

26. Richards, "Tracy W. McGregor."

CHAPTER 9

1. See Thursday Noon Group file, MC-RL. According to William Norton, McGregor conceived the idea for the Thursday Noon Group around 1910. Norton, "Tracy McGregor Dedication Address."

2. Tracy McGregor, "Purposes of Thursday Noon Group," 1913, Thursday Noon Group file, MC-RL.

3. Lovett, *Detroit Rules Itself,* 69.

4. McGregor, Journal, 1911–1913, January 18, 1913, MC-RL.

5. Thursday Noon Group file, MC-RL.

6. James Ingles, *A Sketch of My Life, for the Benefit of My Grandchildren* (Detroit: n.p., 1947), 28–29.

7. "Biography in Brief: Judge Henry S. Hulbert," *Detroit Free Press,* April 13, 1941; *Detroit Free Press,* June 5, 1959.

8. Albert N. Marquis, ed., *The Book of Detroiters* (Chicago: A. N. Marquis, 1914), 90.

9. Ibid.

10. Ingles, *Sketch of My Life*; Marquis, *Book of Detroiters.*

11. Ibid.; Burton, *City of Detroit,* 4:408–12.

12. Ibid.

13. For brief biographical accounts of Francis McMath, Edwin Denby, Clarence Lightener, and James Holden, see *Who's Who in the Midwest* (Chicago: A. N. Marquis, 1918); Marquis, *Book of Detroiters;* and *Michigan and Bar of Michigan* (Detroit: Bench and Bar, 1918).

14. Detroit Citizens League file, Series 1, Box 3, BHC.

15. Tracy McGregor to Pliny Marsh, March 18–May 20, 1914, Detroit Citizens League file, Series 1, Box 2, BHC.

16. Murray McGregor, Oral history interview, 27–28; Norton, "Tracy McGregor Dedication Address"; Ingles, *Sketch of My Life,* 29–30; Thursday Noon Group Papers, MC-RL.

17. Richards, "Tracy W. McGregor"; Hulbert, *Tracy W. McGregor,* 13; Detroit Citizens League, Minute Book, March 14, 1913, Box 1, BHC; Katherine M. Whitney, *A State Hospital School for Epileptic Children* (Michigan, 1944), reprinted from *Journal of Exceptional Children* 10, no. 7 (April 1944): 173–79, and vol. 11 (October 1944): 7–11; "Michigan Farm Colony for Epileptics at Wahjamega," *Biennial Report of Board of Control and officers of Michigan Farm Colony for Epileptics at Wahjamega* (Lansing, MI: Wynkoop, Hollenbeck, Crawford, 1916).

18. Michigan, *Public Acts 1915,* Public Act 173.

19. Edith Jacot, *Development and Demise of an Institution for the Treatment of Epileptics* (March 1974), 10, Record Group 79-11 B12 F2, State Archives of Michigan.

20. Zunz, *Changing Face of Inequality,* 310; Holli, *Detroit,* 122; *Detroiter,* January 11, 1915; December 21, 1915.

21. Kruesi, *Report on Unemployment.*

22. Walter Kruesi, *Who Was Who in America, 1974–1976* (Chicago: A. N. Marquis Co., 1976), 234.

23. Kruesi, *Report on Unemployed,* 30.

24. Ibid., 7–8.

25. Ibid., 9.

26. Ibid., 9–10.

27. Ibid., 8.

28. Ibid., 9.

29. Ibid.

30. Ibid., 10–11.

31. Zunz, *Changing Face of Inequality,* 152–76; Richards, "Tracy W. McGregor," 12; "Members Vote to Aid Housing Situation," *Detroiter,* August 14, 1920.

32. Tracy McGregor diary, January 8, 1912.

33. *Detroiter,* September 13, 1915).

34. Richards, "Tracy W. McGregor"; Zunz, *Changing Face of Inequality,* 156–57, 326; Hulbert, *Tracy W. McGregor,* 20

35. Richards, "Tracy W. McGregor."

36. The Detroit Housing Association file includes the list of contributors to Todd's salary. Among the major contributors in addition to McGregor were Alexis Angell, Arthur McGraw, Henry Stevens, Willard Pope, Henry Leland, James Holden, David C. Whitney, and Truman Newberry. Detroit Housing Association file, MC-RL.

37. *Detroit News,* December 12, 30, 1916. The plan for the hotel is in the Detroit Housing file, MC-RL.

38. Men's Hotel Company, Financial statements, 1919–21, MC-RL.

39. Men's Hotel file, MC-RL.

40. Gregory Mason, "Americans First: How the People of Detroit Are Making Americans of Foreigners," *New Outlook,* September 27, 1916, 193–96, 200–201; Holli, *Detroit,* 120.

41. Zunz, *Changing Face of Inequality,* 312–14; Cynthia Korolov, "Help the Other Fellow: Henry Ford and the Ford English School" (master's thesis, Wayne State University, 2002), 20.

42. Lovett, *Detroit Rules Itself,* 69; "Americanization and the Work of Detroit Public Evening Schools," *Detroiter,* November 24, 1919; *Detroiter,* September 13, 20, 1915; May 22, June 5, August 16, 27, September 17, 1916.

43. Holli, *Reform in Detroit,* 27–29.

44. Hulbert, *Tracy W. McGregor,* 20; Richards, "Tracy W. McGregor."

45. Lovett, *Detroit Rules Itself,* 20–21; Richards, "Tracy W. McGregor"; *Civic Search Light* 4 (February 1917).

46. Lovett, *Detroit Rules Itself,* 108.

47. Richards, "Tracy W. McGregor"; Thursday Noon Group, Account Book, 1916–24, 162, MC-RL; Detroit Board of Education, *Proceedings,* December 23, 1920, 267; February 24, 1921, 367; January 9, 1921, 552; July 1, 1922.

48. Thursday Noon Group, Account Book, 1916–24, MC-RL.

49. *Detroit Journal,* April 28, 29, 1915.

50. Hulbert, *Tracy W. McGregor,* 18–21; *Detroit Journal,* May 5, 6, 8, 1915.

51. "Proposed New $2,500,000 Belle Isle Bridge," *Detroiter,* June 4, 1917.

52. Hulbert, *Tracy W. McGregor,* 18–20.

53. Ibid., 20.

54. Lovett, *Detroit Rules Itself,* 23, 27–29.

55. Ibid., 51–52, 93, 108; Fragnoli, "Progressive Coalitions," 96; *Civic Search Light* (November 1916), (June 1918).

56. Lovett, *Detroit Rules Itself,* 23–24, 108.

57. Ibid., 133.

58. Fragnoli, "Progressive Coalitions," 192–95; Richards, "Tracy W. McGregor"; Lovett, *Detroit Rules Itself,* 154.

59. Marsh, Oral history interview, 24–25; Hulbert, *Tracy W. McGregor,* 17.

60. Marsh, Oral history interview, 24–25.

61. *Civic Search Light* 9 (May 1922); Fragnoli, "Progressive Coalitions," 211.

62. Hulbert, *Tracy W. McGregor,* 17.

63. Lovett, *Detroit Rules Itself,* 154.

64. Hulbert, *Tracy W. McGregor,* 16, 17.

65. Tracy McGregor diary, January 13, 18, 1913; Thursday Noon Group, Campaign Funding file, July 13, 1918, MC-RL.

66. James Couzens Papers.

67. Thursday Noon Group, "Political Endorsements," March 5, 1917, MC-RL.

68. Thursday Noon Group, "Political Endorsements," March 5, 1917; Thursday Noon Group, Account Book, 1916–24, 150, MC-RL; McGregor, Financial journal, January 6, 1916.

69. McGregor, Financial journal, July 10, 1919; W. H. Bishop to M. Hubert O'Brien, October 11, 1922, MC-RL.

70. George Stark, "Thursday Group Carries on Work Started by McGregor," *Detroit News,* May 8, 1936.

71. Marsh, Oral history interview.

72. Ingles to Joseph Crowley, March 11, 1919, MC-RL; Ingles, *Sketch of My Life,* 29–30.

73. Norton, "Tracy McGregor Dedication Address," May 10, 1955.

74. Marsh, Oral history interview.

75. Ibid.

76. Kirby White to McGregor, February 21, 1930, MC-RL.

77. Ibid.

78. McGregor to Henry S. Hulbert, February 8, 1935; McGregor to Hugo Freund, February 11, 1935, MC-RL.

79. McGregor to Hulbert, February 8, 1935, MC-RL.

80. Butzel to McGregor, December 20, 1935, MC-RL.

81. Stark, "Thursday Group."

CHAPTER 10

1. For an overview of the history of the Merrill-Palmer Institute, I am indebted to my colleague, Dr. Stanley D. Solvick. Professor Solvick has completed a yet unpublished, superb study of that institute, especially under the leadership of Edna Noble White.

2. Pauline Wilson Knapp, "All about Edna Noble White," October 1961, MPC-RL.

3. Ibid.

4. Detroit Bureau of Governmental Research, "Memorandum in Re Palmer Will to Establish A School of Motherhood and Household Arts" (March 1919).

5. Ibid.

6. Lizzie M. Palmer, W., "Last Will and Testament," May 17, 1916, MC-RL; and Merrill-Palmer Corporation, *First Annual Report,* 1920, MPC-RL.

7. Corporate Records of the Merrill-Palmer Motherhood and Home Training School, Series 1, Box 1, MPC-RL.

8. Ibid., January, 1919, Series 1, Box 1, MPC-RL.

9. George Canfield to Tracy McGregor, November 17, 1919, Series 1, Box 2, MPC-RL.

10. Detroit Bureau of Governmental Research, "Memorandum."

11. Ibid.

12. Ibid.

13. Ibid.

14. Ibid.

15. Dr. Benjamin R. Schenck to R. McClelland Brady, Extract of letter in Brady to Harry Stevens, August 13, 1918, MC-RL; Merrill-Palmer Motherhood and Home Training School, Board of Trustees, Minutes, November 25, 1918, MPC-RL [hereafter Merrill-Palmer Motherhood and Home Training School, Minutes, date].

16. Dr. Benjamin R. Schenck to R. McClelland Brady, Extract of letter in Brady to Harry Stevens, August 13, 1918, MC-RL.

17. Edna Noble White, "Notes on the Early History of the School," n.d., MC-RL; *The Merrill-Palmer School: An Account of Its First Twenty Years, 1920–1940.* (Detroit: Merrill-Palmer School, 1940).

18. White, "Notes."

19. George Canfield to Tracy McGregor, November 17, 1919, MPC-RL.

20. Merrill-Palmer Motherhood and Home Training School, Minutes, November 21, 1918.

21. Ibid., May 19, June 5, 1919.

22. Ibid., December 30, 1918.

23. Ibid., December 23, 1918; Henrietta Calvin to Tracy McGregor, January 13, 1919, MPC-RL.

24. Henrietta Calvin to Tracy McGregor, January 13, 1919, MPC-RL.

25. Knapp, "All about Edna Noble White."

26. Ibid.

27. Ibid.; White, "Notes"; Merrill-Palmer Motherhood and Home Training School, Minutes, September 25, October 23, November 10, 1919.

28. Knapp, "All about Edna Noble White," 4–5.

29. Merrill-Palmer Corporation, First Annual Report, 1920, MPC-RL.

30. Ibid., 4–5.

31. Ibid., 8.

32. Ibid.

33. Ibid.

34. "History and Development of the Merrill-Palmer School," 1955, 2, MC-RL.

35. Ibid., 3; Merrill-Palmer Motherhood and Home Training School, Minutes, January 21, 1921.

36. "History and Development of the Merrill-Palmer School," 4.

37. Ibid., 5–6.

38. Dorothy Tyler, "Edna Noble White," 1954, 4–6, MC-RL; Knapp, "All about Edna Noble White," 4–6.

39. Merrill-Palmer Motherhood and Home Training School, Minutes, November 18, 1918.

40. "History and Development of the Merrill-Palmer School," 1.

41. Ibid., 3–4.

42. Ibid., 3; Merrill-Palmer Motherhood and Home Training School, Minutes, November 25, 1918; Merrill-Palmer Corporation, First Annual Report, 1920.

43. Merrill-Palmer Motherhood and Home Training School, Minutes, September 30, 1921.

44. Ibid.

45. Merrill-Palmer Motherhood and Home Training School, Annual Report, 1921; Twelfth Report, 1935–37.

46. Merrill-Palmer Corporation, Annual Report, 1922; Annual Reports for 1935–37; Merrill-Palmer Motherhood and Home Training School, "Minutes of Special Meeting," September 30, October 3, 7, 24, 1921.

47. At most of the meetings of the board of trustees starting in 1918, the agenda included deliberations involving the sale of Merrill properties and the reinvestment of the proceeds. See, for example, the board meetings of November 18, 25, 1918; September 29, October 27, 1919; September 20, 1920; and June 14, 1921. See also the Merrill-Palmer Financial Ledgers, MPC-RL.

48. *Detroit Historical Society Bulletin,* 1965, BHC.

49. Merrill-Palmer Motherhood and Home Training School, Minutes, March 3, 1919; July 22, 1921; November 28, 1922.

50. Sidney Miller to Tracy McGregor, June 21, 1929; Cleveland Thurber to Tracy McGregor, November 7, 1929; Henry Rosin to Tracy McGregor, December 21, 1929; Tracy McGregor to Cleveland Thurber, August 12, 1931; and John Spaulding to Merrill-Palmer Motherhood and Home Training School, February 16, 1932, MC-RL.

51. "Tracy W. McGregor, In Memoriam," Merrill-Palmer Corporation, Annual Report, 1936–37; Merrill-Palmer Motherhood and Home Training School, Minutes, June 2, 1936.

CHAPTER 11

1. See Michigan Secretary of State, Whitney Realty Company, Annual Reports, 1912, 1923, 1924, State Archives of Michigan.

2. The extensive files of the Warren Farms Land Company and the LaSalle Land Company are in MC-RL.

3. Fugate, *For the Benefit of All,* 46, 48, 50.

4. Ibid., 80.

5. "View of the Work of the McGregor Fund for the Period beginning January 1, 1932, to January 1, 1937," 2–3; and McGregor Fund, Minutes, December 21, 1925, MFA.

6. McGregor Fund, Minutes, January 16, 1929.

7. "View of Work of the McGregor Fund," 2.

8. Ibid.

9. Tracy McGregor diary, May 1, 1930.

10. "View of Work of the McGregor Fund," 2.

11. "Memorandum to K," in Tracy McGregor diary, May 1, 1930.

12. Ibid.

13. McGregor Fund, Minutes, October 8, 1934.

14. McGregor Fund, Minutes, June 20, 1932.

15. McGregor Fund, Minutes, November 10, 1932.

16. Ibid., June 20, 1932; "View of Work of the McGregor Fund," 3–4.

17. McGregor Fund, Minutes, November 10, 1932.

18. Ibid., March 2, 1933.

19. "View of Work of the McGregor Fund," 9.
20. McGregor Fund, Minutes, March 2, 1933.
21. Ibid., June 12, 1933.
22. "View of Work of the McGregor Fund," 5.
23. Ibid.
24. McGregor Fund, *Seven-Year Report, 1931–1937* (Detroit: McGregor Fund, 1937), 10–13.
25. Ibid., 13.
26. Ibid.
27. Ibid., 14.
28. Ibid., 9–10.
29. Ibid.
30. Ibid.
31. "View of Work of the McGregor Fund," 7.
32. Ibid.
33. McGregor Fund, *Seven-Year Report,* 8.
34. Ibid.
35. Ibid., 12; "View of Work of the McGregor Fund," 10.
36. Ibid.
37. Ibid.

CHAPTER 12

1. Tracy McGregor, "Books and Reading for Men of the Mission Brotherhood," MC-RL.
2. Ibid.
3. Ibid.
4. Tracy McGregor diary, December 23, 1921–January 19, 1922.
5. *Detroit News,* March 13, 1927.
6. *Highland Parker,* March 18, 1926, 7.
7. Marsh, Oral history interview.
8. Ibid.
9. Ibid.
10. Ibid.
11. "Copy of Deed Executed between Katherine McGregor and the City of Highland Park for the Library Property," MC-RL.
12. *Detroit News,* October 18, 1925; Norton, "Tracy McGregor Dedication Address."
13. *Highland Parker,* March 18, 1926; McGregor Public Library, "McGregor Library Dedication Program," March 5, 1926, MC-RL.
14. Ibid.
15. Marsh, Oral history interview, 12.
16. Ibid.

17. Ibid.

18. McGregor Public Library, "Dedication Program"; "Exercises: Laying of the Cornerstone, May 28, 1925," MC-RL.

19. McGregor Public Library, "Dedication Program."

20. Ibid.

21. Tracy McGregor diary, September 20, 1925; McGregor to Van Tyne, September 19, 20, 25, 1925; November 8, 1929, MC-RL.

22. McGregor to Van Tyne, September 23, 1925, Van Tyne Collection, Bentley Library, University of Michigan, Ann Arbor.

23. Adams, "Report on the College Plan of the Late Tracy W. McGregor," 1936, AHA Archives, Manuscript Collection, Library of Congress, Washington, DC.

24. Ibid.

25. McGregor to William Hammond, April 21, 1932, MC-RL.

26. Tracy McGregor diary, March 19, 1931; April 19, December 1932.

27. Ibid., June 23, 1930.

28. McGregor to Clements, January 23, 1933, Clements Library, University of Michigan, Ann Arbor.

29. Clements to McGregor, March 27, 1933, Clements Library, University of Michigan, Ann Arbor.

30. McGregor to Clements, April 14, 1933, Clements Library, University of Michigan, Ann Arbor.

31. Lawrence Wroth to McGregor, February 4, 1932, MC-RL.

32. Meyer to McGregor, March 9, 1931, MC-RL.

33. McGregor to Karpinski, March 2, 1932, McGregor Collection, Clements Library Archives, Bentley Library, University of Michigan, Ann Arbor; Tracy McGregor diary, December 27, 1929.

34. McGregor's diary entries provide detailed information on his visits to various bookstores and dealers.

35. Wyman Parker, *Henry Stevens of Vermont: An American Rare Book Dealer in London, 1845–1886* (Amsterdam: Nico Israel, 1963), 306.

36. Henry Stevens to McGregor, August 15, 1929, MC-RL.

37. In 1932 more than two hundred letters, telegrams, and cables passed between McGregor and Stevens and Stiles. See Book file, MC-RL.

38. John Dann, *One Hundred and One Treasures* (Ann Arbor: University of Michigan, 1998), 26.

39. Henry Stevens to McGregor, November 27, 1931, MC-RL.

40. Harper to McGregor, December 16, 1933, MC-RL.

41. Adams to McGregor, March 7, 1933, MC-RL.

42. L. Wroth to McGregor, April 28, 1931, MC-RL.

43. Lawrence Martin to McGregor, April 21, 1933; Andrew Long to McGregor, August 2, 1933; and H. M. Lydenberg to McGregor, April 27, 1933, all in MC-RL.

44. See Book file, 1930–34, MC-RL.

45. Douglas Parsonage to McGregor, November 24, 1931, MC-RL. Parsonage was Harper's assistant manager.

46. Harper to McGregor, July 22, 1932; May 26, 1933, MC-RL.

47. Harper to McGregor, July 25, 1932.

48. Ibid.

49. *De Ora Antartica Per Regem Portugallic Pridem Muenta* (Strasburg, Mathiam: Hupsuss, 1503).

50. William Runge, "The Tracy McGregor Library and Its Founder," University of Virginia *Newsletter* 39 (July 15, 1963), 42.

51. Ibid.

52. John Smith, *The True Relation of Such Occurances and Accidents of Noate as Hath Hapned in Virginia Since the First Planting of That Colony* (London, 1608).

53. See Book file, MC-RL.

54. William G. Mather to Henry S. Hulbert, February 26, 1938, Hulbert file, MC-RL.

55. Runge, "Tracy McGregor Library," 44.

56. McGregor to Slagle, November 8, 1934, MC-RL.

57. June 3, 1935, MC-RL.

58. June 4, 1935, MC-RL.

59. Slagle to Kenneth Moore, October 5, 1936, MC-RL.

60. Margaret Maxwell, *Shaping a Library: William L. Clements as Collector* (Amsterdam: Nico Israel, 1973), 230.

61. Ibid., 254.

62. Ibid., 337; William Clements to Albert Kahn, December 9, 1931, Clements Library Archives, Bentley Library, University of Michigan, Ann Arbor.

63. *Dictionary of American Biography,* Supplement, 21, 181.

64. Adams to W. W. Bishop, September 5, 1934, Clements Library Archives, Bentley Library, University of Michigan, Ann Arbor; Maxwell, *Shaping a Library,* 343n3.

65. Maxwell, *Shaping a Library,* 338.

66. Clements Library, Committee of Management, Minutes November 13, 1934, Clements Library Archives [hereafter Committee of Management, Minutes, date].

67. Ibid., 2.

68. McGregor Fund, "Minutes," November 11, 1934.

69. McGregor to Alexander Ruthven, February 25, 1935, MC-RL.

70. McGregor Fund, *Seven-Year Report,* 8.

71. Ruthven to McGregor, January 2, February 23, 1935, MC-RL.

72. Ruthven to McGregor, March 1, 1935, MC-RL.

73. Committee of Management, Minutes, November 1935.

74. Renville Wheat to McGregor, February 17, 1936, MC-RL.

75. McGregor to Adams, February 29, 1936. MC-RL.

76. Maxwell, *Shaping a Library,* 339; McGregor Fund, Minutes, December 22, 1936; March 31, 1937. University of Michigan, Board of Regents, *Proceedings,* March 26, 1937, 189–92.

CHAPTER 13

1. *The McGregor Plan for the Encouragement of Book Collecting by American College Libraries* (Washington, DC: American Historical Association, 1937).

2. Ibid.; Adams, "Report on the College Plan," 3–4.

3. Adams, "Report on the College Plan," 4, 9–11.

4. Randolph Adams, "Librarians as Enemies of Books," *Library Quarterly* 7 (July 1937): 317–31.

5. Adams, "Report on the College Plan."

6. McGregor to Conyers Read, October 29, 1934; and McGregor to Dexter Perkins, January 8, 1934, American Historical Association Collection, Manuscripts Division, Library of Congress, Washington, DC [hereafter cited as AHA Collection]. See also AHA File on McGregor Plan.

7. McGregor Fund, Minutes, June 12, 1933; June 5, November 14, 1934.

8. American Historical Association, "Report of Committee on Americana for College Libraries," 1935, AHA Collection.

9. Ibid., 3.

10. Ibid.

11. Ibid.

12. Adams to Trustees of the McGregor Fund, June 10, 1937, AHA Collection.

13. *McGregor Plan*, 13.

14. American Historical Association, Committee on Americana for College Libraries, Minutes, May 17, 1933, 2, AHA Collection.

15. Ibid., May 13, 1933; September 27, December 23, 1934; December 22, 1936; March 15, 1937.

16. Adams, "Report on the College Plan," Appendix B.

17. Ibid., Appendix A.

18. American Historical Association, Committee on Americana for College Libraries, Minutes, June 1936, AHA Collection.

19. Conyers Read to Mildred White, June 30, 1937, MC-RL.

20. Adams to McGregor Fund Trustees, June 10, November 3, 1937, MC-RL.

21. Adams to AHA Committee, January 18, 1945, AHA Collection.

22. Ibid.

23. Adams, "Report on the College Plan," 10.

24. Ibid., 14–15.

CHAPTER 14

1. Randolph Adams to J. Franklin Jameson, May 20, 1936, AHA Collection.

2. Ibid.

3. Jameson to Wheat, July 2, 1936, MC-RL.

4. Clemens to Slagle, September 11, 1936; McGregor to Clemens, March 18, 1936, MC-RL.

5. Ibid.
6. Slagle to Wheat, September 16, 1936, MC-RL.
7. Ibid.
8. Harry Clemens to Henry Hulbert, September 4, 1936, MC-RL.
9. Thurber to Henry Hulbert, October 12, 1937, MC-RL.
10. Wheat to Hulbert, November 11, 1937, MC-RL.
11. Adams to J. Franklin Jameson, May 20, 1936, AHA Collection; Clarence Brigham to Renville Wheat, April 28, 1928, MC-RL. The McGregor Fund gave five thousand dollars to the American Antiquarian Society in 1936 for a publication on the works of Cotton Mather. McGregor Fund, Minutes, June 23, 1936.
12. Henry Hulbert to Conyers Read, September 23, 1937; and Read to Hulbert, September 25, 1937, AHA Collection.
13. Jameson to Hulbert, September 25, 1937, AHA Collection.
14. Read to Hulbert, September 25, 1937, MC-RL.
15. J. Newcomb to Henry Hulbert, September 13, 1937, MC-RL.
16. McGregor Fund, Minutes, June 14, 1937.
17. William G. Mather to Hulbert, February 26, 1938, MC-RL.
18. McGregor Fund, Minutes, June 14, 1937.
19. Ibid., January 25, 1938.
20. McGregor Fund, Minutes, March 18, 1938. See also J. Newcomb to Hulbert, February 28, 1938, March 31, May 6, May 11, 1938, MC-RL.
21. McGregor Fund, Minutes, March 18, 1938.
22. Renville Wheat to Clarence Brigham, May 10, 1938, MC-RL.
23. McGregor Fund, Minutes, April 20, May 16, October 13, December 16, 1938.
24. McGregor Fund, Minutes, December 16, 1938.
25. Ibid., September 22, 1938.
26. University of Virginia, *Alumni News* 27 (May 1939): 162.
27. Hulbert's remarks were published in a separate booklet. See *Tracy W. McGregor.*
28. McGregor Fund, Minutes, June 17, October 13, 1938; "Dropout Leaves a Literary Legacy," *Book Marks,* June 14, 1940. In 1940 the trustees purchased from Pewabic Pottery a selection of its tiles for installation in the McGregor Room of the Alderman Library. Mary Chase Stratton to Henry Hulbert, June 19, 1940, MC-RL.

EPILOGUE

1. Katherine McGregor to Murray and Jessie McGregor, April 28, 1936, MC-RL.
2. Ibid.
3. Ibid.
4. Tracy wrote in September 1929, "'K' is running down in health . . . and her burdens are too much for her." Tracy McGregor diary, September 16, 1929.
5. Henry S. Hulbert, "Memorandum, 1938," MC-RL.
6. Tracy and Katherine McGregor constantly discussed their plans to give financial support to national and local charitable institutions. In addition to the McGregor Fund,

they both had private financial resources that they used for their favorite charities and humanitarian projects.

7. See correspondence relating to Katherine McGregor's health in the Henry Hulbert and Murray McGregor files in MC-RL.

8. McGregor Fund, Minutes, June 20, 1932.

9. White and Bowen died before McGregor in 1933 and 1935, respectively. Moore had worked very closely with McGregor on his business affairs and had managed the LaSalle and Warren farms ventures.

10. In 1931 McGregor gave financial assistance to Murray McGregor and George Brown for the mortgages on their homes. Mildred R. White to Renville Wheat, July 9, 1937; and McGregor Will, Section II, 5, MC-RL.

11. McGregor Will, Section II, MC-RL [hereafter cited McGregor Will, followed by section number].

12. Ibid.

13. Ibid., Section V.

14. Ibid.

15. Ibid., Section III.

16. McGregor Fund, Minutes, November 10, 30, December 1, 1932; June 16, 1933; October 8, 1934.

17. McGregor Will, Section IV. McGregor excluded from the gift "any books bequested to my wife."

18. Kathryn Slagle to Kenneth Moore, July 28, 1936, MC-RL.

19. K. Moore to Katherine McGregor, August 2, 1937, MC-RL.

20. "Contents of Large Storage Box, Turned over by Miss Slagle," December 12, 1936, MC-RL.

21. Ibid.

22. Mildred White to Henry Hulbert, March 3, 1942, MC-RL.

23. McGregor Fund, *Seven-Year Report,* 16.

24. McGregor Fund, Minutes, May 9, 11, 27, 1936.

25. Ibid., May 11, 27, 1936.

26. Mildred White to Henry Hulbert, Renville Wheat, Kenneth Moore, January 31, 1927, MC-RL.

27. Ibid.

28. McGregor Fund, *Seven-Year Report,* 6.

29. Ibid., 7.

30. Ibid.

31. Ibid., 8–9.

32. Ibid., 8–10.

33. Ibid., 10.

34. Ibid.; McGregor Fund, *Ten Year Report, 1940–1949* (Detroit: McGregor Fund, 1950), 7–8.

35. McGregor Fund, *Seven-Year Report,* 10–12.

36. Ibid., 13–14.

37. Ibid.; McGregor Fund, *Report for 1938–39,* 8.

38. McGregor Fund, *Report for 1931–37,* 14–15.

39. McGregor Fund, Minutes, June 30, 1937.

40. Slagle to Kenneth Moore, July 28, 1936, MC-RL.

41. Ibid.

42. McGregor Fund, *Seven-Year Report,* 12.

43. McGregor Fund, Minutes, May 16, 1938; March 31, 1939; Internal Revenue Agent George E. Neal to McGregor Fund, March 25, 1938, MC-RL. See also IRS file, MC-RL.

44. McGregor Fund, *Ten-Year Report,* 5.

45. McGregor Fund, *Seven-Year Report,* 6.

46. Renville Wheat to Conyers Read, February 2, 1937, MC-RL.

47. McGregor Fund, Minutes, December 22, 1936; June 14, 1937; June 30, 1938, September 14, 1953.

48. Mildred White to Henry Hulbert, March 3, 1942, MC-RL.

49. McGregor Fund, Minutes, March 10, November 10, 1952; April 13, 1953. The fund also arranged for a second bas-relief of McGregor to be placed in the McGregor Room of the Alderman Library at the University of Virginia.

50. Mildred White to Henry Hulbert, March 3, 1942, MC-RL.

51. Mildred White to Murray McGregor, December 3, 1954, MC-RL.

52. Mildred White to "Friends of Tracy and Katherine McGregor, deceased," December 1, 1954, MC-RL.

53. Mildred White to Murray McGregor, December 3, 1954, MC-RL.

54. Ibid.

55. Ibid.

56. Mildred White to "Friends of Tracy and Katherine McGregor, deceased," December 1, 1954, MC-RL.

57. Mildred White to Murray McGregor, December 3, 1954, MC-RL.

58. McGregor Fund, Minutes, March 8, April 12, June 14, 1954. The tapes of the interviews with Murray McGregor, James Redhouse, and Pliny Marsh are in the William J. Norton Collection, Bentley Library, University of Michigan, Ann Arbor.

59. McGregor Fund, Minutes, May 8, 1944.

60. Ibid., January 8, November 8, 1954; March 14, 1955.

61. Ibid., April 11, 1955.

62. Ibid., May 9, 1955.

63. Ibid., May 9, 1955.

64. Ibid., November 23, December 12, 1955; February 6, 1956.

65. Ibid., January 15, February 10, 1955.

A NOTE ON THE ARCHIVAL AND MANUSCRIPT SOURCES

As noted in the introduction, the Tracy W. McGregor Collection in the Archives of Labor and Urban Affairs at Wayne State University was the main source for this study. McGregor was meticulous in the preservation of his papers that covered every aspect of his life and career. Other relevant collections at Wayne State University include the archives of the Associated Charities of Detroit, the Detroit Community Union, the Detroit Community Fund, and the United Community Services. The extensive files of the Merrill-Palmer Institute were also helpful. The Prismatic Club Archives contain important material relating to close associates of McGregor.

The Burton Historical Collection of the Detroit Public Library has numerous collections relating to Detroit leaders and organizations affiliated with McGregor and his colleagues. The Detroit Citizens League papers provide a clear picture of Detroit during the early decades of the twentieth century and this organization's campaign to reform Detroit's political system. The records of the Jewish Welfare Federation of Detroit supplement the United Community Services Collection at Wayne State University. The papers of Hazen Pingree, Thomas Palmer, John C. Lodge, and the extensive biographical files maintained at the Burton Historical Collection were especially helpful. The Henry Leland Collection in the Automotive History Collection of the Detroit Public Library illustrated the important role McGregor played as one of Detroit's reform advocates.

The Bentley Library of the University of Michigan contains several important sources, including the papers of William J. Norton, Dexter M. Ferry, Carleton Wells, and Henry B. Joy. The inactive archives of the William L. Clements Library at the Bentley Library, as well as the Randolph Adams papers at the Clements Library shed light on McGregor's activities as a collector of

Americana and his important role as a member of the Committee of Management of the Clements Library.

The American Historical Association (AHA) collection in the Manuscripts Division of the Library of Congress provides detailed information on the establishment of the McGregor Plan under the auspices of the AHA to encourage colleges and universities to establish rare book collections. McGregor's correspondence with J. Franklin Jameson, Conyers Read, and other leading historians document his plans to place his Americana collection in a major university.

The James Couzens papers at the Library of Congress are also of interest in relation to McGregor's role as the chair of the fund-raising committee of the Detroit Community Fund.

The McGregor Fund Archives covers in detail the work of the fund during its formative years. The minutes of the board of trustees and especially the files of Henry S. Hulbert, who served as a member of the board from 1925 to 1959 and as president of the fund from 1936 to 1955, are important to a study of the inner workings of the fund. Following Tracy McGregor's death, the board carried on his legacy.

INTERVIEWS

The oral history interviews conducted by William J. Norton were of great value as a source on the McGregors. The interview with Murray McGregor provided insights into his brother's mission in life. Also of great value were the interviews with Pliny Marsh and James Redhouse.

BIBLIOGRAPHY

Adams, Randolph. "Librarians as Enemies of Books." *Library Quarterly* 7 (July 1937): 317–31.

———. *Political Ideas of the American Revolution.* Durham, NC: Trinity College Press, 1922.

———. "Remarks on the Operation of the McGregor Plan, 1934 to 1942." Clements Library Archives, Bentley Library, University of Michigan, Ann Arbor.

———. "Report on the College Plan of the Late Tracy W. McGregor," 1936. AHA Archives, Manuscript Collection, Library of Congress, Washington, DC.

American Historical Association. "Report of Committee on Americana for College Libraries," 1935, AHA Collection, Manuscripts Division, Library of Congress, Washington, DC.

"Americana: Tracy McGregor Collection of Rare Books Is Valuable Library Asset." *Emory Alumnus* (June 1937).

"An American Palace." *Detroit Free Press,* February 4, 1895.

Angell, A. C. "Eulogy of E. W. Pendleton." MC-RL.

Associated Charities of Detroit. "General Hints and Suggestions to Visitors of the ACD." *Proceedings of the Second Annual Meeting.* Detroit: n.p., 1882.

Arnove, Robert, ed. *Philanthropy and Cultural Imperialism.* Bloomington: Indiana University Press, 1982.

Bald, F. Clever. *Michigan in Four Centuries.* New York: Harper, 1954.

Barnard, Harry. *Independent Man: The Life of Senator James Couzens.* New York: Scribners, 1958.

Benson, Robert. "Yamasaki's Legacy." *Detroit News,* February 18, 1986.

Bingay, Malcolm W. *Detroit Is My Hometown.* New York: Bobbs-Merrill, 1946.

Bowen, Lem W. "Obituary," September 9, 1925. BHC.

Boyle, Kevin. *Arc of Justice: A Saga of Race, Civil Rights, and Murder in the Jazz Age.* New York: Henry Holt & Co., 2004.

Brandt, E. N. *Chairman of the Board: A Biography of Carl A. Gerstacker.* East Lansing: Michigan State University Press, 2003.

Bremmer, Robert. *American Philanthropy.* Chicago: University of Chicago Press, 1960.

Burton, Clarence. *The City of Detroit, Michigan, 1701–1922.* Detroit: S. J. Clarke, 1922.

Carnegie, Andrew. *Gospel of Wealth North American Review* 148 (June 1889): 653–64.

Catlin, George B. *The Story of Detroit.* Detroit: *Detroit News,* 1923.

Chernow, Ron. *The Life of John D. Rockefeller, Sr.* New York: Random House, 1998.

Crosby, Alfred. *America's Forgotten Pandemic: The Influenza of 1918.* Cambridge: Cambridge University Press, 1989.

Curti, Merle, and Roderick Nash. *Philanthropy in the Shaping of American Higher Education.* New Brunswick, NJ: Rutgers, 1965.

Dancy, John. *Sand against the Wind: The Memories of John Dancy.* Detroit: Wayne State University Press, 1966.

Dann, John. *One Hundred and One Treasures.* Ann Arbor: University of Michigan, 1998.

Della Torre, Sonia. "The Merrill-Palmer Institute of Human Development and Family Life." Unpublished manuscript. ALUA.

De Ora Antartica Per Regem Portugallic Pridem Muenta. Strasburg, Mathiam: Hupsuss, 1503.

Detroit Bureau of Governmental Research. *The Detroit House of Correction.* Detroit: The Council, 1934.

———. "Memorandum in Re Palmer Will to Establish a School of Motherhood and Household Arts," March 1919.

Detroit City Directory. 1913. Burton Historical Collection, State Library of Michigan and other research libraries.

Detroit Community Fund. The First Sixty Years. Detroit, 1917.

———. *Social Services Directory of Detroit.* Detroit: Detroit Community Union, 1917.

Detroit Community Fund, Board of Directors. Minutes, 1917–32. ALUA.

Detroit Historical Society Bulletin, 1965, BHC.

Detroit Patriotic Fund, Board of Directors. Minutes, February 6, 1918, MC-RL.

Detroit Rescue Mission. First Annual Report. Detroit, 1910. MC-RL.

"Detroit's Big Landowners." *Detroit News-Tribune,* June 30, 1895.

"Dexter M. Ferry, Jr.: A Detroiter." *The Detroiter,* November 5, 1928, 9, 14, 18.

"Dropout Leaves a Literary Legacy." *Book Marks,* June 14, 1940.

Dunbar, Willis, and George May. *Michigan: A History of the Wolverine State.* Grand Rapids, MI: Erdman, 1980.

Elenbaas, Jack D. "Detroit and the Progressive Era: A Study of Urban Reform, 1900–1914." Ph.D. diss., Wayne State University, 1968.

Ehrlick, John. "William J. Norton." Unpublished mss. Prismatic Club Archives, ALUA.

"The Fellowship Club Season, 1908–9." MC-RL.

Ferry, Hawkins. *Buildings of Detroit: A History.* Detroit: Wayne State University Press, 1968.

Fine, Sidney. *Frank Murphy: Detroit Years.* Ann Arbor: University of Michigan Press, 1975.

Fragnoli, Raymond. "Progressive Coalitions and Municipal Reforms." *Detroit in Perspective* 4 (Spring 1980).

———. *The Transformation of Reform in Detroit—and After, 1912–1933.* New York: Garland, 1982.

Fugate, Sandy. *For the Benefit of All*: A History of Philanthropy in Michigan. Battle Creek, MI: W. K. Kellogg Foundation, 1997.

Gaber, Andrea. *The Capitalist Philosophers.* New York: Times Books, 2000.

Gavrilovich, Peter, and Bill McGraw. *The Detroit Almanac.* Detroit: Detroit Free Press, 2000.

Glazer, Sidney. *Detroit: A Study in Urban Development.* New York: Bookman Associates, 1965.

Glenn, John, Lillian Browdt, and F. Emerson Andrews. *The Russell Sage Foundation, 1907–1947.* New York: Russell Sage Foundation, 1947.

Greusel, John. "Tracy McGregor, Practical Philanthropist." *Detroit Free Press,* October 8, 1905.

Hall, Peter D. *Inventing the Nonprofit Sector and Other Essays on Philanthropy, Voluntarism, and Nonprofit Organizations.* Baltimore: Johns Hopkins University Press, 2001.

Handbook of the Washington Street Congregational Church and Sunday School. Toledo, OH: St. John Printing, 1884.

Hauer, Sister Marie Pacelli. "Tracy McGregor as a Leader of Social Reform." Seminar paper, University of Detroit, 1967.

Helping Hand Mission. Home Report, 1893. MC-RL.

Holli, Melvin G. *Detroit.* New York: Franklin Watts, 1976.

———. *Reform in Detroit: Hazen S. Pingree and Urban Politics.* New York: Oxford University Press, 1969.

Hopkins, Charles H. *The Rise of the Social Gospel in American Protestantism, 1865–1915.* New Haven, CT: Yale University Press, 1940.

Howarth, Jolin, "J. L. Hudson, An Appreciation." *Detroit Saturday Night,* July 20, 1912.

Hudson, Joseph L. "Address at Opening of McGregor Institute Building," June 9, 1901. MC-RL.

Hulbert, Henry. McGregor "Obituary," MC-RL.

———. "Memorandum, 1938." MC-RL.

———. *Tracy W. McGregor.* Detroit: McGregor Fund, 1939.

Independent Sector. *Giving and Volunteering 1992.* Washington, DC: Independent Sector, 1992.

Ingles, James. *A Sketch of My Life, for the Benefit of My Grandchildren.* Detroit, n.p., 1947.

Jackson, Harry. *The Michigan State Prison at Jackson.* Jackson: Michigan State Prison, 1928.

Jacot, Edith. *Development and Demise of an Institution for the Treatment of Epileptics,* March 1974. Record Group 79-11 B12 F2. State Archives of Michigan, Lansing, MI.

Josephen, Matthew. "Dynamic Detroit." *Harper's,* December 30, 1930. Reproduced in Melvin G. Holli, *Detroit,* 177–22. New York: Franklin Watts, 1976.

Katzman, David. *Before the Ghetto: Black Detroit in the Nineteenth Century.* Urbana: University of Illinois Press, 1973.

W. K. Kellogg Foundation. *The First Eleven Years.* Battle Creek, MI: Kellogg Foundation, 1942.

———. *The First Fifty Years.* Battle Creek, MI: Kellogg Foundation, 1980.

———. *I'll Invest My Money in People.* Battle Creek, MI: Kellogg Foundation, 1990.

Kelsey, Gladys H. "A Haven for Jobless." *Detroit Saturday Night,* June 28, 1930.

Knapp, Pauline Wilson. "All about Edna Noble White," 1961. MPC-RL.

Kolata, Gina. Flu: *The Story of the Great Influenza Pandemic of 1918 and the Search for the Virus That Caused It.* New York: Farrar, Straus and Giroux, 1999.

Korolov, Cynthia. "Help the Other Fellow: Henry Ford and the Ford English School." Master's thesis, Wayne State University, 2002.

Kresge, Stanley S. *The S. S. Kresge Story.* Racine, WI: Western Publishing, 1979.

Kresge Foundation. *The First Fifty-Year Report, 1924–1974.* Detroit: Kresge Foundation, 1974.

Kruesi, Walter. *Who Was Who in America, 1974–1976.* Chicago: A. N. Marquis Co., 1976.

Kruesi, Walter F. *Report on Unemployment in the Winter of 1914–1915 in Detroit, and the Institutions and Measures of Relief.* Detroit, n.p., 1915.

Lagemann, Ellen C. *Private Power for Private Good: A History of the Carnegie Foundation for the Advancement of Teaching.* Middletown, CT: Wesleyan University Press, 1989.

Leland, Henry. *Master of Precision.* Detroit: Wayne State University Press, 1966.

Lewis, David. *The Public Image of Henry Ford.* Detroit: Wayne State University Press, 1976.

Lodge, John. *I Remember Detroit.* Detroit: Wayne State University Press, 1949.

Lovett, William P. *Detroit Rules Itself.* Boston: Garland, 1930.

Macdonald, Dwight. *The Ford Foundation.* New York: Reynal, 1956.

Madigan, Charles M. *Robert R. McCormick: A Celebration of the Life and Legacy.* Chicago: McCormick Tribute Foundation, 2005.

Maget, Richard, ed. *An Agile Servant: Community Leadership by Community Foundations.* New York: Foundation Center, 1989.

Marquis, Albert. *The Book of Detroiters.* Chicago: A. N. Marquis, 1914.

Marquis, Samuel S. *Henry Ford: An Interpretation.* Boston: Little Brown, 1923.

Marsh, Pliny. Oral history interview conducted by William J. Norton William. J. Norton Collection, Bentley Library, University of Michigan, Ann Arbor.

Martin, Elizabeth A. *Detroit and the Great Migration, 1916–1929.* Ann Arbor, MI: Bentley Historical Library, 1993.

Mason, Gregory. "Americans First: How the People of Detroit Are Making Americans of Foreigners." *New Outlook,* September 27, 1916.

Mason, Philip P. *Rum Running and the Roaring Twenties.* Detroit: Wayne State University, 1995.

Maxwell, Margaret. *Shaping a Library: William L. Clements as Collector.* Amsterdam: Nico Israel, 1973.

McGregor, Douglas. "Why Is A Homeless Man," 1931. MC-RL.

McGregor, Murray. "Founding of the Toledo and Detroit Missions." MC-RL.

———. Oral history interview conducted by William J. Norton and Mark Beach, 1954, 1–3. MC-RL.

McGregor, Thomas. "Autobiographical Sketch." MC-RL.

———. "The Detroit Mission." MC-RL.

———. "Gospel for the Masses." Unpublished Mss. MC-RL.

———. "History of Mission Manuscript" [1930]. MC-RL.

———. "J. L. Hudson." MC-RL.

McGregor, T. W. "Transients and Homeless," Address, National Conference of Social Work, Detroit, June 1933. MC-RL.

McGregor, Tracy. Financial journals, 1900-1918. MC-RL.

———. "Purposes of Thursday Noon Group." 1913. Thursday Noon Group file. MC-RL.

———."Speech before Michigan Senate." March 1911. MC-RL.

———. *The Story of a Man without a Home.* Detroit: McGregor Institute, 1910.

———. *Toward a Philosophy of Inner Life.* Detroit: n.p. 1934.

———. *Twenty Thousand Men.* Detroit: McGregor Institute, 1916.

McGregor, Tracy W. "Books and Reading for Men of T & F Club." MC-RL.

———. "The Effects of Prohibition on Homeless Men." Speech given over Radio CKOK, October 11, 1932. MC-RL.

McGregor Fund. Annual Reports, 1931–2005. MFA and MC-RL.

———. *Seven-Year Report, 1931–1937.* Detroit: McGregor Fund, 1937.

———. *Ten-Year Report, 1940–1949.* Detroit: McGregor Fund, 1950.

McGregor Fund, Board of Trustees. Minutes, 1925–1956, MFA.

McGregor Helping Hand Mission after One Year. Detroit, 1892. MC-RL.

McGregor Helping Hand Mission after Two Years. Detroit, 1892. MC-RL.

McGregor Institute. "25th Anniversary." February 1916. MC-RL.

———. Annual Reports. Detroit: McGregor Institute, 1891–1935. MC-RL.

———. "McGregor Institute: A Review of Forty Years." *Annual Report for 1930.* MC-RL.

———. "Monthly Newsletter." MC-RL.

———. "Statement for the Year 1911." MC-RL.

McGregor Institute, Board of Trustees. Minutes, 1899–1940.

"McGregor Library." *Highland Parker,* March 18, 1926. MC-RL.

"McGregor Memorial: A Community Conference Center." Dedication program, May 18, 1958. MC-RL.

"McGregor Memorial Conference Center." *Inside Wayne* 20 (August 13, 1958).

McGregor Mission. "Statement for the Year 1904." MC-RL.

———. *The Year 1900 at The McGregor Mission.* MC-RL.

"The McGregor Mission." *Detroit Free Press,* June 23, 1895.

McGregor Mission Brotherhood. Programme. May 2, 1910. MC-RL.

The McGregor Plan for the Encouragement of Book Collecting by American College Libraries. Washington, DC: American Historical Association, 1937.

McGregor Public Library. "McGregor Library Dedication Program." Detroit, March 5, 1926. MC-RL.

McRae, Norman, and Shirley McRae. *Detroit: The First City of the Midwest.* Carlsbad, CA: Heritage Media, 2001.

Merrill-Palmer Corp. *First Annual Report.* 1920. MPC-RL.

Merrill-Palmer Institution, Board of Trustees. Minutes, 1918–36. MPC-RL.

Merrill-Palmer Motherhood and Home Training School, Board of Trustees. Minutes, November 25, 1918. MPC-RL.

The Merrill-Palmer School: An Account of Its First Twenty Years, 1920–1940 (Detroit: Merrill-Palmer School, 1940).

Michigan, *Public Acts 1915*, Public Act 173.

Michigan and Bar of Michigan (Detroit: Bench and Bar, 1918).

Michigan Farm Colony for Epileptics at Wahjamega, Board of Control. Annual Reports. Lansing, MI: Wynkoop, Hallenbed, Crawford, 1914–21.

"Michigan Farm Colony for Epileptics at Wahjamega." *Biennial Report of Board of Control of Michigan Farm Colony for Epileptics at Wahjamega.* Lansing, MI: Wyankoop. Hallenbeck, Crawford, 1916.

Michigan Secretary of State. Whitney Realty Company, Annual Reports, 1912, 1923, 1924. State Archives of Michigan.

Miller, Sidney T. "The McGregor Mission in Detroit," 1901. MC-RL.

"Mission Churches of Detroit." *Detroit News*, April 16, 1893.

Morton, Elizabeth Ann. *Detroit and the Great Migration, 1916–1929.* Ann Arbor, MI: Bentley Historical Library, 1993.

Nevins, Allan, and Frank Hill. *Ford: The Times, the Man, the Company.* New York: Charles Scribner, 1954.

Nielsen, Waldemar A. *The Big Foundations.* New York: Columbia University Press, 1972.

Norton, James. "Persons and Problems of Many Years Ago," February 1968. Prismatic Club Archives, ALUA.

Norton, James N. "A History of the Detroit Community Fund and the Council of Social Agencies of Metropolitan Detroit, 1917–1938." Master's thesis, University of Michigan, 1940.

Norton, William J. *The Cooperative Movement in Social Work.* New York: Macmillan, 1927.

———. "The Saga of a Foundation Executive," November 6, 1954. Prismatic Club Archives, ALUA.

———. "Tracy W. McGregor Dedication Address," May 10, 1955. MC-RL.

Palmer, Lizzie M. "Last Will and Testament." May 17, 1916. MC-RL.

Parker, Wyman. *Henry Stevens of Vermont: An American Rare Book Dealer in London, 1845–1886.* Amsterdam: Nico Israel, 1963.

Patch, Carolyn. *Grace Whitney Hoff: The Story of an Abundant Life.* Cambridge, MA: Riverside Press, 1933.

Patterson, Calvin. "Tracy W. McGregor: Exemplar." Unpublished Mss. MFA.

Perman, W. J. "Thomas McGregor As I Knew Him." MC-RL.

Petrone, Jean. *Hudson's: Hub of America's Heartland.* West Bloomfield, MI: Altwerger and Mandel, 1991.

Pingree, Hazen. "Mayor Pingree Reforms in Detroit." *Outlook* 55 (February 6, 1897), 437–42. Cited in Melvin G. Holli. *Detroit*, 110–16. New York: Franklin Watts, 1976.

Poremba, David L. *Detroit and Its World Setting.* Detroit: Wayne State University Press, 2001.

Preston, Minnie. "Thomas McGregor." MC-RL.

Rabinowitz, Alan. *Social Change Philanthropy in America.* Westport, CT: Quorum, 1990.

Re, Vittorio. *Michigan's Italian Community: A Historical Perspective.* Detroit: Wayne State University, 1981.

Redhouse, James. Oral history interview conducted by William J. Norton and Mark Beach. William J. Norton Collection, Bentley Library, University of Michigan, Ann Arbor.

Report of Commission to Investigate the Extent of Feeblemindedness, Epilepsy, and other Conditions of Mental Defectiveness in Michigan. Lansing, MI: Wynkoop, Hallenbeck, Crawford, 1915.

"Report of Word Done at Toledo Helping Hand Mission from February 19 to March 31, 1890." MC-RL.

Richards, William. "Tracy W. McGregor." *Detroiter,* February 20, 1928.

Richards, William C. *Biography of a Fund: The Story of the Children's Fund of Michigan, 1929–1954.* Detroit: Children's Fund, 1957.

Riis, Jacob A. *How the Other Half Lives: Studies among the Tenements of New York.* New York: Charles Scribner's, 1890.

Robbins, Daniel M. "Eloise, the Finest Poorhouse in the World." *Michigan Christian Advocate,* February 15, 1934.

Runge, William. "The Tracy McGregor Library and Its Founder." University of Virginia *Newsletter* 39 (July 15, 1963).

Smith, John. *The True Relation of Such Occurances and Accidents of Noate as Hath Hapned in Virginia Since the First Planting of That Colony.* London, 1608.

Stark, George. "Thursday Group Carries on Work Started by McGregor." *Detroit News,* May 8, 1936.

———. "Tracy McGregor." *Detroit News,* May 4, 1936.

Starring, Charles. "Hazen S. Pingree: Another Forgotten Eagle." *Michigan History* 32 (June 1948).

Stromberg, Warren. "A Scot's Arithmetic: McGregor in Spirit, Still Busy Helping Mankind." *Detroit Free Press,* April 2, 1961.

Sullivan, Martin. "On the Dole: The Relief Issue in Detroit, 1929–1939." Ph.D. thesis, University of Notre Dame, 1974.

"Survey of Mission Men," March 1892–March 1894 (Detroit, March 1894). MC-RL.

Sward, Keith. *The Legend of Henry Ford.* New York: Rinehart, 1948.

Taitt, James D. "Historical Reminiscences of the Presbyterian Church at Oxbow, New York." *Early History of Oxbow and the Scotch Settlement* (Oxbow: Presbyterian Church of Oxbow, 1921), 10, 15.

"Ten Years of Civic Service." *The Civic Search Light* 9 (May 1922).

Toledo Helping Hand Mission. *A Home for Men.* Toledo, OH: Helping Hand Mission, n.d.

Toledo High School. Class of 1886, *Graduation Booklet,* June 1886. MC-RL.

Toledo High School. Programs, 1886–87.

The Tracy W. McGregor Library: Three Decades of Development, 1939–1969. Charlottesville: University of Virginia, 1970.

"T. W. McGregor Heads Inner-Racial Board." *Detroit Free Press,* September 16, 1925.

"Tracy W. McGregor, In Memoriam." Merrill-Palmer Motherhood and Home Training School, *Annual Report for 1936–37.*

"A Tramps' Paradise." *Detroit Journal,* December 20, 1890.

Tyler, Dorothy. "Edna Noble White," 1954. MC-RL.

United Community Services of Metropolitan Detroit, 1917–1967. Detroit: UCS, 1992.

United Jewish Charities. *50 Years of Community Service.* Detroit, Jewish Welfare Federation, 1950.

University of Michigan, Board of Regents. *Proceedings,* 1923–40.

University of Virginia Library. "Tracy W. McGregor Library: Three Decades of Development, 1939–1969." MC-RL.

Upson, Lent D. *The Growth of City Government.* Detroit, Bureau of Government Research, 1942.

Van Tyne, Claude. *The Loyalists in the American Revolution.* New York: Macmillan, 1902.

Washington, Forrester B. *The Negro in Detroit: Survey of the Conditions of a Negro Group in a Northern Industrial Center during the War Prosperity Period.* Detroit: n.p., 1920.

Washington Congregational Church. *Handbook: Church and Sunday School.* Toledo: Washington Congregational Church, 1884

———. *The Helper of the Washington Congregational Church.* Toledo, OH, February 1892.

Washington Street Congregational Church (Toledo, Ohio). *Programme,* 1887. MC-RL.

Wayne County Training School. *Annual Reports,* 1927–37. BHC.

White, Edna Noble. "Notes on the Early History of the School," n.d. MC-RL.

Whitney, Katherine M. *A State Hospital School for Epileptic Children.* Michigan, 1944. Reprinted from *Journal of Exceptional Children* 10, no. 7 (April 1944): 173–79, and vol. 11 (October 1944): 7–11.

Who's Who in the Midwest. Chicago: A. N. Marquis, 1918.

Widger, Benjamin. "McGregor Institute Will Pay Tribute to Memory of the Founder of Home for Men 'Up Against It.'" Detroit *Free Press,* April 26, 1925.

Woodford, Arthur. *American Urban Renaissance.* Detroit: Greater Detroit Chamber of Commerce, 1979.

Woodford, Frank, and Arthur Woodford. *All Our Yesterdays.* Detroit: Wayne State University Press, 1969.

"The Year 1932 at the Institute." MC-RL.

Young, Clarence, and William A. Quinn. *Foundation for Living: The Story of Charles Stewart Mott and Flint.* New York: McGraw-Hill, 1963.

Zunz, Oliver. *The Changing Face of Inequality: Urbanization, Industrial Development, and Immigrants in Detroit, 1880–1920.* Chicago: University of Chicago Press, 1982.

INDEX

www.ingramcontent.com/pod-product-compliance
Lightning Source LLC
LaVergne TN
LVHW011203090826
844660LV00063B/979/J
* 9 7 8 0 8 1 4 3 3 3 7 6 1 *